Lecture Notes in Computer Science 6823

Commenced Publication in 1973
Founding and Former Series Editors:
Gerhard Goos, Juris Hartmanis, and Jan van Leeuwen

Alex Groce
Madanlal Musuvathi (Eds.)

Model Checking Software

18th International SPIN Workshop
Snowbird, UT, USA, July 14-15, 2011
Proceedings

 Springer

Volume Editors

Alex Groce
Oregon State University
1148 Kelley Engineering Center
Corvallis, OR 97331-5501, USA
E-mail: alex@eecs.oregonstate.edu

Madanlal Musuvathi
Microsoft Research
One Microsoft Way
Redmond, WA 98052, USA
E-mail: madanm@microsoft.com

ISSN 0302-9743   e-ISSN 1611-3349
ISBN 978-3-642-22305-1   e-ISBN 978-3-642-22306-8
DOI 10.1007/978-3-642-22306-8
Springer Heidelberg Dordrecht London New York

Library of Congress Control Number: 2011930657

CR Subject Classification (1998): F.3, D.2.4, D.3.1, D.2, F.4.1, C.2.4

LNCS Sublibrary: SL 1 – Theoretical Computer Science and General Issues

Typesetting: Camera-ready by author, data conversion by Scientific Publishing Services, Chennai, India

Printed on acid-free paper

Springer is part of Springer Science+Business Media (www.springer.com)

Preface

This volume contains the proceedings of the 18th International SPIN Workshop on Model Checking of Software (SPIN 2011). SPIN 2011 took place during July 14–15, at Cliff Lodge in Snowbird, Utah, co-located with the 23rd International Conference on Computer-Aided Verification (CAV 2011). The SPIN Workshop series is an annual forum for researchers and practitioners, with a general focus on specifying and checking properties of (software) systems. The more specific focus of the SPIN workshops is on explict-state techniques, as implemented in SPIN and other tools, or techniques based on a combination of explicit representation with other approaches.

SPIN 2011 featured two invited speakers. Jasmin Fisher of Microsoft Research Cambridge is an expert on "excutable biology," the design and analysis of computer algorithms describing biological phenomena, an approach with great promise for new discoveries, global dynamic pictures of system behavior, and cost-efficient preliminary studies that save laboratory time and resources. John Regehr of the University of Utah leads a research group that works to improve the quality of embedded software via static analysis, stress testing, formal verification, and sometimes the graceful tolerance of runtime bugs. SPIN also shared speakers with the EC^2 Workshop on Exploiting Concurrency Efficiently and Correctly.

SPIN 2011 attracted 29 submissions, and accepted 10 regular papers and 3 tool demonstration papers. All papers received at least three rigorous reviews. The reviewers discussed papers with neither overwhelmingly positive nor overwhelmingly negative reviews until a consensus was reached. Program Committee members with conflicts of interest were excluded from all discussions of relevant submissions. The editors are extremely grateful to the members of the Program Committee and their subreviewers for working under a very tight deadline (one of the tightest review deadlines in the history of SPIN) and to accepted paper authors for the quick turnaround in producing camera-ready copies.

The Chairs are also indebted to the members of the SPIN Steering Committee, particularly Stefan Leue and Gerard Holzmann (creator of this year's eye-catching publicity poster), and the Chairs of previous SPIN events for their assistance in organizing this year's workshop. We are also grateful for the efforts of the CAV Chairs, Ganesh Gopalakrishnan and Shaz Qadeer, and the CAV Workshops Chair Neha Rungta, in making the logistics of holding SPIN as simple and pleasant as possible.

July 2011   Alex Groce
                                                                    Madanlal Musuvathi

Organization

Steering Committee

Dragan Bosnacki   Eindhoven University of Technology, The Netherlands
Susanne Graf   Verimag, France
Gerard Holzmann   Jet Propulsion Laboratory, Pasadena, USA
Stefan Leue   University of Konstanz, Germany
Willem Visser   University of Stellenbosch, South Africa

Program Chairs

Alex Groce   Oregon State University, USA
Madanlal Musuvathi   Microsoft Research, Redmond, USA

Program Committee

James Andrews   University of Western Ontario, Canada
Dragan Bosnacki   Eindhoven University of Technology, The Netherlands
Sebastian Burckhardt   Microsoft Research, Redmond, USA
Cristian Cadar   Imperial College, London, UK
George Candea   EPFL, Switzerland
Sagar Chaki   Software Engineering Institute, Pittsburgh, USA
Supratik Chakraborty   I.I.T. Bombay, India
Azadeh Farzan   University of Toronto, Canada
Susanne Graf   Verimag, France
Alex Groce   Oregon State University, USA
Aarti Gupta   NEC Labs, USA
Klaus Havelund   Jet Propulsion Laboratory, Pasadena, USA
Gerard Holzmann   Jet Propulsion Laboratory, Pasadena, USA
Gerwin Klein   NICTA and UNSW, Sydney, Australia
Akash Lal   Microsoft Research, India
Alberto Lluch Lafuente   IMT Institute for Advanced Studies, Lucca, Italy
Rupak Majumdar   Max Planck Institute for Software Systems, Germany
Darko Marinov   University of Illinois, Urbana-Champaign, USA
Madanlal Musuvathi   Microsoft Research, Redmond, USA
David Parker   University of Oxford, UK

Corina Pasareanu   Carnegie Mellon/NASA Ames, USA
Doron Peled   Bar-Ilan University, Israel
Koushik Sen   University of California, Berkeley, USA
Scott Stoller   Stony Brook University, USA
Murali Talupur   SCL, Intel, USA

Subreviewers

Andreas Bauer	Baris Kasikci	Indranil Saha
Bruno Blanchet	Johannes Kinder	Sai Deep Tetali
Stefan Bucur	Volodymyr Kuznetsov	Abhishek Udupa
Jacob Burnim	Michele Loreti	Andrea Vandin
Anupam Datta	Jasen Markovski	Simon Winwood
Tayfun Elmas	Matthieu Moy	Yu Yang
Milos Gligoric	Maximilian R. Odenbrett	

Table of Contents

Tool Demonstrations

Model Checking Cell Fate Decisions

Jasmin Fisher

Microsoft Research Cambridge, UK

Abstract. As time goes by, it becomes more and more apparent that the puzzles of life involve more and more molecular pieces that fit together in increasingly complex ways. Biology is not an exact science. It is messy and noisy, and most often vague and ambiguous. We cannot assign clear rules to the way cells behave and interact with one another, and we often cannot quantify the exact amounts of molecules, such as genes and proteins, in the resolution of a single cell. To make matters worse (so to speak), the combinatorial complexity observed in biological networks is staggering, which renders the comprehension and analysis of such systems a major challenge. Recent efforts to create executable models of complex biological phenomena - an approach called Executable Biology - entail great promise for new scientific discoveries, shading new light on the puzzle of life. At the same time, this 'new wave of the future' forces Computer Science to stretch far and beyond, and in ways never considered before, in order to deal with the enormous complexity observed in biology. In this talk, I will summarize some of the success stories in using formal verification to reason about mechanistic models in biology. In particular, I will focus on models of cell fate decisions during normal development, organogenesis, and cancer, and their analysis using model checking. If time permits, I will also mention some of the major milestones on the way to conquer biological complexity.

A. Groce and M. Musuvathi (Eds.): SPIN 2011, LNCS 6823, p. 1, 2011.
© Springer-Verlag Berlin Heidelberg 2011

Property-Dependent Reductions
for the Modal Mu-Calculus

Radu Mateescu[1] and Anton Wijs[2]

[1] INRIA Grenoble – Rhône-Alpes / VASY project-team / LIG, Inovallée
655, av. de l'Europe, Montbonnot, F-38334 Saint Ismier, France
Radu.Mateescu@inria.fr
[2] Technische Universiteit Eindhoven, Postbus 513
5600 MB Eindhoven, The Netherlands
A.J.Wijs@tue.nl

Abstract. When analyzing the behavior of finite-state concurrent systems by model checking, one way of fighting state explosion is to reduce the model as much as possible whilst preserving the properties under verification. We consider the framework of action-based systems, whose behaviors can be represented by labeled transition systems (LTSs), and whose temporal properties of interest can be formulated in modal μ-calculus (L_μ). First, we determine, for any L_μ formula, the maximal set of actions that can be hidden in the LTS without changing the interpretation of the formula. Then, we define L_μ^{dsbr}, a fragment of L_μ which is compatible with divergence-sensitive branching bisimulation. This enables us to apply the maximal hiding and to reduce the LTS on-the-fly using divergence-sensitive τ-confluence during the verification of any L_μ^{dsbr} formula. The experiments that we performed on various examples of communication protocols and distributed systems show that this reduction approach can significantly improve the performance of on-the-fly verification.

1 Introduction

Model checking [5] is a technique to systematically verify whether a system specification meets a given temporal property. Although successfully applied in many cases, its usefulness in practice is still hampered by the state explosion phenomenon, which may entail high memory and CPU requirements in order to carry out the verification.

One way to improve the performance of model checking is to check the property at a higher level of abstraction; by abstracting parts of the system behavior away from the specification, its corresponding state space will be smaller, thereby easier to check. This can either be done globally, i.e., before verifying the property, or on-the-fly, i.e., during verification. However, one needs to be careful not to abstract away any details crucial for the outcome of the check, i.e., relevant for the property. This is known as *action abstraction* in action-based formalisms,

A. Groce and M. Musuvathi (Eds.): SPIN 2011, LNCS 6823, pp. 2–19, 2011.

where state spaces are represented by *Labeled Transition Systems* (LTSs), specifications are written using some flavor of *process algebra* [2], and temporal properties are described using a temporal logic such as the *μ-calculus (L_μ)* [18,28]. Abstracted behavior is then represented by some predefined action, denoted τ in process algebras. In the past, the main focus in this area has been on devising μ-calculus variants adequate with specific relations, such as μACTL\X [9], which is adequate w.r.t. divergence-sensitive branching bisimulation [15,14], or weak μ-calculus [28], which is adequate w.r.t. weak bisimulation [25]. For such fragments, the minimization of an LTS modulo the specific relation preserves the truth value of all formulas written in the adequate μ-calculus. Other works focused on devising reductions targeted to specific formulas, such as those written in the *selective μ-calculus* [3]. For each selective μ-calculus formula, it is possible to hide all actions not occurring in the formula, and subsequently minimize the LTS modulo $\tau^*.a$ bisimulation [10] before verifying the formula.

In this paper, we propose two enhancements with respect to existing work. Firstly, starting from an arbitrary L_μ formula, we determine automatically the maximal set of actions which can be hidden in an LTS without affecting the outcome of the verification of that formula. This yields the maximum potential for reduction, and therefore for improving the performance of model checking. After hiding, the LTS can be minimized modulo strong bisimulation without disturbing the truth value of the formula. This method is not intrusive, in the sense that it does not force the user to write formulas in a certain way. Secondly, we identify a fragment of L_μ, called L_μ^{dsbr}, which is compatible with divergence-sensitive branching bisimulation. We show that this fragment subsumes μACTL\X, the modalities of selective μ-calculus, and the weak μ-calculus. Compared to these μ-calculi, which require that action formulas contain only names of visible actions, our L_μ^{dsbr} fragment also allows the presence of the invisible action τ, therefore providing additional flexibility in the specification of properties.

The reduction approach for L_μ^{dsbr} is now supported within the CADP[1] verification toolbox [13]. The model checking of a L_μ^{dsbr} formula can be optimized generally in two ways: globally, by generating the LTS, then hiding the maximal set of actions according to the formula, and minimizing the LTS modulo strong or divergence-sensitive branching bisimulation before checking the formula; and on-the-fly, by applying maximal hiding and reduction modulo divergence-sensitive τ-confluence simultaneously with the verification. The experiments we carried out on several examples of protocols and distributed systems show that these optimizations can lead to significant performance improvements.

Section 2 defines the formalisms and relations considered in this paper. Section 3 studies the maximal hiding of actions in an LTS w.r.t. a given L_μ formula. Section 4 introduces the L_μ^{dsbr} fragment, shows its compatibility with divergence-sensitive branching bisimulation, and compares its expressiveness with other logics. Section 5 describes and illustrates experimentally the model checking optimizations obtained by applying maximal hiding and reductions for L_μ^{dsbr} formulas. Section 6 gives concluding remarks and directions of future work.

---

[1] http://www.inrialpes.fr/vasy/cadp

2   Background

Labeled transition system. We consider as interpretation model the classical LTS, which underlies process algebras and related action-based description languages. An LTS is a tuple $\langle S, A, T, s_0 \rangle$, where S is the set of states, A is the set of actions (including the invisible action τ), $T \subseteq S \times A \times S$ is the transition relation, and $s_0 \in S$ is the initial state. The visible actions in $A \setminus \{\tau\}$ are noted a and the actions in A are noted b. A transition $\langle s_1, b, s_2 \rangle \in T$ (also noted $s_1 \xrightarrow{b} s_2$) means that the system can move from state s_1 to state s_2 by performing action b. The reflexive transitive closure of $\xrightarrow{\tau}$ is denoted by $\Rightarrow$. A finite path is denoted by $s_0 \xrightarrow{b_0 \cdots b_{k-1}} s_k$, which is a finite sequence $s_0, s_1, \ldots, s_k$, such that there exist actions $b_0, \ldots, b_{k-1}$ with $\forall 0 \leq i < k.s_i \xrightarrow{b_i} s_{i+1}$. We assume below the existence of an LTS $M = \langle S, A, T, s_0 \rangle$ on which temporal formulas will be interpreted.

Modal μ-calculus. The variant of L_μ that we consider here consists of action formulas (noted α) and state formulas (noted φ), which characterize subsets of LTS actions and states, respectively. The syntax and semantics of these formulas are defined in Figure 1. Action formulas are built over the set of actions by using Boolean connectors in a way similar to ACTL (Action-based CTL) [26], which is a slight extension w.r.t. the original definition of L_μ [18]. Derived action operators can be defined as usual: true = $\neg$false, $\alpha_1 \wedge \alpha_2 = \neg(\neg\alpha_1 \vee \neg\alpha_2)$, etc. State formulas are built from Boolean connectors, the possibility modality ($\langle\ \rangle$), and the minimal fixed point operator (μ) defined over propositional variables X belonging to a set $\mathcal{X}$. Derived state operators can be defined as usual: true = $\neg$false, $\varphi_1 \wedge \varphi_2 = \neg(\neg\varphi_1 \vee \neg\varphi_2)$, $[\alpha]\,\varphi = \neg\,\langle\alpha\rangle\,\neg\varphi$ is the necessity modality, and $\nu X.\varphi = \neg\mu X.\neg\varphi[\neg X/X]$ is the maximal fixed point operator ($\varphi[\neg X/X]$ stands for φ in which all free occurrences of X have been negated).

The interpretation $[\![\alpha]\!]_A$ of an action formula on the set of actions of an LTS denotes the subset of actions satisfying α. An action b satisfies a formula α (also

---

Action formulas:

$$\alpha ::= b \qquad\qquad [\![b]\!]_A = \{b\}$$
$$|\ \ \text{false} \qquad\qquad [\![\text{false}]\!]_A = \emptyset$$
$$|\ \ \neg\alpha_1 \qquad\qquad [\![\neg\alpha_1]\!]_A = A \setminus [\![\alpha_1]\!]_A$$
$$|\ \ \alpha_1 \vee \alpha_2 \qquad\qquad [\![\alpha_1 \vee \alpha_2]\!]_A = [\![\alpha_1]\!]_A \cup [\![\alpha_2]\!]_A$$

State formulas:

$$\varphi ::= \text{false} \qquad\qquad [\![\text{false}]\!]_M\,\rho = \emptyset$$
$$|\ \ \neg\varphi_1 \qquad\qquad [\![\neg\varphi_1]\!]_M\,\rho = S \setminus [\![\varphi_1]\!]_M\,\rho$$
$$|\ \ \varphi_1 \vee \varphi_2 \qquad\qquad [\![\varphi_1 \vee \varphi_2]\!]_M\,\rho = [\![\varphi_1]\!]_M\,\rho \cup [\![\varphi_2]\!]_M\,\rho$$
$$|\ \ \langle\alpha\rangle\,\varphi_1 \qquad\qquad [\![\langle\alpha\rangle\,\varphi_1]\!]_M\,\rho = \{s \in S \mid \exists s \xrightarrow{b} s' \in T.b \in [\![\alpha]\!]_A \wedge s' \in [\![\varphi_1]\!]_M\,\rho\}$$
$$|\ \ X \qquad\qquad [\![X]\!]_M\,\rho = \rho(X)$$
$$|\ \ \mu X.\varphi_1 \qquad\qquad [\![\mu X.\varphi_1]\!]_M\,\rho = \bigcap\{U \subseteq S \mid [\![\varphi_1]\!]_M\,(\rho \oslash [U/X]) \subseteq U\}$$

Fig. 1. Syntax and semantics of L_μ

noted $b \models_A \alpha$) if and only if $b \in [\![\alpha]\!]_A$. A transition $s_1 \xrightarrow{b} s_2$ such that $b \models_A \alpha$ is called an α-transition. A propositional context $\rho : \mathcal{X} \to 2^S$ is a partial function mapping propositional variables to subsets of states. The notation $\rho \oslash [U/X]$ stands for a propositional context identical to ρ except for variable X, which is mapped to the state subset U. The interpretation $[\![\varphi]\!]_M \rho$ of a state formula on an LTS M and a propositional context ρ (which assigns a set of states to each propositional variable occurring free in φ) denotes the subset of states satisfying φ in that context. The Boolean connectors are interpreted as usual in terms of set operations. The possibility modality $\langle \alpha \rangle \varphi_1$ (resp. the necessity modality $[\alpha] \varphi_1$) denotes the states for which some (resp. all) of their outgoing transitions labeled by actions satisfying α lead to states satisfying φ_1. The minimal fixed point operator $\mu X.\varphi_1$ (resp. the maximal fixed point operator $\nu X.\varphi_1$) denotes the least (resp. greatest) solution of the equation $X = \varphi_1$ interpreted over the complete lattice $\langle 2^S, \emptyset, S, \cap, \cup, \subseteq \rangle$. A state s satisfies a closed formula φ (also noted $s \models_M \varphi$) if and only if $s \in [\![\varphi]\!]_M$ (the propositional context ρ can be omitted since φ does not contain free variables).

Propositional Dynamic Logic with Looping. In addition to plain L_μ operators, we will use the modalities of PDL-Δ (*Propositional Dynamic Logic with Looping*) [29], which characterize finite (resp. infinite) sequences of transitions whose concatenated actions form words belonging to regular (resp. ω-regular) languages. The syntax and semantics of PDL-Δ (defined by translation to L_μ) are given in Figure 2. Regular formulas (noted β) are built from action formulas and the testing (?), concatenation (.), choice (|), and transitive reflexive closure (*) operators. Apart from Boolean connectors, state formulas are built from the possibility modality ($\langle\ \rangle$) and the infinite looping operator ($\langle\ \rangle @$), both containing regular formulas. Derived state operators are defined as follows: $[\beta] \varphi = \neg \langle \beta \rangle \neg \varphi$ is the necessity modality, and $[\beta] \dashv = \neg \langle \beta \rangle @$ is the saturation operator.

A transition sequence satisfies a formula β if the word obtained by concatenating all actions of the sequence belongs to the regular language defined by β. The testing operator makes it possible to specify state formulas that must hold in the intermediate states of a transition sequence. The possibility modality $\langle \beta \rangle \varphi_1$ (resp. the necessity modality $[\beta] \varphi_1$) denotes the states for which some (resp. all) of their outgoing transition sequences satisfying β lead to states satisfying φ_1.

$$\beta ::= \alpha \mid \varphi? \mid \beta_1.\beta_2 \mid \beta_1|\beta_2 \mid \beta_1^*$$
$$\varphi ::= \mathsf{false} \mid \neg\varphi_1 \mid \varphi_1 \vee \varphi_2 \mid \langle \beta \rangle \varphi_1 \mid \langle \beta \rangle @$$

$$\langle \varphi'? \rangle \varphi = \varphi' \wedge \varphi$$
$$\langle \beta_1.\beta_2 \rangle \varphi = \langle \beta_1 \rangle \langle \beta_2 \rangle \varphi$$
$$\langle \beta_1|\beta_2 \rangle \varphi = \langle \beta_1 \rangle \varphi \vee \langle \beta_2 \rangle \varphi$$
$$\langle \beta^* \rangle \varphi = \mu X.(\varphi \vee \langle \beta \rangle X)$$
$$\langle \beta \rangle @ = \nu X. \langle \beta \rangle X$$

Fig. 2. Syntax and semantics of PDL-Δ

The infinite looping operator $\langle\beta\rangle$ @ (resp. the saturation operator $[\beta]$ ⊣) denotes the states having some (resp. no) outgoing transition sequence consisting of an infinite concatenation of sub-sequences satisfying β.

The operators of PDL-Δ can be freely mixed with those of L_μ, and in practice they allow a much more concise and intuitive description of properties. The variant of L_μ extended with PDL-Δ operators, noted L_μ^{reg}, has been considered and efficiently implemented in [21] (in fact, the syntax used for PDL-Δ operators in Fig. 2 is that of L_μ^{reg} and not the original one). In the remainder of the paper, we will use L_μ^{reg} whenever possible for specifying properties.

Divergence-sensitive branching bisimulation. As equivalence relation between LTSs, we consider divergence-sensitive branching bisimulation [15,14], which preserves branching-time properties such as inevitable reachability and also the existence of divergences (τ-cycles), while still making possible substantial reductions of LTSs. This relation is finer than plain branching bisimulation and weak bisimulation [25] (none of which preserves divergences), therefore being a good candidate for comparing the behaviour of concurrent systems.

Definition 1 (Divergence-Sensitive Branching Bisimulation [15]). *A binary relation R on the set of states S is a divergence-sensitive branching bisimulation if R is symmetric and $s\ R\ t$ implies that*

- *if $s \xrightarrow{b} s'$ then*
    - *either $b = \tau$ with $s'\ R\ t$;*
    - *or $t \Rightarrow \hat{t} \xrightarrow{b} t'$ with $s\ R\ \hat{t}$ and $s'\ R\ t'$.*
- *if for all $k \geq 0$ and $s = s_0$, $s_k \xrightarrow{\tau} s_{k+1}$ then for all $\ell \geq 0$ and $t = t_0$, $t_\ell \xrightarrow{\tau} t_{\ell+1}$ and $s_k\ R\ t_\ell$ for all k,ℓ.*

Two states s and t are divergence-sensitive branching bisimilar, noted $s \approx_{br}^{ds} t$, if there is a divergence-sensitive branching bisimulation R with $s\ R\ t$.

When expressing certain properties (e.g., inevitable reachability), it is necessary to characterize deadlock states in the LTS, i.e., states from which the execution cannot progress anymore. From the $\approx_{br}^{ds}$ point of view, deadlock states are precisely those states leading eventually to sink states (i.e., states without successors) after a finite number of τ-transitions. These states can be characterized by the PDL-Δ formula below:

$$deadlock = [\text{true}^*.\neg\tau]\ \text{false} \wedge [\tau]\ \dashv$$

where the box modality forbids the reachability of visible actions and the saturation operator forbids the presence of divergences.

3   Maximal Hiding

When checking a state formula φ over an LTS, some actions of the LTS can be hidden (i.e., renamed into τ) without disturbing the interpretation of φ.

Definition 2 (Hiding Set). *Let α be an action formula interpreted over a set of actions A. The* hiding set *of α w.r.t. A is defined as follows:*

$$h_A(\alpha) = \begin{cases} [\![\alpha]\!]_A & \text{if } \tau \models \alpha \\ A \setminus [\![\alpha]\!]_A & \text{if } \tau \not\models \alpha \end{cases}$$

The hiding set *of a state formula φ w.r.t. A, noted $h_A(\varphi)$, is defined as the intersection of $h_A(\alpha)$ for all action subformulas α of φ.*

Definition 3 (Hiding). *Let A be a set of actions and $B \subseteq A$. The* hiding *of an action $b \in A$ w.r.t. B is defined as follows:*

$$hide_B(b) = \begin{cases} b & \text{if } b \notin B \\ \tau & \text{if } b \in B \end{cases}$$

The hiding *of an* LTS *$M = \langle S, A, T, s_0 \rangle$ w.r.t. B is defined as follows:*

$$hide_B(\langle S, A, T, s_0 \rangle) = \left\langle S, (A \setminus B) \cup \{\tau\}, \{s_1 \stackrel{hide_B(b)}{\to} s_2 \mid s_1 \stackrel{b}{\to} s_2 \in T\}, s_0 \right\rangle.$$

The following lemma states that hiding an action b w.r.t. the hiding set of an action formula α does not disturb the satisfaction of α by b.

Lemma 1. *Let α be an action formula interpreted over a set of actions A. Then, the hiding set $h_A(\alpha)$ is the maximal set $B \subseteq A$ such that:*

$$b \models_A \alpha \Leftrightarrow hide_B(b) \models_A \alpha$$

for any action $b \in A$.

Proof. We show first that $h_A(\alpha)$ satisfies the statement in the lemma. Let $b \in h_A(\alpha)$. By Definition 3, this means $hide_{h_A(\alpha)}(b) = \tau$. Two cases are possible. If $\tau \models \alpha$, then $h_A(\alpha) = [\![\alpha]\!]_A$ by Definition 2, and therefore $b \models_A \alpha$. If $\tau \not\models \alpha$, then $h_A(\alpha) = A \setminus [\![\alpha]\!]_A$ by Definition 2, and therefore $b \not\models_A \alpha$.

To show the maximality of $h_A(\alpha)$, suppose there exists $b \in A \setminus h_A(\alpha)$ such that $b \models_A \alpha \Leftrightarrow \tau \models_A \alpha$. Two cases are possible, both leading to a contradiction. If $\tau \models \alpha$, then $h_A(\alpha) = [\![\alpha]\!]_A$ by Definition 2, and since $b \notin h_A(\alpha)$, this means $b \not\models \alpha$. If $\tau \not\models \alpha$, then $h_A(\alpha) = A \setminus [\![\alpha]\!]_A$ by Definition 2, and since $b \notin h_A(\alpha)$, this means $b \models \alpha$. □

To enable LTS reductions prior to (or simultaneously with) the verification of a state formula φ, it is desirable to hide as many actions as possible in the LTS, i.e., all actions in $h_A(\varphi)$. The following proposition ensures that this hiding preserves the interpretation of φ.

Proposition 1 (Maximal Hiding). *Let $M = \langle S, A, T, s_0 \rangle$ be an* LTS, *φ be a state formula, and $B \subseteq h_A(\varphi)$. Then:*

$$[\![\varphi]\!]_M \, \rho = [\![\varphi]\!]_{hide_B(M)} \, \rho$$

for any propositional context ρ.

Proof. We proceed by structural induction on φ. We give here the most interesting case $\varphi ::= \langle \alpha \rangle \varphi_1$, the other cases being handled similarly. Since $B \subseteq h_A(\langle \alpha \rangle \varphi_1)$ by hypothesis and $h_A(\langle \alpha \rangle \varphi_1) = h_A(\alpha) \cap h_A(\varphi_1)$ by Definition 2, it follows that $B \subseteq h_A(\alpha)$ and $B \subseteq h_A(\varphi_1)$. Therefore, we can apply the induction hypothesis for φ_1, B and Lemma 1 for α, B, which yields:

$\llbracket \langle \alpha \rangle \varphi_1 \rrbracket_{hide_B(M)} \rho$ = by definition of $\llbracket \ \rrbracket$ and $hide_B(M)$
$\{s \in S \mid \exists s \xrightarrow{hide_B(b)} s'.hide_B(b) \models_A \alpha \wedge$
$\qquad s' \in \llbracket \varphi_1 \rrbracket_{hide_B(M)} \rho\}$ = by induction hyp. and Lemma 1
$\{s \in S \mid \exists s \xrightarrow{b} s'.b \models_A \alpha \wedge s' \in \llbracket \varphi_1 \rrbracket_M \rho\}$ = by definition of $\llbracket \ \rrbracket$
$\llbracket \langle \alpha \rangle \varphi_1 \rrbracket_M \rho$. $\square$

In general, for a given property, there are several μ-calculus formulas φ specifying it, with different hiding sets $h_A(\varphi)$. To take advantage of Proposition 1, one must choose a formula φ with a hiding set as large as possible. Intuitively, in such a *well-specified* formula φ, all action subformulas are relevant for the interpretation of φ on an LTS. For example, the following formula is not well-specified:

$$\varphi = \mu X.(\langle a_1 \rangle \text{ true} \vee (([a_2] \text{ false} \vee \langle a_2 \rangle \text{ true}) \wedge \langle a_3 \rangle X))$$

because its subformula $[a_2]$ false $\vee \langle a_2 \rangle$ true is a tautology and could be deleted from φ without changing its meaning. The presence of this subformula yields the hiding set $h_A(\varphi) = A \setminus \{a_1, a_2, a_3\}$, whereas deleting it yields a larger hiding set $h_A(\varphi) = A \setminus \{a_1, a_3\}$. We do not attempt here to check well-specifiedness automatically, and will assume below that state formulas are well-specified.

For instance, consider the L_μ^{reg} formula below, expressing the inevitable reachability of a *recv* action after every *send* action:

$$\varphi = [\text{true}^*.send] \, \mu X.(\neg deadlock \wedge [\neg recv] \, X)$$

When checking φ on an LTS, one can hide all actions in $h_A(\varphi) = h_A(send) \cap h_A(\neg recv) = (A \setminus \llbracket send \rrbracket_A) \cap \llbracket \neg recv \rrbracket_A = (A \setminus \{send\}) \cap (A \setminus \{recv\}) = A \setminus \{send, recv\}$, i.e., all actions other than *send* and *recv*, without changing the interpretation of the formula.

4   Mu-Calculus Fragment Compatible with $\approx_{br}^{ds}$

When minimizing an LTS modulo a weak bisimulation relation, such as $\approx_{br}^{ds}$ [15], the degree of reduction achieved is often directly proportional to the percentage of τ-transitions contained in the original LTS. Therefore, Proposition 1 provides, for a given L_μ formula, the highest potential for reduction, by enabling as many actions as possible to be hidden in the LTS. However, this proposition does not indicate which L_μ formulas are *compatible* with $\approx_{br}^{ds}$, i.e., are preserved by reduction modulo this relation. We propose below a fragment of L_μ satisfying this property.

4.1 Mu-Calculus Fragment L_μ^{dsbr}

The L_μ fragment we consider here, called L_μ^{dsbr}, is defined in Figure 3. Compared to standard L_μ, this fragment differs in two respects.

(1) It introduces two new weak operators $\langle(\varphi_1?.\alpha_1)^*\rangle\,\psi$ and $\langle\varphi_1?.\alpha_1\rangle\,@$ expressed in PDL-Δ, where the action formulas α_1 must capture the invisible action. The weak possibility modality $\langle(\varphi_1?.\alpha_1)^*\rangle\,\psi$ characterizes the states having an outgoing sequence of (0 or more) α_1-transitions whose intermediate states satisfy φ_1 and whose terminal state satisfies ψ. The weak infinite looping operator $\langle\varphi_1?.\alpha_1\rangle\,@$ characterizes the states having an infinite outgoing sequence of α_1-transitions whose intermediate states satisfy φ_1. When the φ_1 subformula occurring in a weak operator is true, it can be omitted, because in this case the operator becomes $\langle\alpha_1^*\rangle\,\psi$ or $\langle\alpha_1\rangle\,@$.

(2) The occurrence of strong modalities $\langle\alpha_2\rangle\,\varphi$ and $[\alpha_2]\,\varphi$ is restricted syntactically such that these modalities must contain action formulas α_2 denoting visible actions only, and that they can appear only after a weak possibility modality $\langle(\varphi_1?.\alpha_1)^*\rangle$ or weak necessity modality $[(\varphi_1?.\alpha_1)^*]$. The intuition is that visible transitions matched by a strong modality will remain in the LTS after maximal hiding and $\approx_{br}^{ds}$ minimization, and the transition sequences preceding them can become invisible or even disappear in the minimized LTS without affecting the interpretation of the formula, because these sequences are still captured by the weak modality immediately preceding the current strong modality.

The deadlock formula defined in Section 2 belongs to L_μ^{dsbr}, since it can be rewritten as follows by eliminating the concatenation operator:

$$deadlock = [\mathsf{true}^*.\neg\tau]\,\mathsf{false} \wedge [\tau]\,\dashv = [\mathsf{true}^*]\,[\neg\tau]\,\mathsf{false} \wedge [\tau]\,\dashv$$

The response formula given in Section 3 can also be reformulated in L_μ^{dsbr}:

$$[\mathsf{true}^*.send]\,\mu X.(\neg deadlock \wedge [\neg recv]\,X) =$$
$$[\mathsf{true}^*]\,[send]\,([(\neg recv)^*]\,\neg deadlock \wedge [\neg recv]\,\dashv)$$

The subformula stating the inevitable reachability of a *recv* action, initially expressed using a minimal fixed point operator, was replaced by the conjunction of a weak necessity modality forbidding the occurrence of deadlocks before a *recv*

$\varphi ::= \langle(\varphi_1?.\alpha_1)^*\rangle\,\psi \mid \langle\varphi_1?.\alpha_1\rangle\,@ \mid \mathsf{false} \mid \neg\varphi_1 \mid \varphi_1 \vee \varphi_2 \mid X \mid \mu X.\varphi_1$

$\psi ::= \varphi \mid \langle\alpha_2\rangle\,\varphi \mid \neg\psi_1 \mid \psi_1 \vee \psi_2$

where $\tau \in [\![\alpha_1]\!]_A$ and $\tau \notin [\![\alpha_2]\!]_A$

$[\![\langle(\varphi_1?.\alpha_1)^*\rangle\,\psi]\!]_M\,\rho = \{s \in S \mid \exists m \geq 0.s = s_0 \wedge (\forall 0 \leq i < m.s_i \overset{b_{i+1}}{\to} s_{i+1} \in T$
$\wedge\ b_{i+1} \in [\![\alpha_1]\!]_A \wedge\ s_i \in [\![\varphi_1]\!]_M\,\rho) \wedge\ s_m \in [\![\psi]\!]_M\,\rho\}$

$[\![\langle\varphi_1?.\alpha_1\rangle\,@]\!]_M\,\rho = \{s \in S \mid s = s_0 \wedge \forall i \geq 0.(s_i \overset{b_{i+1}}{\to} s_{i+1} \in T \wedge b_{i+1} \in [\![\alpha]\!]_A$
$\wedge\ s_i \in [\![\varphi_1]\!]_M\,\rho)\}$

Fig. 3. Syntax and semantics of the L_μ^{dsbr} fragment

action has been reached, and a weak saturation operator forbidding the presence
of cycles not passing through a *recv* action.

In [14, Corollary 4.4], it was shown that $\approx_{br}^{ds}$ is an equivalence with the so-called *stuttering property*:

Definition 4 (Stuttering). *Let* $M = \langle S, A, T, s_0 \rangle$ *be an* LTS *and let* $s_1, s_2 \in S$
such that $s_1 \approx_{br}^{ds} s_2$. *If* $s_1 \xrightarrow{\tau} s_1^1 \xrightarrow{\tau} \cdots \xrightarrow{\tau} s_1^m \xrightarrow{\tau} s_1'$ ($m \geq 0$) *and* $s_1' \approx_{br}^{ds} s_2$, *then*
$\forall 1 \leq i \leq m.s_1^i \approx_{br}^{ds} s_2$.

Using the stuttering property, we can prove the following lemma.

Lemma 2. *Let* $M = \langle S, A, T, s_0 \rangle$ *be an* LTS *and let* $A' \subseteq A$ *with* $\tau \in A'$ *and*
$s_1, s_2 \in S$ *such that* $s_1 \approx_{br}^{ds} s_2$. *Then for all* $m \geq 0$ *with* $s_1 = s_1^0$ *and* $\forall 0 \leq
i < m.s_1^i \xrightarrow{b_i} s_1^{i+1} \in T$ ($b_i \in A'$), *there exists* $k \geq 0$ *such that* $s_2 = s_2^0$ *and*
$\forall 0 \leq j < k.(s_2^j \xrightarrow{b_j'} s_2^{j+1} \in T$ ($b_j' \in A'$) $\wedge \exists 0 \leq i < m.s_1^i \approx_{br}^{ds} s_2^j$), *and* $s_1^m \approx_{br}^{ds} s_2^k$.

Proof. We proceed by induction on m.

1. *Base case:* $m = 0$, hence $s_1 = s_1^0 = s_1^m$. Clearly, we can choose $k = 0$ and $s_2 = s_2^0 = s_2^k$.
2. *Inductive case:* $s_1^0 \xrightarrow{b_1} s_1^1 \cdots s_1^{m-1} \xrightarrow{b_m} s_1^m \xrightarrow{b_{m+1}} s_1^{m+1}$. By the induction hypothesis, there exists $k \geq 0$ such that $s_2 = s_2^0$ and $\forall 0 \leq j < k.(s_2^j \xrightarrow{b_j'} s_2^{j+1} \in T$ ($b_j' \in A'$) $\wedge \exists 0 \leq i < m.s_1^i \approx_{br}^{ds} s_2^j$), and $s_1^m \approx_{br}^{ds} s_2^k$. We show that it also holds for $m + 1$. We distinguish two cases for $s_1^m \xrightarrow{b_{m+1}} s_1^{m+1}$:
   (a) $b_{m+1} = \tau$. Since $s_1^m \approx_{br}^{ds} s_2^k$, by Definition 1, also $s_1^{m+1} \approx_{br}^{ds} s_2^k$.
   (b) $b_{m+1} \neq \tau$. Since $s_1^m \approx_{br}^{ds} s_2^k$, by Definition 1, $s_2^k \Rightarrow \hat{s}_2 \xrightarrow{b_{m+1}} s_2'$, with $s_1^m \approx_{br}^{ds} \hat{s}_2$, and $s_1^{m+1} \approx_{br}^{ds} s_2'$. Say that $s_2^k \Rightarrow \hat{s}_2$ consists of c τ-steps $s_2^k \xrightarrow{\tau_1} s_2^{k+1} \cdots s_2^{k+c-1} \xrightarrow{\tau_c} s_2^{k+c}$ with $s_2^{k+c} = \hat{s}_2$. By Definition 4, for all $k \leq i \leq k+c$, we have $s_1^m \approx_{br}^{ds} s_2^i$. Hence, there exists a matching sequence from s_2 of length $k + c + 1$ with $s_2^{k+c+1} = s_2'$. Note that $\tau_1, \ldots, \tau_c \in A'$. $\qquad\square$

A propositional context $\rho : \mathcal{X} \to 2^S$ is said to be $\approx_{br}^{ds}$-*closed* if for all states
$s_1, s_2 \in S$ such that $s_1 \approx_{br}^{ds} s_2$ and for any propositional variable $X \in \mathcal{X}$,
$s_1 \in \rho(X) \Leftrightarrow s_2 \in \rho(X)$. Now we can state the main result about L_μ^{dsbr}, namely
that this fragment is compatible with the $\approx_{br}^{ds}$ relation.

Proposition 2 (Compatibility with $\approx_{br}^{ds}$). *Let* $M = \langle S, A, T, s_0 \rangle$ *be an* LTS
and let $s_1, s_2 \in S$ *such that* $s_1 \approx_{br}^{ds} s_2$. *Then:*

$$s_1 \in \llbracket \varphi \rrbracket_M \rho \Leftrightarrow s_2 \in \llbracket \varphi \rrbracket_M \rho$$

for any state formula φ *of* L_μ^{dsbr} *and any* $\approx_{br}^{ds}$-*closed propositional context* ρ.

Proof. We proceed by structural induction on φ. We give here the most interesting cases, the other being handled similarly.

Case $\varphi ::= \langle (\varphi_1?.\alpha_1)^* \rangle \, \psi$. Let $s_1, s_2 \in S$ such that $s_1 \approx_{br}^{ds} s_2$ and assume that $s_1 \in [\![\langle (\varphi_1?.\alpha_1)^* \rangle \, \psi]\!]_M \, \rho$, i.e., $s_1 \in \{ s \in S \mid \exists m \geq 0.s = s_0 \land (\forall 0 \leq i < m.s_i \overset{b_{i+1}}{\to} s_{i+1} \in T \land b_{i+1} \in [\![\alpha_1]\!]_A \land \ s_i \in [\![\varphi_1]\!]_M \, \rho) \land \ s_m \in [\![\psi]\!]_M \, \rho \}$. This means that:

$$\exists m \geq 0.s_1 = s_0' \ \land \ (\forall 0 \leq i < m.s_i' \overset{b_{i+1}}{\to} s_{i+1}' \in T \tag{1}$$
$$\land \ b_{i+1} \in [\![\alpha_1]\!]_A \land \ s_i' \in [\![\varphi_1]\!]_M \, \rho) \land \ s_m' \in [\![\psi]\!]_M \, \rho \}$$

We have to prove that $s_2 \in [\![\langle (\varphi_1?.\alpha_1)^* \rangle \, \psi]\!]_M \, \rho$, which means that:

$$\exists k \geq 0.s_2 = s_0'' \ \land \ (\forall 0 \leq j < k.s_i'' \overset{b_{j+1}'}{\to} s_{i+1}'' \in T \tag{2}$$
$$\land \ b_{j+1}' \in [\![\alpha_1]\!]_A \land \ s_i'' \in [\![\varphi_1]\!]_M \, \rho) \land \ s_k'' \in [\![\psi]\!]_M \, \rho \}$$

First, since $s_1 \approx_{br}^{ds} s_2$, $\tau \in [\![\alpha_1]\!]_A$, and (1), by Lemma 2 with $A' = [\![\alpha_1]\!]_A$, there exists $k \geq 0$ with $s_2 = s_0''$ such that $\forall 0 \leq j < k.(s_j'' \overset{b_{j+1}'}{\to} s_{j+1}'' \in T (b_{j+1}' \in [\![\alpha_1]\!]_A) \land \exists 0 \leq i < m.s_i' \approx_{br}^{ds} s_j'')$ and $s_m' \approx_{br}^{ds} s_k''$. Furthermore, for all $0 \leq j < k$, since there exists $0 \leq i < m.s_i' \approx_{br}^{ds} s_j''$ and $s_i' \in [\![\varphi_1]\!]_M \, \rho$, by the induction hypothesis, it follows that $s_j'' \in [\![\varphi_1]\!]_M \, \rho$. Finally, since $s_m' \approx_{br}^{ds} s_k''$ and $s_m' \in [\![\psi]\!]_M \, \rho$, we will show that $s_k'' \in [\![\psi]\!]_M \, \rho$ by induction on the structure of ψ. First, we can assume that there is no $\hat{s}'' \in S$ such that $s_k'' \overset{\tau}{\to} \hat{s}'' \in T$. If this is not true, since $\tau \in [\![\alpha_1]\!]_A$, we can choose $s_{k+1}'' = \hat{s}''$ and increase k by one. This can be repeated until there is no $\hat{s}'' \in S$ such that $s_k'' \overset{\tau}{\to} \hat{s}'' \in T$. For ψ, we distinguish four cases:

- $\psi ::= \varphi$. By the induction hypothesis, $s_k'' \in [\![\psi]\!]_M \, \rho$.
- $\psi ::= \langle \alpha_2 \rangle \, \varphi$. Since $s_m' \in [\![\langle \alpha_2 \rangle \, \varphi]\!]_M \, \rho$, we have $s_m' \in \{ s \in S \mid \exists s \overset{a}{\to} s' \in T.a \in [\![\alpha_2]\!]_A \land \ s' \in [\![\varphi]\!]_M \, \rho \}$, hence there exists $s_m' \overset{a}{\to} s' \in T$ with $a \in [\![\alpha_2]\!]_A$. Since $s_m' \approx_{br}^{ds} s_k''$, $\tau \notin [\![\alpha_2]\!]_A$, and $s_k'' \overset{\tau}{\to} \hat{s}'' \notin T$, by Definition 1, there must exist $s_k'' \overset{a}{\to} \hat{s}'' \in T$ with $s' \approx_{br}^{ds} \hat{s}''$. Since $s' \in [\![\varphi]\!]_M \, \rho$, by the induction hypothesis, $\hat{s}'' \in [\![\varphi]\!]_M \, \rho$, hence $s_k'' \in \{ s \in S \mid \exists s \overset{a}{\to} s' \in T.a \in [\![\alpha_2]\!]_A \land \ s' \in [\![\varphi]\!]_M \, \rho \}$, i.e., $s_k'' \in [\![\psi]\!]_M \, \rho$.
- $\psi ::= \neg \psi_1$. Since $s_m' \in [\![\neg \psi_1]\!]_M \, \rho$, we have $s_m' \in S \setminus [\![\psi_1]\!]_M \, \rho$. By the induction hypothesis for ψ, also $s_k'' \in S \setminus [\![\psi_1]\!]_M \, \rho$, hence $s_k'' \in [\![\neg \psi_1]\!]_M \, \rho$.
- $\psi ::= \psi_1 \lor \psi_2$. Since $s_m' \in [\![\psi_1 \lor \psi_2]\!]_M \, \rho$, i.e., $s_m' \in [\![\psi_1]\!]_M \, \rho \cup [\![\psi_2]\!]_M \, \rho$, i.e., $s_m' \in [\![\psi_1]\!]_M \, \rho \lor s_m' \in [\![\psi_2]\!]_M \, \rho$, by the induction hypothesis for ψ, we have $s_k'' \in [\![\psi_1]\!]_M \, \rho \lor s_k'' \in [\![\psi_2]\!]_M \, \rho$, i.e., $s_k'' \in [\![\psi_1]\!]_M \, \rho \cup [\![\psi_2]\!]_M \, \rho$, i.e., $s_k'' \in [\![\psi_1 \lor \psi_2]\!]_M \, \rho$.

Hence, (2) holds. The converse implication (by considering $s_2 \in [\![\langle (\varphi_1?.\alpha_1)^* \rangle \, \psi]\!]_M \, \rho$) holds by a symmetric argument.

Case $\varphi ::= \langle \varphi_1?.\alpha_1 \rangle @$. Let $s_1, s_2 \in S$ such that $s_1 \approx_{br}^{ds} s_2$ and assume that $s_1 \in [\![\langle \varphi_1?.\alpha_1 \rangle @]\!]_M \, \rho$, i.e., $s_1 \in \{ s \in S \mid s = s_0 \land \forall i \geq 0.(s_i \overset{b_i}{\to} s_{i+1} \land b_i \in [\![\alpha_1]\!]_A \land \ s_i \in [\![\varphi_1]\!]_M \, \rho) \}$. This means that:

$$s_1 = s_0' \land \forall i \geq 0.(s_i' \overset{b_i}{\to} s_{i+1}' \land b_i \in [\![\alpha_1]\!]_A \land \ s_i' \in [\![\varphi_1]\!]_M \, \rho) \tag{3}$$

We have to prove that $s_2 \in [\![\langle \varphi_1?.\alpha_1 \rangle @]\!]_M \rho$, which means that:

$$s_2 = s_0'' \wedge \forall j \geq 0.(s_j'' \xrightarrow{b_j'} s_{j+1}'' \wedge b_j' \in [\![\alpha_1]\!]_A \wedge s_j'' \in [\![\varphi_1]\!]_M \rho) \qquad (4)$$

Since $s_1 \approx_{br}^{ds} s_2$, $\tau \in [\![\alpha_1]\!]_A$, and (3), by Lemma 2 with $A' = [\![\alpha_1]\!]_A$, for any finite prefix of length $m \geq 0$ of the infinite path π from s_1, there exists a finite path of length $k \geq 0$ from s_2 such that $s_2 = s_0'' \wedge \forall 0 \leq j < k.(s_j'' \xrightarrow{b_j'} s_{j+1}'' \wedge b_j' \in [\![\alpha_1]\!]_A \wedge \exists 0 \leq i < m.s_i' \approx_{br}^{ds} s_j'')$ and $s_m' \approx_{br}^{ds} s_k''$, hence, by the induction hypothesis, for all $0 \leq j \leq k$, we have $s_j'' \in [\![\varphi_1]\!]_M \rho$. We distinguish two cases:

1. π contains an infinite number of transitions with a label in $[\![\alpha_1]\!]_A \setminus \{\tau\}$. Repeatedly applying the above reasoning for intermediate states in π yields that (4) holds for s_2.
2. π contains a finite number of transitions with a label in $[\![\alpha_1]\!]_A \setminus \{\tau\}$. Then, there exists an $\hat{s}$ reachable from s_1 such that from $\hat{s}$, an infinite τ-path exists. By the earlier reasoning, there exists an $\hat{s}'$ reachable from s_2 such that $\hat{s} \approx_{br}^{ds} \hat{s}'$ and for all states s_j'' in the path from s_2 to $\hat{s}'$, we have $s_j'' \in [\![\varphi_1]\!]_M \rho$. Finally, since $\hat{s} \approx_{br}^{ds} \hat{s}'$, by the second clause of Definition 1, there also exists an infinite τ-path π' from $\hat{s}'$. Finally, by Definition 1 and repeated application of Definition 4, it follows that for all states s_j'' in π', $\hat{s} \approx_{br}^{ds} s_j''$, hence by the induction hypothesis, $s_j'' \in [\![\varphi_1]\!]_M \rho$. Therefore, (4) holds for s_2.

The converse implication (by considering $s_2 \in [\![\langle \varphi_1?.\alpha_1 \rangle @]\!]_M \rho$) holds by a symmetric argument.   □

Proposition 2 makes it possible to reduce an LTS (after applying maximal hiding) modulo $\approx_{br}^{ds}$ before the verification of a closed L_μ^{dsbr} formula. It follows that L_μ^{dsbr} is also compatible with all equivalence relations weaker than $\approx_{br}^{ds}$, such as $\tau^*.a$ [10] and weak [25] bisimulations. For practical purposes, it is desirable to use a temporal logic sufficiently expressive to capture the essential classes of properties (safety, liveness, fairness). Thus, the question is whether L_μ^{dsbr} subsumes the existing temporal logics compatible with $\tau^*.a$ and weak bisimulations; in Subsections 4.2 and 4.3, we show that this is indeed the case.

4.2   Subsuming μACTL\X

ACTL [26] is a branching-time logic similar to CTL [4], but interpreted on LTSs. It consists of action formulas (noted α) and state formulas (noted φ) expressing properties about actions and states of an LTS, respectively. The temporal operators of ACTL\X (the fragment of the logic without the next-time operators) are defined in Table 1 by means of their encodings in L_μ proposed in [9]. The operator $\mathsf{E}[\varphi_1{}_\alpha \mathsf{U}\varphi_2]$ (resp. $\mathsf{A}[\varphi_1{}_\alpha \mathsf{U}\varphi_2]$) denotes the states from which some (resp. all) outgoing sequences lead, after 0 or more α-transitions (or τ-transitions) whose source states satisfy φ_1, to a state satisfying φ_2. The operator $\mathsf{E}[\varphi_1{}_{\alpha_1} \mathsf{U}_{\alpha_2}\varphi_2]$ (resp. $\mathsf{A}[\varphi_1{}_{\alpha_1} \mathsf{U}_{\alpha_2}\varphi_2]$) denotes the states from which some (resp. all) outgoing

Table 1. Syntax and semantics of the ACTL\X temporal operators

Operator	Translation
$\mathsf{E}[\varphi_{1\ \alpha}\mathsf{U}\varphi_2]$	$\mu X.(\varphi_2 \vee (\varphi_1 \wedge \langle \alpha \vee \tau \rangle X))$
$\mathsf{E}[\varphi_{1\ \alpha_1}\mathsf{U}_{\alpha_2}\varphi_2]$	$\mu X.(\varphi_1 \wedge (\langle \alpha_2 \rangle \varphi_2 \vee \langle \alpha_1 \vee \tau \rangle X))$
$\mathsf{A}[\varphi_{1\ \alpha}\mathsf{U}\varphi_2]$	$\mu X.(\varphi_2 \vee (\varphi_1 \wedge \neg deadlock \wedge [\neg(\alpha \vee \tau)]\,\mathsf{false} \wedge [\alpha \vee \tau]\,X))$
$\mathsf{A}[\varphi_{1\ \alpha_1}\mathsf{U}_{\alpha_2}\varphi_2]$	$\mu X.(\varphi_1 \wedge \neg deadlock \wedge [\neg(\alpha_1 \vee \alpha_2 \vee \tau)]\,\mathsf{false} \wedge [\alpha_2 \wedge \neg\alpha_1]\,\varphi_2 \wedge$ $[\alpha_1 \wedge \alpha_2]\,(\varphi_2 \vee X) \wedge [\neg\alpha_2]\,X)$

sequences lead, after 0 or more α_1-transitions (or τ-transitions) whose source states satisfy φ_1, to an α_2-transition whose source state satisfies φ_1 and whose target state satisfies φ_2. The action subformulas α, α_1, and α_2 denote visible actions only.

ACTL\X was shown to be adequate with $\approx_{br}^{ds}$ [26]. Moreover, this logic was extended in [9] with fixed point operators, yielding a fragment of L_μ called μACTL\X, which is still adequate with $\approx_{br}^{ds}$. The temporal operators of ACTL\X can be translated in L_μ^{dsbr}, as stated by the following proposition.

Proposition 3 (Translation from ACTL\X to $\mathbf{L}_\mu^{dsbr}$). *The following identities relating formulas of L_μ and formulas of L_μ^{dsbr} hold:*

$$\mu X.(\varphi_2 \vee (\varphi_1 \wedge \langle \alpha \vee \tau \rangle X)) = \langle (\varphi_1?.\alpha \vee \tau)^* \rangle\,\varphi_2$$

$$\mu X.(\varphi_1 \wedge (\langle \alpha_2 \rangle\,\varphi_2 \vee \langle \alpha_1 \vee \tau \rangle X)) = \langle (\varphi_1?.\alpha \vee \tau)^* \rangle\,(\varphi_1 \wedge \langle \alpha_2 \rangle\,\varphi_2)$$

$$\mu X.(\varphi_2 \vee (\varphi_1 \wedge \neg deadlock \wedge [\neg(\alpha \vee \tau)]\,\mathsf{false} \wedge [\alpha \vee \tau]\,X)) =$$
$$[(\neg\varphi_2?.\alpha \vee \tau)^*]\,(\varphi_2 \vee (\varphi_1 \wedge \neg deadlock \wedge [\neg(\alpha \vee \tau)]\,\mathsf{false})) \wedge [\neg\varphi_2?.\alpha \vee \tau]\,\dashv$$

$$\mu X.(\varphi_1 \wedge \neg deadlock \wedge [\neg(\alpha_1 \vee \alpha_2 \vee \tau)]\,\mathsf{false} \wedge [\alpha_2 \wedge \neg\alpha_1]\,\varphi_2 \wedge$$
$$[\alpha_1 \wedge \alpha_2]\,(\varphi_2 \vee X) \wedge [\neg\alpha_2]\,X) =$$
$$\nu X.\,[(\neg\alpha_2)^*]\,(\varphi_1 \wedge \neg deadlock \wedge [\neg(\alpha_1 \vee \alpha_2 \vee \tau)]\,\mathsf{false} \wedge [\alpha_2 \wedge \neg\alpha_1]\,\varphi_2 \wedge$$
$$[\alpha_1 \wedge \alpha_2]\,(\varphi_2 \vee X) \wedge X) \wedge$$
$$\nu X.([\neg\alpha_2]\,\dashv \wedge [(\neg\alpha_2)^*]\,[\alpha_1 \wedge \alpha_2]\,(\varphi_2 \vee X)) \wedge \mu X.\,[(\neg\alpha_2)^*]\,[\alpha_1 \wedge \alpha_2]\,(\varphi_2 \vee X).$$

Proposition 3 also ensures that μACTL\X is subsumed by L_μ^{dsbr}, since the fixed point operators are present in both logics. The L_μ^{dsbr} formulas corresponding to the $\mathsf{A}[\varphi_{1\ \alpha_1}\mathsf{U}\varphi_2]$ and $\mathsf{A}[\varphi_{1\ \alpha_1}\mathsf{U}_{\alpha_2}\varphi_2]$ operators are complex, and they serve solely for the purpose of establishing the translation to L_μ^{dsbr}. In practice, we will use the simpler L_μ encodings of the ACTL\X operators given in Table 1.

The response formula given in Section 3 can also be expressed in ACTL\X:

$$\mathsf{AG}_{\mathsf{true},send}\mathsf{A}[\mathsf{true}_{\mathsf{true}}\mathsf{U}_{recv}\mathsf{true}]$$

where $\mathsf{AG}_{\alpha_1,\alpha_2}\varphi = \neg\mathsf{EF}_{\alpha_1,\alpha_2}\neg\varphi = \neg\mathsf{E}[\mathsf{true}_{\alpha_1}\mathsf{U}_{\alpha_2}\neg\varphi]$ is the ACTL counterpart of the AG operator of CTL.

Finally, we claim that L_μ^{dsbr} is more powerful than μACTL\X. Indeed, the formula $\langle (\neg a)^* \rangle\,(\langle b \rangle\,\mathsf{true} \wedge \langle c \rangle\,\mathsf{true})$ does not seem to be expressible in μACTL\X because the occurrences of strong modalities expressing the existence of neighbor b- and c-transitions cannot be coupled individually with the preceding weak modality in order to use only the four temporal operators given in Table 1.

4.3   Subsuming Selective and Weak μ-Calculus

The selective μ-calculus [3] introduces modalities indexed by sets of actions (represented here as action formulas) specifying the reachability of certain actions after sequences of (0 or more) actions not belonging to the indexing set. The selective possibility modality can be encoded in L_μ^{dsbr} as follows:

$$\langle \alpha_1 \rangle_\alpha \, \varphi = \langle (\neg(\alpha_1 \vee \alpha))^* \rangle \langle \alpha_1 \rangle \, \varphi$$

where α, α_1 denote visible actions only. Selective μ-calculus is adequate w.r.t. the $\tau^*.a$ bisimulation: for each selective formula φ, one can hide all LTS actions other than those occurring in the modalities of φ and their index sets, and then minimize the LTS modulo $\tau^*.a$ without changing the interpretation of φ.

Selective μ-calculus was shown to be equivalent to L_μ, because the strong possibility modality of L_μ can be expressed in terms of the selective one: $\langle \alpha \rangle \, \varphi = \langle \alpha \rangle_{\text{true}} \, \varphi$. However, this way of translating would yield no possibility of hiding actions, because the index sets would contain all actions of the LTS. For instance, the response formula given in Section 3 can be reformulated in selective μ-calculus as follows:

$$[send]_{\text{false}} \, \mu X.(\langle \text{true} \rangle_{\text{true}} \, \text{true} \wedge [\neg recv]_{\text{true}} \, X)$$

The minimal fixed point subformula expressing the inevitable reachability of a $recv$ action cannot be mapped to selective μ-calculus modalities, which forces the use of strong modalities (represented by selective modalities indexed by true). Therefore, the set of actions that can be hidden according to [3] without disturbing the interpretation of this formula is $A \setminus (\{ send, recv \} \cup A) = \emptyset$, i.e., no hiding of actions prior to verification would be possible in that setting.

The weak (or observational) μ-calculus [28] is a fragment of L_μ adequate w.r.t. weak bisimulation. It introduces weak modalities specifying the reachability of certain actions preceded and followed by 0 or more τ-transitions. These weak modalities can be encoded in L_μ^{dsbr} as follows:

$$\langle\langle \alpha \rangle\rangle \, \varphi = \langle \tau^* \rangle \langle \alpha \rangle \langle \tau^* \rangle \, \varphi \qquad \langle\langle \rangle\rangle \, \varphi = \langle \tau^* \rangle \, \varphi$$

where α denotes visible actions only. The weak μ-calculus is able to express only weak safety and liveness properties; in particular, it does not capture the inevitable reachability of $recv$ actions present in the example above.

5   Implementation and Experiments

We have implemented the maximal hiding and associated on-the-fly reduction machinery within the CADP verification toolbox [13]. We experimented on the effect of these optimizations on the EVALUATOR [21,22] model checker, which evaluates formulas of the alternation-free fragment of L_μ^{reg} on LTSs on-the-fly. The tool works by first translating the L_μ^{reg} formulas into plain L_μ by eliminating the PDL regular operators, and then reformulating the verification problem as the resolution of a Boolean equation system (BES) [1], which is solved locally using the algorithms of the CÆSAR_SOLVE library [20] of CADP. EVALUATOR makes possible the definition of reusable libraries of derived operators (e.g., those of ACTL) and property patterns (e.g., the pattern system of [8]).

For the sake of efficiency, we focus on L_μ^{dsbr} formulas having a linear-time model checking complexity, namely the alternation-free fragment [6] extended with the infinite looping and saturation operators of PDL-Δ [29], which can be evaluated in linear time using the algorithms proposed in [22]. In the formulas below, we use the operators of PDL and ACTL\X, and the L_μ^{dsbr} formula $inev(a) = [(\neg a)^*] \neg deadlock \wedge [\neg a] \dashv$ as a shorthand for expressing the inevitable execution of an action a. For each verification experiment, we applied maximal hiding as stated in Proposition 1, and then carried out LTS reductions either prior to, or simultaneously with, the verification of the formula.

Strong bisimulation reduction. We considered first global verification, which consists in generating the LTS, applying maximal hiding, minimizing the LTS modulo strong bisimulation, and then verifying the properties on the minimized LTS. LTSs are represented as files in the compact BCG (*Binary Coded Graphs*) format of CADP. Hiding and minimization were carried out using the BCG_LABELS and BCG_MIN tools [7], the whole process being automated using SVL [12] scripts.

We considered a token ring leader election protocol, implemented in LOTOS (experiment 6 in demo 17 of CADP), and checked the following property, stating that each station i on the ring accesses a shared resource (actions $open_i$ and $close_i$) in mutual exclusion with the other stations and each access is reachable (modulo the divergences due to unreliable communication channels):

$$[\text{true}^*] ([open_i.(\neg close_i)^*.open_j]\text{false} \wedge \mathsf{A}[\text{true}_{\text{true}}\mathsf{U}\langle(\langle\text{true}^*.open_i\rangle \text{true})?.\tau\rangle @])$$

This formula belongs to L_μ^{dsbr} (after eliminating the concatenation operators and expanding the A[U] operator) and allows hiding of every action other than *open* and *close*. The "$\langle...\rangle$ @" subformula of A[U] expresses the existence of infinite τ-sequences whose intermediate states enable the potential reachability of an $open_i$ action.

The overall time and peak memory needed for verification are shown in Figure 4 for increasingly larger configurations of the protocol. When strong bisimulation minimization is carried out before verification, we observe gains both in speedup and memory (factors 2.8 and 2.5 for the LTS corresponding to 7 stations, having $53,848,492$ states and $214,528,176$ transitions), which become larger with the size of the LTS.

Divergence-sensitive branching bisimulation reduction. To study the effect of $\approx_{br}^{ds}$ minimization, we considered Philips' Bounded Retransmission Protocol, implemented in LOTOS (demo 16 of CADP), and checked the following response property, expressing that every emission of a data chunk from a packet is eventually

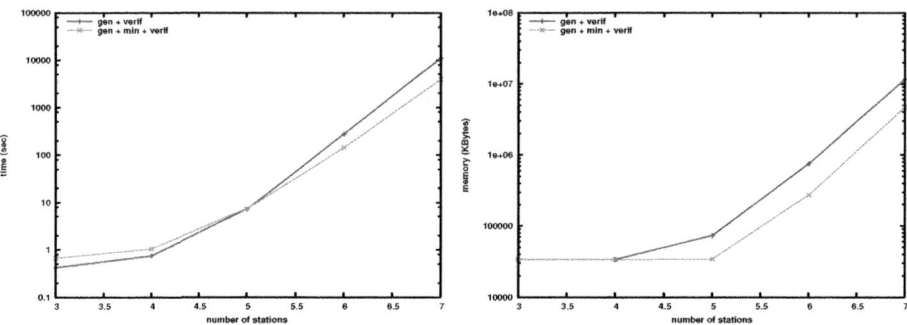

Fig. 4. Effect of strong bisimulation minimization (Token Ring Protocol)

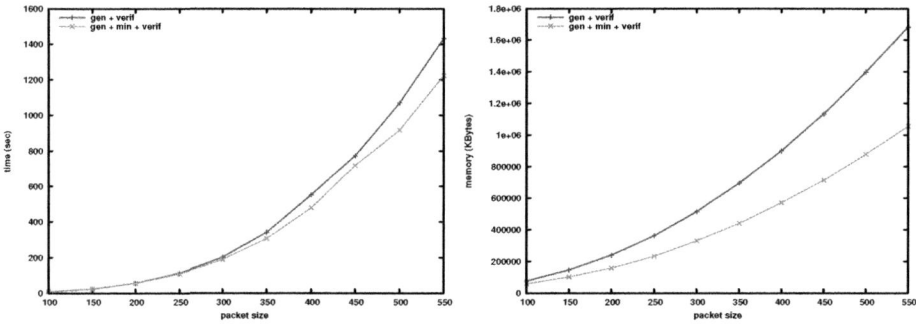

Fig. 5. Effect of $\approx_{br}^{ds}$ minimization (Bounded Retransmission Protocol)

followed by the reception of a confirmation:

$$[\text{true}^*.in\_data]\, \mathsf{A}[\text{true}_{\neg in\_data}\, \mathsf{U}_{in\_conf}\, \text{true}]$$

This formula belongs to L_μ^{dsbr} (after eliminating the concatenation operator and expanding the $\mathsf{A}[\mathsf{U}]$ operator) and allows hiding of every action other than in_data and in_conf.

The overall time and peak memory needed for verification are shown in Figure 5 for increasingly larger configurations of the protocol. For this example, the presence of $\approx_{br}^{ds}$ bisimulation minimization yields mainly memory reductions (factor 1.6 for the LTS corresponding to data packets of length 550 and two retransmissions, having $12, 450, 383$ states and $14, 880, 828$ transitions).

On-the-fly τ-confluence reduction. Lastly, we examined the effect of τ-confluence reduction [16] carried out on-the-fly during the verification of formulas. This reduction, which preserves branching bisimulation, consists in identifying confluent τ-transitions (i.e., whose execution does not alter the observable behavior of the system), and giving them priority over their neighbors during the LTS traversal. The detection of confluent τ-transitions is done on-the-fly by reformulating the

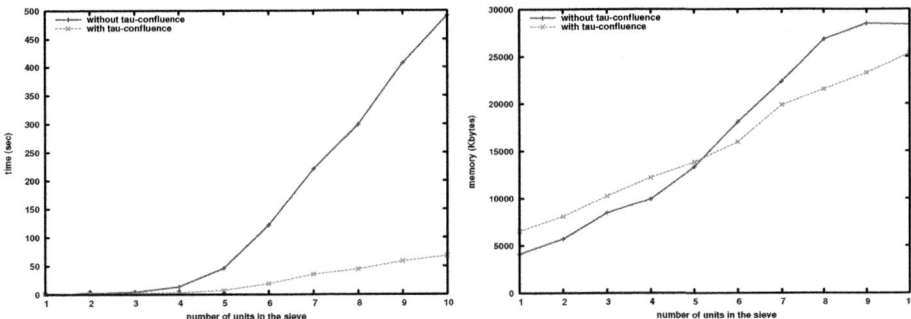

Fig. 6. Effect of on-the-fly τ-confluence reduction (Erathostene's sieve)

problem as a BES resolution [27,23], which is performed locally using the algorithms of CÆSAR_SOLVE. In order to make the reduction compatible with $\approx_{br}^{ds}$, we enhanced the τ-confluence detection with the bookkeeping of divergence, by exploiting the τ-cycle compression algorithm proposed in [19].

We considered the distributed version of Erathosthene's sieve, implemented using LOTOS processes and EXP networks of automata (demo 36 of CADP). We checked the following formula, expressing that each prime number p fed as input to the sieve will be eventually delivered as output and each non-prime number q will be filtered:

$$[\mathsf{true}^*]\,([gen_p]inev(output_p) \wedge [gen_q.\mathsf{true}^*.\neg output_q]\mathsf{false})$$

This formula belongs to L_μ^{dsbr} (after eliminating the concatenation operators) and allows hiding of every action other than gen and $output$.

The overall time and peak memory needed for verification are shown in Figure 6 for increasingly larger configurations of the sieve. We observe a substantial increase in speed in the presence of τ-confluence reduction (about one order of magnitude for a sieve with 10 units). The reduction in memory usage becomes apparent once the size of the system becomes sufficiently large, such that the memory overhead induced by the presence of the on-the-fly reduction machinery is compensated by the memory required for verifying the formula.

6   Conclusion and Future Work

We have presented two automatic techniques to improve the effectiveness of LTS reductions, both before and during system verification. The first technique involves maximal hiding of LTSs based on given L_μ formulas, such that the LTSs can be minimized modulo strong bisimulation. This technique is not intrusive, meaning that the user is not forced to write formulas in a specific way. In the second technique, formulas written in a specific fragment of L_μ, called L_μ^{dsbr}, are used to maximally hide LTSs such that they can be minimized modulo $\approx_{br}^{ds}$. Experimental results show the effectiveness of these techniques.

In future work, we plan to study which property patterns of the system [8] can be translated in L_μ^{dsbr}, so as to provide useful information about the possible reductions modulo $\approx_{br}^{ds}$. We also plan to continue experimenting with maximal hiding and on-the-fly reduction by using *weak* forms of divergence-sensitive τ-confluence implemented in a distributed setting [24], i.e., by employing clusters of machines for both LTS reduction and verification.

References

1. Andersen, H.R.: Model checking and boolean graphs. Theoretical Computer Science 126(1), 3–30 (1994)
2. Baeten, J.C.M.: A Brief History of Process Algebra. Theoretical Computer Science 335(2-3), 131–146 (2005)
3. Barbuti, R., de Francesco, N., Santone, A., Vaglini, G.: Selective mu-calculus and formula-based equivalence of transition systems. Journal of Computer and System Science 59(3), 537–556 (1999)
4. Clarke, E.M., Emerson, E.A., Sistla, A.P.: Automatic verification of finite-state concurrent systems using temporal logic specifications. ACM Transactions on Programming Languages and Systems 8(2), 244–263 (1986)
5. Clarke, E.M., Grumberg, O., Peled, D.A.: Model Checking. MIT Press, Cambridge (1999)
6. Cleaveland, R., Steffen, B.: A linear-time model-checking algorithm for the alternation-free modal mu-calculus. Formal Methods in System Design 2(2), 121–147 (1993)
7. Coste, N., Garavel, H., Hermanns, H., Lang, F., Mateescu, R., Serwe, W.: Ten years of performance evaluation for concurrent systems using CADP. In: Margaria, T., Steffen, B. (eds.) ISoLA 2010. LNCS, vol. 6416, pp. 128–142. Springer, Heidelberg (2010)
8. Dwyer, M.B., Avrunin, G.S., Corbett, J.C.: Patterns in property specifications for finite-state verification. In: Proc. of ICSE 1999 (May 1999)
9. Fantechi, A., Gnesi, S., Ristori, G.: From ACTL to Mu-Calculus. In: Proc. of the ERCIM Workshop on Theory and Practice in Verification, IEI-CNR (1992)
10. Fernandez, J.-C., Mounier, L.: On the fly verification of behavioural equivalences and preorders. In: Larsen, K.G., Skou, A. (eds.) CAV 1991. LNCS, vol. 575, Springer, Heidelberg (1992)
11. Fischer, M.J., Ladner, R.E.: Propositional dynamic logic of regular programs. Journal of Computer and System Sciences 18(2), 194–211 (1979)
12. Garavel, H., Lang, F.: Svl: a scripting language for compositional verification. In: Proc. of FORTE 2001, IFIP, pp. 377–392. Kluwer Academic Publishers, Boston (August 2001); Full Version available as INRIA Research Report RR-4223
13. Garavel, H., Lang, F., Mateescu, R., Serwe, W.: Cadp 2010: A toolbox for the construction and analysis of distributed processes. In: Abdulla, P.A., Leino, K.R.M. (eds.) TACAS 2011. LNCS, vol. 6605, pp. 372–387. Springer, Heidelberg (2011)
14. van Glabbeek, R.J., Luttik, B., Trčka, N.: Branching Bisimilarity with Explicit Divergence. Fundamenta Informaticae 93(4), 371–392 (2009)
15. van Glabbeek, R.J., Weijland, W.P.: Branching Time and Abstraction in Bisimulation Semantics. Journal of the ACM 43(3), 555–600 (1996)
16. Groote, J.F., Sellink, M.P.A.: Confluence for process verification. Theoretical Computer Science 170(1-2), 47–81 (1996)

17. Kleene, S.C.: Introduction to Metamathematics. North-Holland, Amsterdam (1952)
18. Kozen, D.: Results on the propositional μ-calculus. Theoretical Computer Science 27, 333–354 (1983)
19. Mateescu, R.: On-the-fly state space reductions for weak equivalences. In: Proc. of FMICS 2005, pp. 80–89. ACM Computer Society Press, New York (2005)
20. Mateescu, R.: Caesar_solve: A generic library for on-the-fly resolution of alternation-free boolean equation systems. Springer International Journal on Software Tools for Technology Transfer (STTT) 8(1), 37–56 (2006); Full version available as INRIA Research Report RR-5948 (July 2006)
21. Mateescu, R., Sighireanu, M.: Efficient on-the-fly model-checking for regular alternation-free mu-calculus. Science of Computer Programming 46(3), 255–281 (2003)
22. Mateescu, R., Thivolle, D.: A model checking language for concurrent value-passing systems. In: Cuellar, J., Sere, K. (eds.) FM 2008. LNCS, vol. 5014, pp. 148–164. Springer, Heidelberg (2008)
23. Mateescu, R., Wijs, A.: Efficient on-the-fly computation of weak tau-confluence. Research Report RR-7000, INRIA (2009)
24. Mateescu, R., Wijs, A.: Sequential and distributed on-the-fly computation of weak tau-confluence. Science of Computer Programming (2011) (to appear)
25. Milner, R.: Communication and Concurrency. Prentice-Hall, Englewood Cliffs (1989)
26. De Nicola, R., Vaandrager, F.W.: Action versus State Based Logics for Transition Systems. In: Guessarian, I. (ed.) LITP 1990. LNCS, vol. 469, pp. 407–419. Springer, Heidelberg (1990)
27. Pace, G.J., Lang, F., Mateescu, R.: Calculating τ-confluence compositionally. In: Hunt Jr., W.A., Somenzi, F. (eds.) CAV 2003. LNCS, vol. 2725, pp. 446–459. Springer, Heidelberg (2003)
28. Stirling, C.: Modal and Temporal Properties of Processes. Springer, Heidelburg (2001)
29. Streett, R.: Propositional dynamic logic of looping and converse. Information and Control (1982)

String Abstractions for String Verification[*]

Fang Yu[1], Tevfik Bultan[2], and Ben Hardekopf[2]

[1] Department of Management Information Systems
National Chengchi University, Taipei, Taiwan
yuf@nccu.edu.tw
[2] University of California, Santa Barbara, CA, USA
{bultan,benh}@cs.ucsb.edu

Abstract. Verifying string manipulating programs is a crucial problem in computer security. String operations are used extensively within web applications to manipulate user input, and their erroneous use is the most common cause of security vulnerabilities in web applications. Unfortunately, verifying string manipulating programs is an undecidable problem in general and any approximate string analysis technique has an inherent tension between efficiency and precision. In this paper we present a set of sound abstractions for strings and string operations that allow for both efficient and precise verification of string manipulating programs. Particularly, we are able to verify properties that involve implicit relations among string variables. We first describe an abstraction called regular abstraction which enables us to perform string analysis using multi-track automata as a symbolic representation. We then introduce two other abstractions—alphabet abstraction and relation abstraction—that can be used in combination to tune the analysis precision and efficiency. We show that these abstractions form an abstraction lattice that generalizes the string analysis techniques studied previously in isolation, such as size analysis or non-relational string analysis. Finally, we empirically evaluate the effectiveness of these abstraction techniques with respect to several benchmarks and an open source application, demonstrating that our techniques can improve the performance without loss of accuracy of the analysis when a suitable abstraction class is selected.

1 Introduction

String manipulation errors are a leading cause of security vulnerabilities. For example, the top three vulnerabilities in the Open Web Application Security Project (OWASP)'s top ten list [12] are Cross-Site Scripting, Injection Flaws (e.g., SQL injection), and Malicious File Execution (MFE), all of which occur due to the erroneous sanitization and manipulation of input strings. This paper focuses on the problem of verifying assertions about a program's string-related properties, e.g., that a string variable at a given program point cannot contain a specific set of characters, or that a string variable must necessarily be a prefix of some other string variable. These types of assertions can be used to prove the absence of the vulnerabilities listed above, among others.

---

[*] This work is supported by an NSC grant 99-2218-E-004-002-MY3 and NSF grants CCF-0916112 and CCF-0716095.

A. Groce and M. Musuvathi (Eds.): SPIN 2011, LNCS 6823, pp. 20–37, 2011.

The string verification problem is undecidable even for simple string manipulating programs [21]. In this paper we present sound abstraction techniques that enable us to verify properties of string manipulating programs. We first present the *regular abstraction* in which values of string variables are represented as multi-track deterministic finite automata. Multi-track automata read tuples of characters as input instead of only single characters. Each string variable corresponds to a particular track (i.e., a particular position in the tuple). This representation enables relational string analysis [21], meaning that it can be used to verify assertions that depend on relationships among the string variables.

Although we use a symbolic automata representation in order to improve the scalability of our analysis, the size of a multi-track automaton representing a given string relation can be exponentially larger than that of traditional single-track automata representing the (less-precise) non-relational projections of that same relation. For example, the 2-track automaton for the relation $X_1 = cX_2$ (where X_1 and X_2 are string variables) is exponential in the length of c, whereas the projection to the single-track automaton for X_2 (which is Σ^*) is constant-size and the projection for X_1 (which is $c\Sigma^*$) is linear in the length of c. Moreover, the size of the alphabet for multi-track automata increases exponentially with the number of program variables.

In order to improve the scalability of our approach, we propose two additional string abstractions: 1) *Relation abstraction* selects sets of string variables to analyze relationally and analyzes the remaining string variables independently. The intent is to detect relationships only for the string variables whose relations are relevant for the assertions being verified. 2) *Alphabet abstraction* selects a subset of alphabet characters to analyze distinctly and merges the remaining alphabet characters into a special symbol. The intent is to track only those characters that are relevant for the assertions being verified.

These two abstractions are parameterized by the choices of which program variables are analyzed in relation to each other versus being analyzed separately and which characters are merged versus being kept distinct; thus, they actually form a family of string abstractions. We show that this family forms an abstraction lattice that generalizes previously existing string analyses into a single, cohesive framework that can be tuned to provide various trade-offs between precision and performance. In addition, we propose a set of heuristics for choosing useful points in this abstraction lattice based on the program being analyzed. Finally, we empirically show that these abstractions meet our goal of increasing the scalability of the relational string analysis while retaining the precision required to verify realistic programs.

2   A Motivating Example

In this section we give a motivating example that shows the need for relational string analysis based on the regular abstraction as well as the usefulness of the relation and alphabet abstractions proposed in this paper. Consider the simple PHP script shown in Figure 1. The script starts with assigning the user account and password provided in _GET array to two string variables $usr and $passwd in line 2 and line 3, respectively. Then, it assigns the result of the concatenation of $usr and $passwd to another string variable $key in line 4. The echo statement in line 6 is a sink statement. Since it uses

```
1  <?php
2      $usr = $_GET["usr"];
3      $passwd = $_GET["passwd"];
4      $key = $usr . $passwd;
5      if($key == "admin1234")
6          echo "You are login as " . $usr ;
7  ?>
```

Fig. 1. A Simple Example

data directly from a user input, a taint analysis will identify this as a Cross Site Scripting (XSS) vulnerability. That is, a malicious user may provide an input that contains the string constant <script and execute a command leading to an XSS attack. However, the assignment in line 4 states that $usr is the prefix of $key. The branch condition in line 5 enforces the value of $key to be admin1234 and the value of $usr to be a prefix of admin1234. This ensures that the echo statement in line 6 cannot take any string that contains the string constant <script as its input. Hence, this simple script is not vulnerable and the taint analysis raises a false alarm.

Non-relational string analyses techniques (e.g., [5, 20]) will also raise a false alarm for this simple script. Such an analysis will first observe that in lines 1 and 2 variables $usr and $passwd can have any string value since they are assigned user input, and then conclude that in line 3, $key can be any string. Note that the relationship among $key, $usr and $passwd can *not* be tracked in non-relational string analysis. Although such an analysis can conclude that the value of $key is admin1234 in line 6, it will still report that $usr can take any string value in line 6. Let the attack pattern for the XSS be specified as the following regular expression: Σ^* <script Σ^* where Σ denotes the alphabet which is the set of all ASCII symbols. A non-relational string analysis will conclude that the echo statement in line 6 is vulnerable, since the echo statement can take a string value that matches the attack pattern if $usr can take any string value in line 6.

In our string analysis we first use a *regular abstraction* to represent possible values of string variables in a program using multi-track automata [21]. To represent values of n string variables, we use an n-track automaton with an alphabet of size $|\Sigma|^n$. Hence, as the number of variables increases, relational analysis becomes intractable. We propose two additional abstraction techniques to improve the scalability of the relational string analysis. We use the *relation abstraction* to reduce n, and the *alphabet abstraction* to reduce $|\Sigma|$, while preserving sufficient precision to prove the required assertions.

The relation abstraction chooses subsets of string variables to track relationally while tracking the remaining variables independently. For the example shown in Figure 1, a relational analysis that tracks $usr and $key together but $passwd independently is sufficient to prevent the false alarm at line 6. The two track automaton for $usr and $key is able to keep the prefix relation between $usr and $key at line 4. At line 6 while $key is restricted to admin1234, $usr is a strict prefix of admin1234, and the relational analysis is able to conclude that the echo statement cannot take a value that matches the attack pattern.

The alphabet abstraction keeps a subset of the alphabet symbols distinct and merges the remaining symbols to a single abstract symbol. For example, the program in Figure 1 can be analyzed more efficiently by keeping only the character $<$ distinct and merging all other ASCII symbols into an abstract symbol $\star$, thus shrinking the alphabet from 256 characters to 2. That is, we can use one bit (instead of eight bits) plus some reserved characters to encode each track of the multi-track automaton. Under this encoding, the analysis can conclude that at line 6, $usr is a string with length 9 that only contains $\star$, and the echo statement cannot take any string value that matches the attack pattern ($\star^*<\star\star\star\star\star(<|\star)^*$ in this case).

The relation and alphabet abstractions can be used only with regular abstraction, or composed together. In the example above, by combining relation abstraction and alphabet abstraction, we are able to decrease the alphabet size of the multi-track automaton, i.e., $|\Sigma|^n$, from 256^3 symbols to $2^2 = 4$ symbols, and still keep sufficient information to prevent the false alarm.

On the other hand, instead of tracing relations among variables, one may simply sanitize user inputs to prevent potential vulnerabilities, e.g., using the following statement at line 2:

```
$usr = str_replace("<", "", $_GET["usr"]);
```

The expression _GET["usr"] returns the string entered by the user, and the str_replace call replaces all $<$ with the empty string. In this case, we can adopt a coarser abstraction for our string analysis. It is sufficient to use single-track automata (abstract away all relations among variables) with abstract alphabet $\{<, \star\}$ to conclude that the echo statement cannot take any string value that matches the attack pattern.

3   String Abstractions

In this section we first present the regular abstraction which allows us to analyze string manipulating programs using multi-track automata as a symbolic representation. Then we show that the relation and alphabet abstractions can be composed with the regular abstraction (and with each other) to obtain a family of abstractions.

3.1   Regular Abstraction

The regular abstraction maps a set of string tuples to a set of string tuples accepted by a multi-track automaton. This enables us to use deterministic finite state automata (DFAs) as a symbolic representation during string analysis. A *multi-track automaton* (or multi-track DFA) is a DFA that transitions on tuples of characters rather than single characters. For a given alphabet Σ let $\Sigma_\lambda = \Sigma \cup \{\lambda\}$, where $\lambda \notin \Sigma$ is a special padding character. An n-track alphabet is defined as $\Sigma^n = \Sigma_\lambda \times \cdots \times \Sigma_\lambda$ (n times). A track corresponds to a particular position in the n-tuple. A multi-track DFA is *aligned* iff for all words w accepted by the DFA, $w \in \Sigma^*\lambda^*$ (i.e., all padding is at the end of the word). Using aligned multi-track automata gives us a representation that is closed under intersection and can be converted to a canonical form after determinization and minimization. In the following, multi-track DFAs are assumed to be aligned unless explicitly stated otherwise.

The statements of a string manipulating program can be represented as word equations. A *word equation* is an equality relation between two terms, each of which is a finite concatenation of string variables and string constants. Regular abstraction abstracts a given program by mapping the word-equations representing the program statements to multi-track DFA. Since word equations can not be precisely represented using multi-track automata, we use the results presented in [21] to construct a sound abstraction of the given program (i.e., in the abstracted program the set of values that a variable can take is a superset of the possible values that a variable can take in the concrete program). Note that, since branch conditions can contain negated terms, we need to be able to construct both an over- and an under-approximation of a given word equation. We construct multi-track automata that precisely represent word equations when possible, and either over- or under-approximate the word equations (as desired) otherwise.

We define a function CONSTRUCT(*exp*:word equation, *b*:bool) that takes a word equation as input and returns a corresponding multi-track DFA, if necessary either over-approximating (if $b = +$) or under-approximating (if $b = -$). We use the CONSTRUCT function to soundly approximate all word equations *and* their boolean combinations, including existentially-quantified word equations. The boolean operations conjunction, disjunction, and negation on word equations are handled using intersection, disjunction, and complementation of the corresponding multi-track DFAs, respectively; existentially-quantified word equations are handled using homomorphisms (by projecting the track that corresponds to the quantified variable).

Given an assignment statement $stmt$ of the form $X := exp$ we first represent it as a word equation of the form $X' = exp$ where exp is an expression on the current state variables, and X' denotes the next state variables. Then we abstract $stmt$ by constructing a multi-track automaton M_{stmt} that over-approximates the corresponding word equation as follows $M_{stmt} = \text{CONSTRUCT}(X' = exp, +)$. A branch condition specified as an expression exp is similarly abstracted using CONSTRUCT($X' = X \wedge exp, +$) for the then branch and CONSTRUCT($X' = X \wedge \neg exp, +$) for the else branch. The result of the regular abstraction consists of the control flow graph of the original program where each statement in the control flow graph is associated with a multi-track DFA that over-approximates the behavior of the corresponding statement.

The abstract domain that results from the regular abstraction is defined as a lattice on multi-track automata over an alphabet Σ^n. We denote this automata lattice as $\mathcal{L}_M = (\overline{M_{\Sigma^n}}, \sqsubseteq, \sqcup, \sqcap, \bot, \top)$, where $\overline{M_{\Sigma^n}}$ is the set of multi-track automata over the alphabet Σ^n. For $M_1, M_2 \in \overline{M_{\Sigma^n}}$, $M_1 \sqsubseteq M_2$ iff $L(M_1) \subseteq L(M_2)$. The bottom element is defined as $L(\bot) = \emptyset$ and the top element is defined as $L(\top) = (\Sigma^n)^*$. There may be multiple automata that accept the same language; the lattice treats these automata as equivalent. If we use minimized DFAs then there is a unique automaton for each point in the lattice up to isomorphism. All of the multi-track automata in this lattice are aligned [21] and hence all operations take aligned automata as input and return aligned automata as output.

The join operator cannot be defined simply as language union since the family of regular languages is not closed under infinite union. Instead, we use the widening operator from [2] as the join operator where $M_1 \sqcup M_2 = M_1 \nabla M_2$. The meet operator can be defined from the join operator using language complement: let $\neg M$ denote an automaton such that $L(\neg M) = \Sigma^* \setminus L(M)$; then $M_1 \sqcap M_2 = \neg(\neg M_1 \nabla \neg M_2)$.

Note that a similar automata lattice can also be defined for single-track automata over a single-track alphabet Σ where $\mathcal{L}_M = (\overline{M_\Sigma}, \sqsubseteq, \sqcup, \sqcap, \bot, \top)$.

Fixpoint Computation for Forward Reachability. The relational string analysis corresponds to a least-fixpoint computation over the multi-track automata lattice. Each program point is associated with a multi-track DFA whose tracks correspond to string variables and the multi-track DFA accepts the string-tuples that correspond to possible values that string variables can take at that particular program point. In order to be able to handle large alphabets of the multi-track DFA, we use the symbolic DFA representation provided by the MONA automata package [9]. In this symbolic automata representation the transition relations of the DFA are represented as Multi-terminal Binary Decision Diagrams (MBDDs).

We use a standard work-queue algorithm to compute the fixpoint. For a program statement *stmt* that is abstracted as the multi-track automaton M_{stmt} the post-image is computed as:

$$\text{POST}(M, stmt) \equiv (\exists X.M \cap M_{stmt})[X' \mapsto X]$$

In other words, we take the intersection of the multi-track DFA that represents the statement with the multi-track DFA representing the current states (M), apply quantifier elimination on the current state variables X (by projection), and rename the next state variables X' as X (by arranging the indices in the MBDD representation) to obtain the post-image DFA.

Since we use the widening operator as the join operator during the fixpoint computation, the analysis is guaranteed to terminate. During the analysis, we report the assertion violations as they are discovered. The analysis is sound, but it is incomplete due to the following approximations: (1) abstraction of word equations as multi-track DFAs, and (2) use of the widening operator which over approximates the language union.

3.2   Alphabet Abstraction

In this section we formally define the alphabet abstraction. This abstraction targets the values taken on by string variables, mapping multiple alphabet symbols to a single abstract symbol. For example, consider a string variable that can take the value $\{ab, abc\}$. Abstracting the symbols b and c yields the value $\{a\star, a \star \star\}$, where $\star$ stands for both b and c. The concretization of this abstract value would yield the value $\{ab, ac, abc, abb, acb, acc\}$. At the extreme this abstraction can abstract out all alphabets symbols (in the above example, this would yield the abstract value $\{\star\star, \star \star \star\}$). In this case the only information retained from the original value is the length of the strings; all information about the content of the strings is lost. This abstraction is still useful in checking properties related to string length—we will return to this point in Section 3.4.

The alphabet abstraction is parameterized by the choice of which symbols to abstract, hence it forms a family of abstractions. This family forms an abstraction lattice $\mathcal{L}_\Sigma$ called the *alphabet lattice* (distinct from the automata lattice introduced earlier). Let Σ, a finite alphabet, be the concrete alphabet, and $\star \notin \Sigma$ be a special symbol to represent characters that are abstracted away. An abstract alphabet of Σ is defined as $\Sigma' \cup \{\star\}$, where $\Sigma' \subseteq \Sigma$. The abstract alphabets of Σ form a complete lattice $\mathcal{L}_\Sigma = (\mathcal{P}(\Sigma \cup \{\star\}), \sqsubseteq_\Sigma, \cup, \cap, \sigma_\perp, \sigma_\top)$ where the bottom element $\sigma_\perp$ is $\Sigma \cup \{\star\}$, the top element $\sigma_\top$ is $\{\star\}$, and the join and meet operations correspond to set intersection and union, respectively. The abstraction $\sigma_\top$ corresponds to mapping all the symbols in the concrete alphabet to a single symbol, whereas $\sigma_\perp$ corresponds to no abstraction at all. The partial order of $\mathcal{L}_\Sigma$ is defined as follows. Let σ_1, σ_2 be two elements in $\mathcal{L}_\Sigma$,

$$\sigma_1 \sqsubseteq_\Sigma \sigma_2, \text{ if } \sigma_2 \subseteq \sigma_1, \quad \text{and} \quad \sigma_1 \sqsubset_\Sigma \sigma_2, \text{ if } \sigma_1 \sqsubseteq_\Sigma \sigma_2 \text{ and } \sigma_1 \neq \sigma_2.$$

Let $\sigma_1 \sqsubseteq_\Sigma \sigma_2$. We define the representation function for alphabet abstraction as follows: $\beta_{\sigma_1,\sigma_2} : \Sigma^* \to \Sigma^*$ where $\beta_{\sigma_1,\sigma_2}(w) = \{w' \mid |w'| = |w|, \forall i \, 1 \le i \le |w|.(w(i) \in \sigma_2 \Rightarrow w'(i) = w(i)) \wedge (w(i) \notin \sigma_2 \Rightarrow w'(i) = \star)\}$. The representation function simply maps the symbols that we wish to abstract to the abstract symbol $\star$, and maps the rest of the symbols to themselves.

Since the symbolic analysis we defined in Section 3.1 uses automata as a symbolic representation, we have to determine how to apply the alphabet abstraction to automata. We define the abstraction function $\alpha_{\sigma_1,\sigma_2}$ on automata using the representation function $\beta_{\sigma_1,\sigma_2}$ as follows: Let M be a single track DFA over σ_1; then $\alpha_{\sigma_1,\sigma_2}(M) = M'$ where M' is a single track DFA over σ_2 such that $L(M') = \{w \mid \exists w' \in L(M).\beta_{\sigma_1,\sigma_2}(w') = w\}$. Note that there may be multiple automata M' that satisfies this constraint. However, since we use minimized multi-track DFAs they will all be equivalent. We define the concretization function $\gamma_{\sigma_2,\sigma_1}$ similarly: Let M be a single track DFA over σ_2; then $\gamma_{\sigma_1,\sigma_2}(M) = M'$ where M' is a single track DFA over σ_1 such that $L(M') = \{w \mid \exists w' \in L(M).\beta_{\sigma_1,\sigma_2}(w) = w'\}$.

The definitions we give above are not constructive. We give a constructive definition of the abstraction and concretization functions by first defining an alphabet-abstraction-transducer that maps symbols that we wish to abstract to the abstract symbol $\star$, and maps the rest of the symbols to themselves.

An alphabet-abstraction-transducer over σ_1 and σ_2 is a 2-track DFA $M_{\sigma_1,\sigma_2} = \langle Q, \sigma_1 \times \sigma_2, \delta, q_0, F \rangle$, where

- $Q = \{q_0, sink\}$, $F = \{q_0\}$, and
- $\forall a \in \sigma_2.\delta(q_0, (a, a)) = q_0$,
- $\forall a \in \sigma_1 \setminus \sigma_2.\delta(q_0, (a, \star)) = q_0$.

Now, using the alphabet-abstraction-transducer, we can compute the abstraction of a DFA as a post-image computation, and we can compute the concretization of DFA as a pre-image computation. Let M be a single track DFA over σ_1 with track X. $M_{\sigma_1,\sigma_2}(X, X')$ denotes the alphabet transducer over σ_1 and σ_2 where X and X' correspond to the input and output tracks, respectively. We define the abstraction and concretization functions on automata as:

- $\alpha_{\sigma_1,\sigma_2}(M) \equiv (\exists X.M \cap M_{\sigma_1,\sigma_2}(X, X'))[X' \mapsto X]$, and
- $\gamma_{\sigma_1,\sigma_2}(M) \equiv \exists X'.(M[X \mapsto X'] \cap M_{\sigma_1,\sigma_2}(X, X'))$.

The definition can be extended to multi-track DFAs. Let M be a multi-track DFA over σ_1^n associated with $\{X_i \mid 1 \le i \le n\}$, $\alpha_{\sigma_1^n,\sigma_2^n}(M)$ returns a multi-track DFA over

σ_2^n. On the other hand, while M is a multi-track DFA over σ_2^n, $\gamma_{\sigma_1^n,\sigma_2^n}(M)$ returns a multi-track DFA over σ_1^n. We use $M_{\sigma_1^n,\sigma_2^n}$ to denote the extension of the alphabet transducer to multi-track alphabet, where we add $\delta(q_0,(\lambda,\lambda)) = q_0$ to $M_{\sigma_1^n,\sigma_2^n}$ to deal with the padding symbol λ and we use $M_{\sigma_1^n,\sigma_2^n}(X_i,X_i')$ to denote the alphabet transducer associated with tracks X_i and X_i'. The abstraction and concretization of a multi-track DFA M is done track by track as follows:

- $\alpha_{\sigma_1^n,\sigma_2^n}(M) \equiv \forall X_i.(\exists X_i.M \cap M_{\sigma_1^n,\sigma_2^n}(X_i,X_i'))[X_i' \mapsto X_i]$, and
- $\gamma_{\sigma_1^n,\sigma_2^n}(M) \equiv \forall X_i.(\exists X_i'.M[X_i \mapsto X_i'] \cap M_{\sigma_1^n,\sigma_2^n}(X_i,X_i'))$.

The abstraction lattice $\mathcal{L}_{\Sigma}$ defines a family of Galois connections between the automata lattices $\mathcal{L}_M$. Each element σ^n in the abstraction lattice $\mathcal{L}_{\Sigma^n}$ is associated with an automata lattice $\mathcal{L}_{\sigma^n}$ corresponding to multi-track automata with the alphabet σ^n. For any pair of elements in the abstraction lattice $\sigma_1^n, \sigma_2^n \in \mathcal{L}_{\Sigma^n}$, if $\sigma_1^n \sqsubseteq_{\Sigma} \sigma_2^n$, then we can define a Galois connection between the corresponding automata lattices $\mathcal{L}_{\sigma_1^n}$ and $\mathcal{L}_{\sigma_2^n}$ using the abstraction and concretization functions $\alpha_{\sigma_1^n,\sigma_2^n}$ and $\gamma_{\sigma_1^n,\sigma_2^n}$. We formalize this with the following property:

For any Σ^n, and $\sigma_1^n, \sigma_2^n \in \mathcal{L}_{\Sigma^n}$, if $\sigma_1^n \sqsubseteq_{\Sigma} \sigma_2^n$, the functions $\alpha_{\sigma_1^n,\sigma_2^n}$ and $\gamma_{\sigma_1^n,\sigma_2^n}$ define a Galois connection between the lattices $\mathcal{L}_{\sigma_1^n}$ and $\mathcal{L}_{\sigma_2^n}$ where for any $M_1 \in \mathcal{L}_{\sigma_1^n}$ and $M_2 \in \mathcal{L}_{\sigma_2^n}$:

$$\alpha_{\sigma_1^n,\sigma_2^n}(M_1) \sqsubseteq M_2 \Leftrightarrow M_1 \sqsubseteq \gamma_{\sigma_1^n,\sigma_2^n}(M_2)$$

3.3   Relation Abstraction

In this section we formally define the relation abstraction. This abstraction targets the relations between string variables. The abstraction determines the sets of variables that will be analyzed in relation to each other; for each such set the analysis computes a multi-track automaton for each program point such that each track of the automaton corresponds to one variable in that set. In the most abstract case no relations are tracked at all—there is a separate single-track automaton for each variable and the analysis is completely non-relational. On the other hand, in the most precise case we have one single multi-track automaton for each program point.

Let $\overline{X} = \{X_1, \ldots X_n\}$ be a finite set of variables. Let $\chi \subseteq 2^{\overline{X}}$ where $\emptyset \notin \chi$. We say χ defines a relation of $\overline{X}$ if (1) for any $\mathbf{x}, \mathbf{x}' \in \chi$, $\mathbf{x} \not\subseteq \mathbf{x}'$, and (2) $\bigcup_{\mathbf{x}\in\chi}\mathbf{x} = \overline{X}$. The set of χ that defines the relations of $\overline{X}$ form a complete lattice, denoted as $\mathcal{L}_{\overline{X}}$.

- The bottom of the abstraction lattice, denoted as $\chi_{\perp}$, is $\{\{X_1, X_2, \ldots, X_n\}\}$. This corresponds to the most precise case where, for each program point, a single multi-track automaton is used to represent the set of values for all string variables where each string variable corresponds to one track. This is the representation used in the symbolic reachability analysis described in Section 3.1.
- The top of the abstraction lattice, denoted as $\chi_{\top}$, is $\{\{X_1\}, \{X_2\}, \{X_3\}, \ldots, \{X_n\}\}$. This corresponds to the most coarse abstraction where, for each program point, n single-track automata are used and each automaton represents the set of values for a single string variable. This approach has been used in some earlier work such as [1, 20].

The partial order of the abstraction lattice $\mathcal{L}_{\overline{X}}$ is defined as follows: Let χ_1, χ_2 be two elements in $\mathcal{L}_{\overline{X}}$,

- $\chi_1 \sqsubseteq_{\overline{X}} \chi_2$, if for any $\mathbf{x} \in \chi_2$, there exists $\mathbf{x}' \in \chi_1$ such that $\mathbf{x} \subseteq \mathbf{x}'$.
- $\chi_1 \sqsubset_{\overline{X}} \chi_2$ if $\chi_1 \sqsubseteq_{\overline{X}} \chi_2$ and $\chi_1 \neq \chi_2$.

The symbolic reachability analysis discussed in Section 3.1 can be generalized to a symbolic reachability analysis that works for each abstraction level in the abstraction lattice $\mathcal{L}_{\overline{X}}$. To conduct symbolic reachability analysis for the relation abstraction $\chi \in \mathcal{L}_{\overline{X}}$, we store $|\chi|$ multi-track automata for each program point, where for each $\mathbf{x} \in \chi$, we have a $|\mathbf{x}|$-track DFA, denoted as $M_{\mathbf{x}}$, where each track is associated with a variable in $\mathbf{x}$.

In order to define the abstraction and the concretization functions, we define the following projection and extension operations on automata. For $\mathbf{x}' \subseteq \mathbf{x}$, the projection of $M_{\mathbf{x}}$ to $\mathbf{x}'$, denoted as $M_{\mathbf{x}} \downarrow_{\mathbf{x}'}$, is defined as the $|\mathbf{x}'|$-track DFA that accepts $\{w' \mid w \in L(M_{\mathbf{x}}), \forall X_i \in \mathbf{x}'.w'[i] = w[i])\}$. Similarly, $\mathbf{x}' \subseteq \mathbf{x}$, the extension of $M_{\mathbf{x}'}$ to $\mathbf{x}$, denoted as $M_{\mathbf{x}'} \uparrow_{\mathbf{x}}$, is defined as the $|\mathbf{x}|$-track DFA that accepts $\{w \mid w' \in L(M_{\mathbf{x}'}), \forall X_i \in \mathbf{x}'.w[i] = w'[i])\}$.

Let $\mathbf{M}_\chi = \{M_{\mathbf{x}} \mid \mathbf{x} \in \chi\}$ be a set of DFAs for the relation χ. The set of string values represented by $\mathbf{M}_\chi$ is defined as: $L(\mathbf{M}_\chi) = L(\bigcap_{\mathbf{x} \in \chi} M_{\mathbf{x}} \uparrow_{\mathbf{x_u}})$, where $\mathbf{x_u} = \{X_1, X_2, \dots, X_n\}$. I.e., we extend the language of every automaton in $\mathbf{M}_\chi$ to all string variables and then take their intersection.

Now, let us define the abstraction and concretization functions for the relation abstraction (which take a set of multi-track automata as input and return a set of multi-track automata as output).

Let $\chi_1 \sqsubset_{\overline{X}} \chi_2$; then $\alpha_{\chi_1, \chi_2}(\mathbf{M}_{\chi_1})$ returns a set of DFAs $\{M_{\mathbf{x}'} \mid \mathbf{x}' \in \chi_2\}$, where for each $\mathbf{x}' \in \chi_2$, $M_{\mathbf{x}'} = (\bigcap_{\mathbf{x} \in \chi_1, \mathbf{x}' \cap \mathbf{x} \neq \emptyset} M_{\mathbf{x}} \uparrow_{\mathbf{x_u}}) \downarrow_{\mathbf{x}'}$, where $\mathbf{x_u} = \{X_i \mid X_i \in \mathbf{x}, \mathbf{x} \in \chi_1, \mathbf{x}' \cap \mathbf{x} \neq \emptyset\}$.

$\gamma_{\chi_1, \chi_2}(\mathbf{M}_{\chi_2})$ returns a set of DFAs $\{M_{\mathbf{x}} \mid \mathbf{x} \in \chi_1\}$, where for each $\mathbf{x} \in \chi_1$, $M_{\mathbf{x}} = (\bigcap_{\mathbf{x}' \in \chi_2, \mathbf{x}' \cap \mathbf{x} \neq \emptyset}(M_{\mathbf{x}'} \uparrow_{\mathbf{x_u}})) \downarrow_{\mathbf{x}}$, where $\mathbf{x_u} = \{X_i \mid X_i \in \mathbf{x}', \mathbf{x}' \in \chi_2, \mathbf{x}' \cap \mathbf{x} \neq \emptyset\}$.

Similar to the alphabet abstraction, the relation abstraction lattice $\mathcal{L}_{\overline{X}}$ also defines a family of Galois connections. Each element of the relation abstraction lattice corresponds to a lattice on sets of automata. For each $\chi \in \mathcal{L}_{\overline{X}}$ we define a lattice $\mathcal{L}_\chi = (\overline{\mathbf{M}_\chi}, \sqsubseteq, \sqcup, \sqcap, \bot, \top)$. Given two sets of automata $\mathbf{M}_\chi, \mathbf{M}'_\chi \in \overline{\mathbf{M}_\chi}$, $\mathbf{M}_\chi \sqsubseteq \mathbf{M}'_\chi$ if and only if $L(\mathbf{M}_\chi) \subseteq L(\mathbf{M}'_\chi)$. The bottom element is defined as $L(\bot) = \emptyset$ and the top element is defined as $L(\top) = (\Sigma^n)^*$. The join operator is defined as: $\mathbf{M}_\chi \sqcup \mathbf{M}'_\chi = \{M_{\mathbf{x}} \nabla M'_{\mathbf{x}} \mid \mathbf{x} \in \chi, M_{\mathbf{x}} \in \mathbf{M}_\chi, M'_{\mathbf{x}} \in \mathbf{M}'_\chi\}$ and the meet operator is defined as: $\mathbf{M}_\chi \sqcap \mathbf{M}'_\chi = \{\neg(\neg M_{\mathbf{x}} \nabla \neg M'_{\mathbf{x}}) \mid \mathbf{x} \in \chi, M_{\mathbf{x}} \in \mathbf{M}_\chi, M'_{\mathbf{x}} \in \mathbf{M}'_\chi\}$.

For any pair of elements in the relation abstraction lattice $\chi_1, \chi_2 \in \mathcal{L}_{\overline{X}}$, if $\chi_1 \sqsubset_{\overline{X}} \chi_2$, then the abstraction and concretization functions α_{χ_1, χ_2} and γ_{χ_1, χ_2} define a Galois connection between $\mathcal{L}_{\chi_1}$ and $\mathcal{L}_{\chi_2}$. We formalize this with the following property:

For any $\chi_1, \chi_2 \in \mathcal{L}_{\overline{X}}$, if $\chi_1 \sqsubset_{\overline{X}} \chi_2$, then the functions α_{χ_1, χ_2} and γ_{χ_1, χ_2} define a Galois connection between $\mathcal{L}_{\chi_1}$ and $\mathcal{L}_{\chi_2}$ where for any $\mathbf{M}_{\chi_1} \in \mathcal{L}_{\chi_1}$ and $\mathbf{M}'_{\chi_2} \in \mathcal{L}_{\chi_2}$:

$$\alpha_{\chi_1, \chi_2}(\mathbf{M}_{\chi_1}) \sqsubseteq \mathbf{M}'_{\chi_2} \Leftrightarrow \mathbf{M}_{\chi_1} \sqsubseteq \gamma_{\sigma_1^n, \sigma_2^n}(\mathbf{M}'_{\chi_2})$$

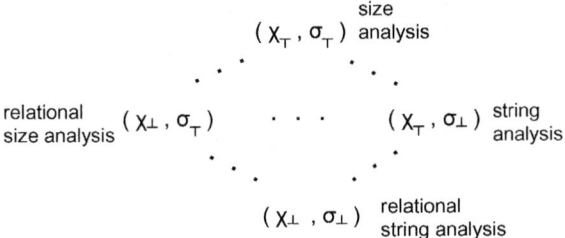

Fig. 2. Some abstractions from the abstraction lattice and corresponding analyses

3.4 Composing Abstractions

As shown in the two previous sections, both alphabet and relation abstractions form abstraction lattices which allow different levels of abstraction. Combining these abstractions leads to a product lattice where each point in this lattice corresponds to the combination of a particular alphabet abstraction with a particular relation abstraction. This creates an even larger set of Galois connections, one for each possible combination of alphabet and relation abstractions. Given Σ and $\overline{X} = \{X_1, \ldots, X_n\}$, we define a point in this product lattice as an *abstraction class* which is a pair (χ, σ) where $\chi \in \mathcal{L}_{\overline{X}}$ and $\sigma \in \mathcal{L}_{\Sigma}$. The abstraction classes of $\overline{X}$ and Σ also form a complete lattice, of which the partial order is defined as: $(\chi_1, \sigma_1) \sqsubseteq (\chi_2, \sigma_2)$ if $\chi_1 \sqsubseteq \chi_2$ and $\sigma_1 \sqsubseteq \sigma_2$.

Given Σ and $\overline{X} = \{X_1, \ldots, X_n\}$, we can select any abstraction class in the product lattice during our analysis. The selected abstraction class (χ, σ) determines the precision and efficiency of our analysis. If we select the abstraction class $(\chi_\perp, \sigma_\perp)$, we conduct our most precise relational string analysis. The relations among $\overline{X}$ will be kept using one n-track DFA at each program point. If we select $(\chi_\top, \sigma_\top)$, we only keep track of the *length* of each string variable individually. Although we abstract away almost all string relations and contents in this case, this kind of path-sensitive (w.r.t length conditions on a single variable) size analysis can be used to detect buffer overflow vulnerabilities [6, 15]. If we select $(\chi_\perp, \sigma_\top)$, then we will be conducting relational size analysis. Finally, earlier string analysis techniques that use DFA, such as [1, 20], correspond to the abstraction class $(\chi_\top, \sigma_\perp)$, where multiple single-track DFAs over Σ are used to encode reachable states. As shown in [1, 20, 17], this type of analysis is useful for detecting XSS and SQLCI vulnerabilities.

Figure 2 summarizes the different types of abstractions that can be obtained using our abstraction framework. The alphabet and relation abstractions can be seen as two knobs that determine the level of the precision of our string analysis. The alphabet abstraction knob determines how much of the string content is abstracted away. In the limit, the only information left about the string values is their lengths. On the other hand, the relation abstraction knob determines which set of variables should be analyzed in relation to each other. In the limit, all values are projected to individual variables. Different abstraction classes can be useful in different cases. An important question is how to choose a *proper* abstraction class for a given verification problem; this is addressed in the next section.

3.5   Heuristics and Refinement for Abstraction Selection

Since the space of total possible abstractions using the relation and alphabet abstractions defined above is very large, we must have some means to decide which specific abstractions to employ in order to prove a given property. Our choice should be as abstract as possible (for efficiency) while remaining precise enough to prove the property in question. In this section we propose a set of heuristics for making this decision.

The intuition behind these heuristics is to let the property under question guide our choice of abstraction. Consider the set of string variables X_i that appear in the assertion of a property. Let G be the dependence graph for X_i generated from the program being verified. Finally, let $\overline{X}$ be the set of string variables appearing in G and $\overline{C}$ be the set of characters used in any string constants that appear in G or in the assertion itself. It is the characters in $\overline{C}$ and the relations between the variables in $\overline{X}$ that are most relevant for proving the given property, and therefore these relations and characters should be preserved by the abstraction—the remaining variables and characters can be safely abstracted away without jeopardizing the verification.

In choosing the alphabet abstraction, our heuristic keeps distinct all characters appearing in $C \subseteq \overline{C}$ and merges all remaining characters of the alphabet together into the special character $\star$. Initially, C is the set of characters that appear in the assertion itself. C can be iteratively refined by adding selected characters in $\overline{C}$.

In choosing the relation abstraction, it is possible to simply group all variables in $\overline{X}$ together and track them relationally while tracking all other variables independently, but this choice might be more precise than necessary. Consider a hypothetical property $(X_1 = X_2 \wedge X_3 = X_4)$. It is not necessary to track the relations between X_1 and either of X_3 or X_4 (and similarly for X_2)—it is sufficient to track the relations between X_1 and X_2 and separately the relations between X_2 and X_3. Therefore our heuristic partitions $\overline{X}$ into distinct groups such that the variables within each group are tracked relationally with each other. To partition $\overline{X}$, our heuristic first groups together variables that appear in the same word equation in the property being verified (e.g., X_1 with X_2 and X_3 with X_4). The partition can be iteratively refined by using the dependency graph G to merge groups containing variables that depend on each other.

This heuristic can also be extended to take into account path sensitivity. Let ϕ be the path condition for the assertion (or the sink statement) and X_ϕ denote the set of string variables appearing in ϕ. We first extend the partition base from $\overline{X}$ to $\overline{X} \cup X_\phi$. Initially, each variable forms an individual group by itself. The partition is then refined by merging these individual groups with groups that contain variables that these new variables depend on. For instance, for the motivating example shown in Figure 1, we have $\overline{X} = \{\$usr\}$ and $X_\phi = \{\$key\}$. The initial partition is $\{\{\$usr\}, \{\$key\}\}$, and the refined partition is $\{\{\$usr, \$key\}\}$ which enables $\$usr$ and $\$key$ to be tracked relationally.

3.6   Handling Complex String Operations

We extend our analysis to other complex string operations that have been previously defined using single-track automata [20, 22], e.g., replacement, prefix, and suffix. We first extract the set of values for each variables from the multi-track DFA $\mathbf{M}_\chi$ as a single track DFA (using projection), then compute the result of the string operation using these single-track DFAs. The post image of $\mathbf{M}_\chi$ can then be computed using the resulting DFAs.

We must modify these operations to ensure the soundness of the alphabet abstraction. Consider REPLACE(M_1, M_2, M_3) [20], which returns the DFA accepting $\{w_1c_1w_2c_2 \ldots w_kc_kw_{k+1} \mid k > 0, w_1x_1w_2x_2 \ldots w_kx_kw_{k+1} \in L(M_1), \forall_i, x_i \in L(M_2), w_i$ does not contain any substring accepted by $M_2, c_i \in L(M_3)\}$. As an instance, let $L(M_1) = \{ab\}$, $L(M_2) = \{c\}$, $L(M_3) = \{a\}$. REPLACE(M_1, M_2, M_3) will return M that accepts $\{ab\}$, the same as M_1, since there is no match appearing in any accepted string. However, let $\{a, \star\}$ be the abstraction alphabet. After applying the alphabet abstraction, we have $L(M_1') = \{a\star\}$, $L(M_2') = \{\star\}$, $L(M_3') = \{a\}$, and REPLACE(M_1', M_2', M_3') will return M' that accepts $\{aa\}$ instead. Since $L(\alpha_\sigma(M)) = \{a\star\} \not\subseteq L(M')$, the result in the concrete domain is not included in the abstract domain after abstraction. It is unsound applying the replace operation directly.

Assume M_1, M_2, M_3 using the same abstraction alphabet σ. To ensure soundness we return $\alpha_\sigma(\text{REPLACE}(\gamma_\sigma(M_1), \gamma_\sigma(M_2), \gamma_\sigma(M_3))$ if $L(M_1) \not\subseteq L(M_{\bar\star})$ and $L(M_2) \not\subseteq L(M_{\bar\star})$, so that all possible results in the concrete domain are included in the abstract domain after abstraction. We return REPLACE(M_1, M_2, M_3), otherwise.

4   Implementation and Experiments

We have incorporated alphabet abstraction to Stranger [18] which is an automata-based string analysis tool for PHP programs. However, Stranger at this point performs string analysis on dependency graphs and is limited to non-relational analysis, i.e., the bottom of the relation abstraction lattice. In order to implement our relational string analysis we extended the symbolic string analysis library that Stranger uses to support (abstract) relational analysis with multi-track automata. We compiled the extended Stranger string analysis library separate from the Stranger front-end to implement the relational string analysis. To evaluate the proposed relation abstraction, we implemented the relational analysis by directly calling the extended Stranger string analysis library functions.

We ran two experiments. In the first experiment we used two sets of benchmarks: 1) Malicious File Execution (MFE) benchmarks, and 2) Cross-Site Scripting (XSS) benchmarks. These benchmarks come from five open source PHP applications. We first used the Stranger front-end to conduct taint analysis on these PHP applications. Stranger taint-analyzer identified the tainted sinks (i.e., sensitive program points that might be vulnerable) for each type of vulnerability and generated the dependency graphs for these potentially vulnerable program segments. We then implemented the relational string analysis for several of these potentially vulnerable program segments by using the extended Stranger string analysis library functions. We implemented the relational string analysis for several abstraction classes to evaluate the effectiveness of the proposed abstractions.

In the second experiment we evaluated the alphabet abstraction by directly using Stranger (that we extended with alphabet abstraction) on an open source web application, called Schoolmate. For this application we looked for XSS (Cross-Site Scripting) vulnerabilities and conducted the string analysis both with and without alphabet abstraction and compared the results. Both experiments were conducted on the Linux 2.6.35

machine equipped with Intel Pentium Dual CPU 2.80 GHz and memory 2.9GB. The
applications used in our experiments are available at:
`http://soslab.nccu.edu.tw/applications`.

MFE benchmarks. This set of benchmarks demonstrates the usefulness of the relational analysis as well as the utility of our relation abstraction. We used 5 benchmarks:

M1: PBLguestbook-1.32, pblguestbook.php (536)   **M2**: MyEasyMarket-4.1, prod.php (94)
M3: MyEasyMarket-4.1, prod.php (189)   **M4**: php-fusion-6.01, db_backup.php (111)
M5: php-fusion-6.01, forums_prune.php (28)

Each benchmark is extracted from an open source web application as described
above and contains a program point that executes a file operation (include, fopen,
etc) whose arguments may be influenced by external inputs. For example, **M1** corresponds to the program point at line 536 in pblguestbook.php distributed in the application PBLguestbook-1.32. Given an abstraction class and a benchmark, we implemented
the corresponding string analysis using the extended Stranger string manipulation library. Our analysis constructs a multi-track DFA for each program point that over-
approximates the set of strings that form the arguments. At the end of the analysis these
DFAs are intersected with a multi-track DFA that characterizes the vulnerable strings
that expose the program to MFE attacks. We report an error if the intersection is nonempty. None of the MFE benchmarks we analyzed contained an actual vulnerability.
The MFE vulnerabilities correspond to scenarios such as a user accessing a file in another user's directory. Such vulnerabilities depend on the relation between two string
values (for example, the user name and the directory name), hence an analysis that does
not track the relations between string variables would raise false alarms.

XSS benchmarks. This set of benchmarks (again extracted from open source web applications) demonstrates the utility of the alphabet abstraction. We use 3 benchmarks:

S1: MyEasyMarket-4.1, trans.php (218)   **S2**: Aphpkb-0.71, saa.php(87)
S3: BloggIT 1.0, admin.php (23)

To identify XSS attacks we use a predetermined set of attack patterns specified as
a regular language. These attack patterns represent strings that potentially make a program vulnerable to XSS attacks. Again, given an abstraction class and a benchmark,
we implemented the corresponding string analysis using the extended Stranger string
manipulation library. Our analysis constructs multi-track DFAs to over-approximate the
set of possible strings values at sinks and intersects these DFAs with the attack patterns
to detect potential vulnerabilities. All three benchmarks we analyzed were vulnerable.
We modified the benchmarks to fix these vulnerabilities and create three new versions
(S1', S2', and S3') that are secure against XSS attacks.

Experimental Results. The results for the MFE benchmarks are summarized in Table 1.
All DFAs are symbolically encoded using MBDDs (where MBDDs are used to represent the transition relation of the DFA). The column labeled "state" shows the number
of states of the DFA while the column labeled "bdd" shows the number of nodes in the
MBDD that encodes the transition relation of the DFA (i.e., it corresponds to the size of
the transition relation of the DFA). Note that the transition relation size decreases when
we use a coarser alphabet abstraction. However, using a coarser alphabet may induce

nondeterministic edges, and as shown in Table 1, in some cases, the number of states may increase after determinization and minimization.

The first set of columns use the abstraction $(\chi_\top, \sigma_\bot)$, i.e., a completely non-relational analysis using a full alphabet (similar to the analyses proposed in [20, 18]). This level of abstraction fails to prove the desired properties and raise false alarms, demonstrating the importance of a relational analysis. The next set of columns uses the abstraction $(\chi, \sigma_\bot)$, using our heuristic to track a subset of variables relationally. This level of abstraction is able to prove all of the desired properties, demonstrating the utility of both the relational analysis and of our heuristic. Finally, the last set of columns uses the abstraction (χ, σ), using our heuristics for both relation and alphabet abstraction. This level of abstraction is also able to verify all the desired properties, and does so with even better time and memory performance than the previous level of abstraction.

The results for the XSS benchmarks are summarized in Table 2. The first three rows show results for the unmodified benchmarks. Since our analysis is sound and all three benchmarks are vulnerable to XSS attacks, we cannot verify the desired properties regardless of the abstractions used. The last three rows show results for the modified benchmarks whose vulnerabilities have been patched, and therefore are secure. The first set of columns uses the abstraction $(\chi_\top, \sigma_\bot)$, i.e., a completely non-relational analysis using a full alphabet. This level of abstraction is sufficient to prove the desired properties, demonstrating that relational analysis is not always necessary and that the ability to selectively remove relational tracking is valuable. The last set of columns uses the abstraction $(\chi_\top, \sigma)$, using our alphabet abstraction to abstract some characters of the alphabet. This level of abstraction is also able to prove the desired properties and does so with improved time and memory performance than the previous level of abstraction, demonstrating again the benefit of our alphabet abstraction.

Detecting XSS Vulnerabilities in an Open-source Web Application. Our second experiment demonstrates the utility of the alphabet abstraction in detecting XSS vulnerabilities in an open source application: Schoolmate. Schoolmate consists of 63 php files with 8620 lines of code in total. The string analysis we report in this experiment is performed fully automatically using the Stranger tool that we extended with the alphabet abstraction.

The experimental results are summarized in Table 3. We first detect XSS vulnerabilities against the original code of schoolmate (denoted as O in Table 3). The first row shows the result of using $(\chi_\top, \sigma_\bot)$, a completely non-relational analysis using full set of ASCII characters as the alphabet. The second row shows the result of $(\chi_\top, \sigma)$, where

Table 1. Experimental results for the MFE benchmarks. DFA: the final DFA associated with the checked program point. state: number of states. bdd: number of BDD nodes. Result: "n" not verified, "y" verified.

		$(\chi_\top, \sigma_\bot)$				$(\chi, \sigma_\bot)$				(χ, σ)		
	Res.	DFA state(bdd)	Time (sec)	Mem (kb)	Res.	DFA state(bdd)	Time (sec)	Mem (kb)	Res.	DFA state(bdd)	Time (sec)	Mem (kb)
M1	n	56(801)	0.030	621	y	50(3551)	0.061	1294	y	54(556)	0.019	517
M2	n	22(495)	0.017	555	y	21(604)	0.044	996	y	22(179)	0.01	538
M3	n	5(113)	0.01	417	y	3(276)	0.019	465	y	3(49)	0.005	298
M4	n	1201(25949)	0.251	9495	y	181(9893)	0.854	19322	y	175(4137)	0.348	5945
M5	n	211(3195)	0.057	1676	y	62(2423)	0.102	1756	y	66(1173)	0.036	782

Table 2. Experimental results for the XSS benchmarks

		$(\chi_T, \sigma_\perp)$				$(\chi, \sigma_\perp)$		
	Res.	DFA state(bdd)	Time (sec)	Mem (kb)	Res.	DFA state(bdd)	Time (sec)	Mem (kb)
S1	n	17(148)	0.012	444	n	65(1629)	0.345	1231
S2	n	27(229)	0.037	895	n	47(2714)	0.161	2684
S3	n	79(633)	0.067	1696	n	79(1900)	0.229	2826
		$(\chi_T, \sigma_\perp)$				(χ_T, σ)		
S1'	y	17(147)	0.012	382	y	17(89)	0.006	287
S2'	y	17(141)	0.252	5686	y	9(48)	0.041	2155
S3'	y	127(1142)	0.444	6201	y	125(743)	0.299	3802

Table 3. Checking XSS Vulnerabilities in Schoolmate

	Abstraction	Result #vuls/#sinks	Time(s) fwd/total	Mem (kb) avg/max	DFA: state/bdd avg	DFA: state/bdd max	Dep. Graph: node/edge avg	Dep. Graph: node/edge max
O	$(\chi_T, \sigma_\perp)$	114/898	1464/1526	62568/191317	764/6894	2709/24382	33/33	123/129
O	(χ_T, σ)	114/898	1052/1104	31987/89488	1051/5255	3593/18005	33/33	123/129
S	$(\chi_T, \sigma_\perp)$	10/898	924/979	52466/145901	725/6564	2164/19553	41/41	143/149
S	(χ_T, σ)	10/898	609/662	27774/82640	1136/5689	3466/17364	41/41	143/149

we apply alphabet abstraction by keeping only the characters appearing in the attack pattern precisely. Each alphabet character is encoded using 3 bits. The coarser abstract analysis discovers 114 potential XSS vulnerabilities out of 898 sinks, using 1052 seconds for the string analysis (fwd) and 1104 seconds in total to explore all entries of 63 PHP scripts. The average size of a dependency graph (for a sink) has 33 nodes (each node represents one string operation) and 33 edges, while the maximum one has 123 nodes and 129 edges (the graph contains cycles). The average memory consumption is 62.5Mb for checking whether a sink is vulnerable, while the maximum consumption is 191Mb. The final DFA on average consists of 1051 states and 5255 bdd nodes to encode the transition relation, and the maximum one consists of 3593 states and 18005 bdd nodes. Compared to $(\chi_T, \sigma_\perp)$, using alphabet abstraction, we introduce zero false alarms (number of reported vulnerabilities are 114 in both analyses) but reduce the analysis time 28% (from 1464 seconds to 1052) and reduce the memory usage 49% (from 62.5Mb to 31.9) on average.

Next we manually inserted 43 sanitization routines in the original code to remove the detected vulnerabilities by sanitizing user inputs and checked the resulting sanitized code against XSS vulnerabilities again (denoted as S in Table 3). The third row shows the result of using $(\chi_T, \sigma_\perp)$, while the fourth row shows the result of (χ_T, σ). For the sanitized code, using alphabet abstraction, we introduce zero false alarms (number of reported vulnerabilities are 10 in both analyses), but reduce the analysis time 34% (from 924 seconds to 609) and reduce the memory usage 47% (from 52.4Mb to 27.7) on average. We have observed that the 10 vulnerabilities that were reported after we inserted the sanitization routines are false positives due to some unmodeled built-in functions (which are conservatively considered to return any possible string value) and path insensitive analysis. The 104 out of 114 vulnerabilities reported in the original version of the Schoolmate application are real vulnerabilities that are eliminated by the sanitization functions that we manually inserted to the application. To summarize, our experimental results demonstrate that using alphabet abstraction, we are able to considerably improve the performance without loss of accuracy of the analysis.

5   Related Work

Symbolic verification using automata have been investigated in other contexts (e.g., Bouajjani et al. [4, 3]). In this paper we focus specifically on verification of string manipulation operations, which is essential to detect and prevent web-related vulnerabilities.

String analysis has been widely studied due to its relevance for security. One influential approach has been *grammar-based* string analysis [5]. This approach uses a context-free grammar to represent the possible string operations and then over-approximates the resulting language by converting the grammar to a regular language. This form of analysis has been used to check for various types of errors in Web applications [8, 11, 16]. This analysis is not relational and cannot verify the simple programs we discussed in Section 2. Both Minamide [11] and Wassermann and Su [16] use multi-track DFAs, known as *transducers*, to model string replacement operations. There are also several recent string analysis tools that use symbolic string analysis based on DFA encodings [14, 7, 20, 22]. Some of these tools employ symbolic execution and use a DFA representation to model and verify string manipulation operations in Java [14, 7]. In our earlier work, we have used a DFA based symbolic reachability analysis to verify the correctness of string sanitization operations in PHP programs [20, 22].

Unlike the relational string analysis approach we use in this paper, (which is based on the results first presented by Yu et al. [21]) all of the above results use single-track DFA and encode the reachable configurations of each string variable separately—i.e., they use a non-relational string analysis. As demonstrated in this paper, a relational analysis enables verification of properties that cannot be verified with these earlier approaches.

However, relational string analysis can generate automata that are exponentially larger than the automata generated during non-relational string analysis. The alphabet and relation abstractions we present in this paper enable us to improve the performance of the relational string analysis by adjusting its precision. The earlier results on relational string analysis presented by Yu et al. [21, 19] do not use any abstraction techniques.

While other work has employed abstraction techniques on automata [3], the novel abstractions we present in this paper are based on string values and relations among string variables. These abstractions allow useful heuristics based on the constants and relations appearing in the input program and the property.

Compared to string analysis techniques based on bounded string constraint solvers (e.g., HAMPI [10] and Kaluza [13]) an important differentiating characteristic of our approach is the fact that it is sound and can, therefore, be used to prove absence of string vulnerabilities.

Finally, this paper shows how string abstraction techniques that can be composed to form an abstraction lattice that subsumes the previous work on string analysis and size analysis. Our previous results, e.g., string analysis [20], composite (string+size) analysis [22], and relational string analysis [21] all become part of this abstraction lattice. This is the first such generalized string analysis result as far as we know.

6 Conclusions

As web applications are becoming more and more dominant, security vulnerabilities in them are becoming increasingly critical. The most common security vulnerabilities in web applications are due to improper sanitization of user inputs, which in turn are due to erroneous or improper use of string manipulation operations. In this paper we have focused on a relational string analysis that can be used to verify string manipulation operations in web applications. We presented two string abstraction techniques called alphabet and relation abstraction. These abstraction techniques enable us to adjust the precision and performance of our string analysis techniques. We also proposed a heuristic to statically determine the abstraction level and empirically demonstrated the effectiveness of our approach on open source web applications.

References

1. Balzarotti, D., Cova, M., Felmetsger, V., Jovanovic, N., Kruegel, C., Kirda, E., Vigna, G.: Saner: Composing Static and Dynamic Analysis to Validate Sanitization in Web Applications. In: Proceedings of the Symposium on Security and Privacy (2008)
2. Bartzis, C., Bultan, T.: Widening arithmetic automata. In: Alur, R., Peled, D.A. (eds.) CAV 2004. LNCS, vol. 3114, pp. 321–333. Springer, Heidelberg (2004)
3. Bouajjani, A., Habermehl, P., Vojnar, T.: Abstract regular model checking. In: Alur, R., Peled, D.A. (eds.) CAV 2004. LNCS, vol. 3114, pp. 372–386. Springer, Heidelberg (2004)
4. Bouajjani, A., Jonsson, B., Nilsson, M., Touili, T.: Regular model checking. In: Emerson, E.A., Sistla, A.P. (eds.) CAV 2000. LNCS, vol. 1855, pp. 403–418. Springer, Heidelberg (2000)
5. Christensen, A.S., Møller, A., Schwartzbach, M.I.: Precise analysis of string expressions. In: Cousot, R. (ed.) SAS 2003. LNCS, vol. 2694, pp. 1–18. Springer, Heidelberg (2003)
6. Dor, N., Rodeh, M., Sagiv, M.: CSSV towards a realistic tool for statically detecting all buffer overflows. C. SIGPLAN Not. 38(5), 155–167 (2003)
7. Fu, X., Lu, X., Peltsverger, B., Chen, S., Qian, K., Tao, L.: A static analysis framework for detecting sql injection vulnerabilities. In: Proc. of the 31st Annual International Computer Software and Applications Conference, Washington, DC, USA, pp. 87–96 (2007)
8. Gould, C., Su, Z., Devanbu, P.: Static checking of dynamically generated queries in database applications. In: Proc. of the 26th International Conference on Software Engineering, pp. 645–654 (2004)
9. Henriksen, J.G., Jensen, J.L., Jørgensen, M.E., Klarlund, N., Paige, R., Rauhe, T., Sandholm, A.: Mona: Monadic second-order logic in practice. In: Brinksma, E., Steffen, B., Cleaveland, W.R., Larsen, K.G., Margaria, T. (eds.) TACAS 1995. LNCS, vol. 1019, pp. 89–110. Springer, Heidelberg (1995)
10. Kiezun, A., Ganesh, V., Guo, P.J., Hooimeijer, P., Ernst, M.D.: Hampi: a solver for string constraints. In: ISSTA, pp. 105–116 (2009)
11. Minamide, Y.: Static approximation of dynamically generated web pages. In: Proc. of the 14th International World Wide Web Conference, pp. 432–441 (2005)
12. Open Web Application Security Project (OWASP). Top ten project (May 2007), http://www.owasp.org/
13. Saxena, P., Akhawe, D., Hanna, S., Mao, F., McCamant, S., Song, D.: A symbolic execution framework for javascript. In: IEEE Symposium on Security and Privacy, pp. 513–528 (2010)
14. Shannon, D., Hajra, S., Lee, A., Zhan, D., Khurshid, S.: Abstracting symbolic execution with string analysis. In: TAICPART-MUTATION 2007, DC, USA, pp. 13–22 (2007)

15. Wagner, D., Foster, J.S., Brewer, E.A., Aiken, A.: A first step towards automated detection of buffer overrun vulnerabilities. In: Proc. of the Network and Distributed System Security Symposium, pp. 3–17 (2000)
16. Wassermann, G., Su, Z.: Sound and precise analysis of web applications for injection vulnerabilities. In: Proc. of the ACM SIGPLAN 2007 Conference on Programming Language Design and Implementation, pp. 32–41 (2007)
17. Yu, F., Alkhalaf, M., Bultan, T.: Generating vulnerability signatures for string manipulating programs using automata-based forward and backward symbolic analyses. In: Proc. of the 24th IEEE/ACM International Conference on Automated Software Engineering (ASE) (2009)
18. Yu, F., Alkhalaf, M., Bultan, T.: STRANGER: An automata-based string analysis tool for PHP. In: Esparza, J., Majumdar, R. (eds.) TACAS 2010. LNCS, vol. 6015, pp. 154–157. Springer, Heidelberg (2010)
19. Yu, F., Alkhalaf, M., Bultan, T.: Patching vulnerabilities with sanitization synthesis. In: Proc. of the 33rd International Conference on Software Engineering (ICSE) (2011)
20. Yu, F., Bultan, T., Cova, M., Ibarra, O.H.: Symbolic string verification: An automata-based approach. In: Havelund, K., Majumdar, R. (eds.) SPIN 2008. LNCS, vol. 5156, pp. 306–324. Springer, Heidelberg (2008)
21. Yu, F., Bultan, T., Ibarra, O.H.: Relational string verification using multi-track automata. In: Domaratzki, M., Salomaa, K. (eds.) CIAA 2010. LNCS, vol. 6482, pp. 290–299. Springer, Heidelberg (2011)
22. Yu, F., Bultan, T., Ibarra, O.H.: Symbolic string verification: Combining string analysis and size analysis. In: Kowalewski, S., Philippou, A. (eds.) TACAS 2009. LNCS, vol. 5505, pp. 322–336. Springer, Heidelberg (2009)

Parallel Recursive State Compression for Free

Alfons Laarman, Jaco van de Pol, and Michael Weber

Formal Methods and Tools, University of Twente, The Netherlands
{a.w.laarman,vdpol,michaelw}@cs.utwente.nl

Abstract. This paper focuses on reducing memory usage in enumerative model checking, while maintaining the multi-core scalability obtained in earlier work. We present a multi-core tree-based compression method, which works by leveraging sharing among sub-vectors of state vectors.

An algorithmic analysis of both worst-case and optimal compression ratios shows the potential to compress even large states to a small constant on average (8 bytes). Our experiments demonstrate that this holds up in practice: the median compression ratio of 279 measured experiments is within 17% of the optimum for tree compression, and five times better than the median compression ratio of SPIN's COLLAPSE compression.

Our algorithms are implemented in the LTSmin tool, and our experiments show that for model checking, multi-core tree compression pays its own way: it comes virtually without overhead compared to the fastest hash table-based methods.

1 Introduction

Many verification problems are computationally intensive tasks that can benefit from extra speedups. Considering recent hardware trends, these speedups do not come automatically for sequential exploration algorithms, but require exploitation of the parallelism within multi-core CPUs. In a previous paper, we have shown how to realize scalable multi-core reachability [14], a basic task shared by many different approaches to verification.

Reachability searches through all the *states* of the program under verification to find errors or deadlocks. It is bound by the number of states that fit into the main memory. Since states typically consist of large *vectors* with one *slot* for each program variable, only small parts are updated for every step in the program. Hence, storing a state in its entirety results in unnecessary and considerable overhead. State compression solves this problem, as this paper will show, at a negligible performance penalty and with better scalability than uncompressed hash tables.

Related work. In the following, we identify compression techniques suitable for (on-the-fly) enumerative model checking. We distinguish between *generic* and *informed* techniques.

A. Groce and M. Musuvathi (Eds.): SPIN 2011, LNCS 6823, pp. 38–56, 2011.
© Springer-Verlag Berlin Heidelberg 2011

Generic compression methods, like Huffman encoding and run length encoding, have been considered for explicit state vectors with meager results [12, 9]. These *entropy encoding* methods reduce *information entropy* [7] by assuming common bit patterns. Such patterns have to be defined statically and cannot be "learned" (as in dynamic Huffman encoding), because the encoding may not change during state space exploration. Otherwise, desirable properties, like fast equivalence checks on states and constant-time state space inclusion checks, will be lost.

Other work focuses on efficient storage in hash tables [6, 10]. The assumption is that a uniformly distributed subset of n elements from the universe U is stored in a hash table. If each element in U hashes to a unique location in the table, only one bit is needed to encode the presence of the element. If, however, the hash function is not so perfect or U is larger than the table, then at least a quotient of the key needs to be stored and collisions need to be dealt with. This technique is therefore known as *key quotienting*. While its benefit is that the compression ratio is constant for any input (not just constant on average), compression is only significant for small universes [10], smaller than we encounter in model checking (this universe consists of all possible combinations of the slot values, not to be confused with the set of reachable states, which is typically much smaller).

The information theoretical lower bound on compression, or the *information entropy*, can be reduced further if the format of the input is known in advance (certain subsets of U become more likely). This is what constitutes the class of *informed compression* techniques. It includes works that provide specialized storage schemes for certain specific state structures, like petri-nets [8] or timed automata [17]. But, also COLLAPSE compression introduced by Holzmann for the model checker SPIN [11]. It takes into account the independent parts of the state vector. Independent parts are identified as the global variables and the local variables belonging to different processes in the SPIN-specific language PROMELA.

Blom et al. [1] present a more generic approach, based on a tree. All variables of a state are treated as independent and stored recursively in a binary tree of hash tables. The method was mainly used to decrease network traffic for distributed model checking. Like COLLAPSE, this is a form of informed compression, because it depends on the assumption that subsequent states only differ slightly.

Problem statement. Information theory dictates that the more information we have on the data that is being compressed, the lower the entropy and the higher the achievable compression. Favorable results from informed compression techniques [8,17,11,1] confirm this. However, the techniques for petri-nets and timed automata employ specific properties of those systems (a deterministic transition relation and symbolic zone encoding respectively), and, therefore, are not applicable to enumerative model checking. COLLAPSE requires local parts of the state vector to be syntactically identifiable and may thus not identify all equivalent parts among state vectors. While tree compression showed more impressive compression ratios by analysis [1] and is more generically applicable, it has never been benchmarked thoroughly and compared to other compression techniques nor has it been parallelized.

Generic compression schemes can be added locally to a parallel reachability algorithm (see Sec. 2). They do not affect any concurrent parts of its implementation and even benefit scalability by lowering memory traffic [12]. While informed compression techniques can deliver better compression, they require additional structures to record uniqueness of state vector parts. With multiple processors constantly accessing these structures, memory bandwidth is again increased and mutual exclusion locks are strained, thereby decreasing performance and scalability. Thus the benefit of informed compression requires considerable design effort on modern multi-core CPUs with steep memory hierarchies.

Therefore, in this paper, we address two research questions: (1) does tree compression perform better than other state-of-the-art on-the-fly compression techniques (most importantly COLLAPSE), (2) can parallel tree compression be implemented efficiently on multi-core CPUs.

Contribution. This paper explains a tree-based structure that enables high compression rates (higher than any other form of explicit-state compression that we could identify) and excellent performance. A parallel algorithm is presented (Sec. 3) that makes this informed compression technique scalable in spite of the multiple accesses to shared memory that it requires, while also introducing *maximal sharing*. With an incremental algorithm, we further improve the performance, reducing contention and memory footprint.

An analysis of compression ratios is provided (Sec. 4) and the results of extensive and realistic experiments (Sec. 5) match closely to the analytical optima. The results also show that the incremental algorithm delivers excellent performance, even compared to uncompressed verification runs with a normal hash table. Benchmarks on multi-core machines show near-perfect scalability, even for cases which are sequentially already faster than the uncompressed run.

2   Background

In Sec. 2.1, we introduce a parallel *reachability* algorithm using a shared hash table. The table's main functionality is the storage of a large set of state vectors of a fixed length k. We call the elements of the vectors *slots* and assume that slots take values from the integers, possibly *references* to complex values stored elsewhere (hash tables or canonization techniques can be used to yield unique values for about any complex value). Subsequently, in Sec. 2.2, we explain two informed compression techniques that exploit similarity between different state vectors. While these techniques can be used to replace the hash table in the reachability algorithm, they are are harder to parallelize as we show in Sec. 2.3.

```
1   S₁.putall(initial_states)
2   parallel_for (id := 1 to N)
3       while (load_balance(S_id))
4           work := 0
5           while (work < max ∧ state := S_id.get())
6               count := 0
7               for (succ ∈ next_state(state))
8                   count := count + 1
9                   work := work + 1
10                  if (¬find_or_put(DB, succ)) then S_id.put(succ)
11              if (0 = count) then ...report deadlock...
```

Alg. 1. Parallel reachability algorithm with shared state storage

2.1 Parallel Reachability

The parallel reachability algorithm (Alg. 1) launches N threads and assigns the initial states of the model under verification only to the *open set* S_1 of the first thread (l.1). The open set can be implemented as a *stack* or a *queue*, depending on the desired search order (note that with $N > 1$, the chosen search order will only be approximated, because the different threads will go through the search space independently). The *closed set* of visited states, DB, is shared, allowing threads executing the search algorithm (l.5-11) to synchronize on the search space and each to explore a (disjoint) part of it [14]. The find_or_put function returns *true* when *succ* is found in DB, and inserts it, when it is not.

Load balancing is needed so that workers that run out of work ($S_{id} = \emptyset$) receive work from others. We implemented the function load_balance as a form of Synchronous Random Polling [20], which also ensures valid termination detection [14]. It returns *false* upon global termination.

DB is generally implemented as a hash table. In [14], we presented a lockless hash table design, with which we were able to obtain almost perfect scalability. However, with 16 cores, the physical memory, 64GB in our case, is filled in a matter of seconds, making memory the new bottleneck. Informed compression techniques can solve this problem with an alternate implementation of DB.

2.2 Collapse and Tree Compression

COLLAPSE compression stores logical parts of the state vector in separate hash tables. A logical part is made up of state slots local to a specific process in the model, therefore the hash tables are called *process tables*. References to the parts in those process tables are then stored in a root hash table. Tree compression is similar, but works on the granularity of slots: tuples of slots are stored in hash tables at the fringe of the tree, which return a reference. References are then bundled as tuples and recursively stored in tables at the nodes of the binary tree. Fig. 1 shows the difference between the process tree and tree compression.

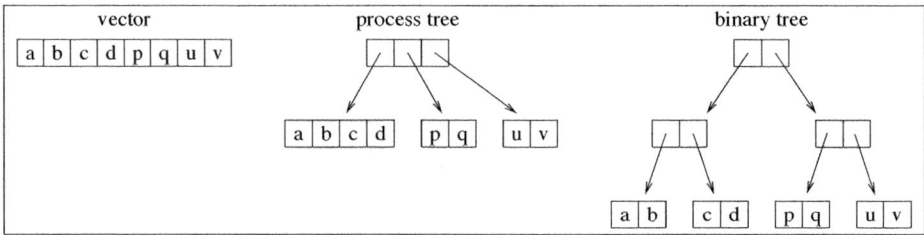

Fig. 1. Process table and (binary) tree for the system $X(a, b, c, d)\|Y(p, q)\|Z(u, v)$. Taken from [4].

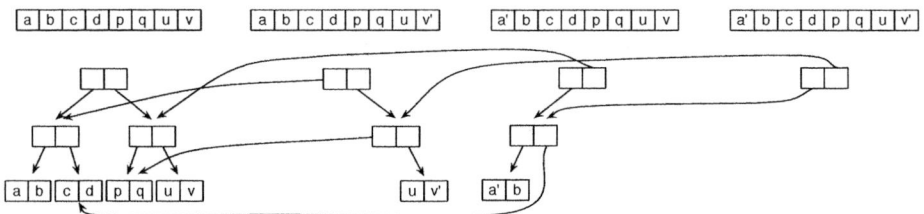

Fig. 2. Sharing of subtrees in tree compression

When using a tree to store equal-length state vectors, compression is realized by the sharing of subtrees among entries. Fig. 2 illustrates this. Assuming that references have the same size as the slot values (say b bits), we can determine the compression rate in this example.

Storing one vector in a tree, requires storing information for the extra tree nodes, resulting in a total of $8b + (4 - 1) \times 2b = 14b$ (not taking into account any implementation overhead from lookup structures). Each additional vector, however, can potentially share parts of the subtree with already-stored vectors. The second and third, in the example, only require a total of $6b$ each and the fourth only $2b$. The four vectors would occupy $4 \times 8b = 32b$ when stored in a normal hash table. This gives a compression ratio of $28b/32b = 7/8$, likely to improve with each additional vector that is stored. Databases that store longer vectors also achieve higher compression rates as we will investigate later.

2.3   Why Parallelization is Not Trivial

Adding generic compression techniques to the above algorithm can be done locally by adding a line $compr := \mathsf{compress}(succ)$ after l.9, and storing $compr$ in DB. This calculation in $compress$ only depends on $succ$ and is therefore easy to parallelize. If, however, a form of *informed* compression is used, like COLLAPSE or tree compression, the compressed value comes to depend on previously inserted state parts, and the *compress* function needs (multiple) accesses to the storage.

Global locking or even locking at finer levels of granularity can be devastating for multi-core performance for single hash table lookups [14]. Informed compression algorithms, however, need multiple accesses and thus require careful attention when paral-

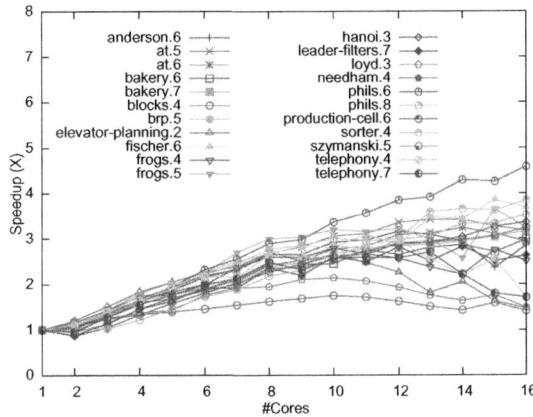

Fig. 3. Speedup with COLLAPSE

lelized. Fig. 3 shows that SPIN's COLLAPSE suffers from scalability problems (experimental settings can be found in Sec. 5).

3   Tree Database

Sec. 3.1 first describes the original tree compression algorithm from [1]. In Sec. 3.2, *maximal sharing* among tree nodes is introduced by merging the multiple hash tables of the tree into a single fixed-size table. By simplifying the data structure in this way, we aid scalability. Furthermore, we prove that it preserves consistency of the database's content. However, as we also show, the new tree will "confuse" tree nodes and erroneously report some vectors as *seen*, while in fact they are *new*. This is corrected by tagging root tree nodes, completing the parallelization.

Sec. 3.3 shows how tree references can also be used to compact the size of the open set in Alg. 1. Now that the necessary space reductions are obtained, the current section is concluded with an algorithm that improves the performance of the tree database by using thread-local incremental information from the reachability search (Sec. 3.4).

3.1   Basic Tree Database

The tuples shown in Fig. 2 are stored in hash tables, creating a *balanced binary tree* of tables. Such a tree has $k - 1$ tree nodes, each of which has a number of siblings of both the left and the right subtree that is equal or off by one. The tree_create function in Alg. 2 generates the Tree structure accordingly, with Nodes storing *left* and *right* subtrees, a Table *table* and the length of the (sub)tree k.

The tree_find_or_put function takes as arguments a Tree and a state vector V (both of the same size $k > 1$), and returns a tuple containing a reference to the inserted value and a boolean indicating whether the value was inserted before (*seen*, or else: *new*). The function is recursively called on half of the state vector (l.9-10) until the vector length is one. The recursion ends here and a single value

---

1 **type** Tree $=$ Node(Tree $left$, Tree $right$, Table $table$, **int** k) | Leaf
2 **proc** Tree tree_create (k)
3   **if** $(k = 1)$
4   **return** Leaf
5   **return** Node(tree_create$(\lceil \frac{k}{2} \rceil)$, tree_create$(\lfloor \frac{k}{2} \rfloor)$, Table(2), k)
6 **proc** (**int**, **bool**) tree_find_or_put (Leaf, V)
7   **return** $(V[0], \_)$
8 **proc** (**int**, **bool**) tree_find_or_put (Node($left$, $right$, $table$, k), V)
9      $(R_{\text{left}}, \_) :=$ tree_find_or_put($left$, lhalf(V))
10     $(R_{\text{right}}, \_) :=$ tree_find_or_put($right$, rhalf(V))
11   **return** table_find_or_put ($table$, $[R_{\text{left}}, R_{\text{right}}]$)

Alg. 2. Tree data structure and algorithm for the tree_find_or_put function

of the vector is returned. At l.11, the returned values of the left and right subtree are stored as a tuple in the hash table using the table_find_and_put operation, which also returns a tuple containing a reference and a *seen/new* boolean.

The function lhalf takes a vector V as argument and returns the first half of the vector: lhalf$(V) = [V_0, \ldots, V_{(\lceil \frac{k}{2} \rceil - 1)}]$, and symmetrically rhalf$(V) = [V_{\lceil \frac{k}{2} \rceil}, \ldots, V_{(k-1)}]$. So, $|\text{lhalf}(V)| = \lceil |V|/2 \rceil$, and $|\text{rhalf}(V)| = \lfloor |V|/2 \rfloor$.

Implementation requirements. A space-efficient implementation of the hash tables is crucial for good compression ratios. Furthermore, resizing hash tables are required, because the unpredictable and widely varying tree node sizes (tables may store a crossproduct of their children as shown in Sec. 4). However, resizing replaces entries, in other words, it breaks *stable indexing*, thus making direct references between tree nodes impossible. Therefore, in [1], stable indices were realized by maintaining a second table with references. Thus solving the problem, but increasing the number of cache misses and the storage costs per entry by 50%.

3.2 Concurrent Tree Database

Three conflicting requirements arise when attempting to parallelize Alg. 2: (1) resizing is needed because the load of individual tables is unknown in advance and varies highly, (2) stable indexing is needed, to allow for references to table entries, and (3) calculating a globally unique index concurrently is costly, while storing it requires extra memory as explained in the previous section.

An ideal solution would be to collapse all hash tables into a single non-resizable table. This would ensure stable indices without any overhead for administering them, while at the same time allowing the use of a scalable hash table design [14]. Moreover, it will enable *maximal sharing* of values between tree nodes, possibly further reducing memory requirements. *But can all tree nodes safely be merged without corrupting the contents of the database?*

```
1 type ConcurrentTree = CTree(Table table, int k)
2 proc (int, bool) tree_find_or_put (tree, V)
3     R := tree_rec(tree, V)
4     B := if CAS(R.tag, non_root, is_also_root) then new else seen
5     return (R, B)
6 proc int tree_rec (CTree(table, k), V)
7     if (k = 1)
8         return V[0]
9     R_left := tree_rec(CTree(table, ⌈k/2⌉), lhalf(V))
10    R_right := tree_rec(CTree(table, ⌊k/2⌋), rhalf(V))
11    (R, _) := table_find_or_put(table, [R_left, R_right])
12    return R
```

Alg. 3. Data structure and algorithm for parallel tree_find_or_put function

We can describe table_find_or_put as a injective function: H_k : $\mathbb{N}^k \rightarrow \mathbb{N}$. The tree_find_or_put function with one hash table can be expressed as a recurrent relation: $T_k(A_0, \ldots, A_{(k-1)}) = H_2(T_{\lceil \frac{k}{2} \rceil}(A_0, \ldots, A_{(\lceil \frac{k}{2} \rceil - 1)}), T_{\lfloor \frac{k}{2} \rfloor}(A_{\lceil \frac{k}{2} \rceil}, \ldots, A_{(k-1)}))$, with $T_1 = I$ (the identity function). We have proven that this is an injective function [16]. Therefore, an insert of a vector $A \in \mathbb{N}^k$ always yields a unique value for the root of the tree (T_k), thus demonstrating that the contents of the tree database are not corrupted by merging the hash tables of the tree nodes.

However, the above also shows that Alg. 2 will not always yield the right answer with merged hash tables. Consider: $T_2(A_0, A_1) = H_2(0,0) = T_k(A_0, \ldots, A_{(k-1)})$. In this case, when the root node T_k is inserted into H, it will return a boolean indicating that the tuple $(0, 0)$ was already seen, as it was inserted for T_2 earlier.

Nonetheless, we can use the fact that T_k is an injection to create a concurrent tree database by adding one bit (a *tag*) to the merged hash table. Alg. 3 defines a new ConcurrentTree structure, only containing the merge *table* and the length of the vectors k. It separates the recursion in the tree_rec function, which only returns a reference to the inserted node. The tree_find_or_put function now atomically flips the tag on the entry (the tuple) pointed to by R in *table* from *non_root* to *is_also_root*, if it was not *non_root* before (see l.4). To this end, it employs the hardware primitive *compare-and-swap* (CAS), which takes three arguments: a memory location (in this case, $R.tag$), an *old* value and a *designated* value. CAS atomically compares the value *val* at the memory location with *old*, if equal, *val* is replaced by *designated* and true is returned, if not, false is returned.

Implementation considerations. Crucial for efficient concurrency is *memory layout*. While a bit array or sparse bit vector may be used to implement the tags (using R as index), its parallelization is hardly efficient for high-throughput applications like reachability analysis. Each modified bit will cause an entire cache line (with typically thousands of other bits) to become *dirty*, causing other CPUs accessing the same memory region to be forced to update the line from main memory. The latter operation is multiple orders of magnitude more expensive than normal (cached) operations. Therefore, we merge the bit array/vector into the hash table *table* as shown in Fig 4, for this increases the spatial locality of node accesses with a factor proportional to the width of tree nodes. The small column on the left represents the bit array with black entries indicating *is_also_root*. The appropriate size of *b* is discussed in Sec. 4.

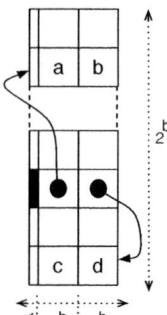

Fig. 4. Memory layout for CTree(Table, 4) with $\langle a, b, c, d \rangle$ inserted

Furthermore, we used the lockless hash table presented in [14], which normally uses *memoized hashes* in order to speed up probing over larger keys. Since the stored tree nodes are relatively small, we dropped the memoize hashes, demonstrating that this hash table design also functions well without additional memory overhead.

3.3   References in the Open Set

Now that tree compression reduces the space required for state storage, we observed that the open sets of the parallel reachability algorithm can become a memory bottleneck [15]. A solution is to store references to the root tree node in the open set as illustrated by Alg. 4, which is a modification of l.5-11 from Alg. 1.

The tree_get function is shown in Alg. 5. It reconstructs the vector from a reference. References are looked up in *table* using the table_get function, which

```
1  while ( ref := S_id.get())
2       state := tree_get (DB, ref)
3       for ( succ ∈ next_state(state))
4            (newref, seen) := tree_find_or_put (DB, succ)
5            if (¬seen)
6                 S_id.put(newref)
```

Alg. 4. Reachability analysis algorithm with references in the open set

```
1  proc int[] tree_get(CTree(table, k), val_or_ref)
2       if (k = 1)
3            return [val_or_ref]
4       [R_left, R_right] := table_get(table, val_or_ref)
5       V_left := tree_get(CTree(table, ⌈k/2⌉), R_left)
6       V_right := tree_get(CTree(table, ⌊k/2⌋), R_right)
7       return concat(V_left, V_right)
```

Alg. 5. Algorithm for tree vector retrieval from a reference

1 **type** ReferenceTree = RTree(ReferenceTree *left*, ReferenceTree *right*, **int** *ref*) | Leaf

2 **proc** (**int**, **bool**) tree_rec (CTree(*table*, k), V, P, Leaf)

3   **return** ($V[0]$, $V[0] = P[0]$)

4 **proc** (**int**, **bool**) tree_rec (CTree(*table*, k), V, P, **inout** RTree(*left*, *right*, *ref*))

5   (R_{left}, B_{left}) := tree_rec(CTree(*table*, $\lceil \frac{k}{2} \rceil$), lhalf($V$), lhalf($P$), *left*)

6   (R_{right}, B_{right}) := tree_rec(CTree(*table*, $\lfloor \frac{k}{2} \rfloor$), rhalf($V$), rhalf($P$), *right*)

7   **if** ($\neg B_{\text{left}} \vee \neg B_{\text{right}}$)

8   (*ref*, _) := table_find_or_put (*table*, $[R_{\text{left}}, R_{\text{right}}]$)

9   **return** (*ref*, $B_{\text{left}} \wedge B_{\text{right}}$)

Alg. 6. ReferenceTree structure and incremental tree_rec function

returns the tuple stored in the table. The algorithm recursively calls itself until $k = 1$, at this point *ref_or_val* is known to be a slot value and is returned as vector of size 1. Results then propagate back up the tree and are concatenated on l.7, until the full vector of length k is restored at the root of the tree.

3.4 Incremental Tree Database

The time complexity of the tree compression algorithm, measured in the number of hash table accesses, is linear in the number of state slots. However, because of today's steep memory hierarchies these random memory accesses are expensive. Luckily, the same principle that tree compression exploits to deliver good state compression, can also be used to speedup the algorithm. The only entries that need to be inserted into the node table are the slots that actually changed with regard to the previous state and the tree paths that lead to these nodes. For a state vector of size k, the number of table accesses can be brought down to $\log_2(k)$ (the height of the tree) assuming only one slot changed. When c slots change, the maximum number of accesses is $c \times \log_2(k)$, but likely fewer if the slots are close to each other in the tree (due to shared paths to the root).

Alg. 6 is the incremental variant of the tree_find_or_put function. The callee has to supply additional arguments: P is the predecessor state of V ($V \in$ next_state(P) in Alg. 1) and RTree is a ReferenceTree containing the balanced binary tree of references created for P. RTree is also updated with the tree node references for V. tree_find_or_put needs to be adapted to pass the arguments accordingly.

The boolean in the return tuple now indicates thread-local similarities between subvectors of V and P (see l.3). This boolean is used on l.7 as a condition for the hash table access; if the left or the right subvectors are not the same, then RTree is updated with a new reference that is looked up in *table*. For initial states, without predecessor states, the algorithm can be initialized with an imaginary predecessor state P and tree RTree containing reserved values, thus forcing updates.

We measured the speedup of
the new incremental algorithm compared to the original (for the experimental setup see Sec. 5). Fig. 5
shows that the speedup is linearly
dependent on $\log(k)$, as expected.

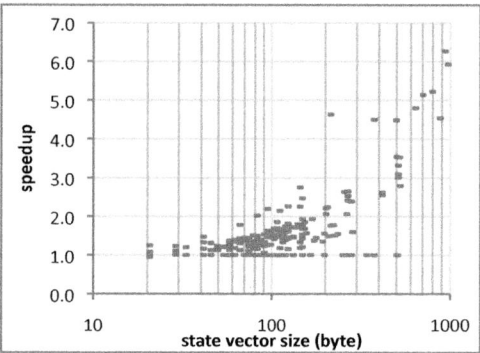

The incremental tree_find_or_put
function changed its interface with
respect to Alg. 3. Alg. 7 presents
a new search algorithm (1.5-11 in
Alg. 1) that also records the reference tree in the open set. RTree
refs has become an input of the tree
database, because it is also an output, it is copied to *new_refs*.

Fig. 5. Speedup of Alg. 6 wrt. Alg. 3

```
1  while  ((prev,  refs) := S_id.get())
2      for  (next ∈ next_state(prev))
3          new_refs := copy(refs)
4          (_, seen) := tree_find_or_put (DB, next, prev, new_refs)
5          if  (¬seen)
6              S_id.put((next, new_refs))
```

Alg. 7. Reachability analysis algorithm with incremental tree database

Because the internal tree node references are stored, Alg.7 increases the size
of the open set by a factor of almost two. To remedy this, either the tree_get
function (Alg. 5) can be adapted to also return the reference trees, or the tree_get
function can be integrated into the incremental algorithm (Alg. 6). (We do not
present such an algorithm due to space limitations.) We measured little slowdown
due to the extra calculations and memory references introduced by the tree_get
algorithm (about 10% across a wide spectrum of input models).

4 Analysis of Compression Ratios

In the current section, we establish the minimum and maximum compression
ratio for tree and COLLAPSE compression. We count references and slots as
stored in tuples at each tree node (a single such *node entry* thus has size 2). We
fix both references and slots to an equal size.[1]

Tree compression. The worst case scenario occurs when storing a set of vectors
S with each k identical slot values ($S = \{\langle s, \ldots, s \rangle \mid s \in \{1, \ldots, |S|\}\}$) [1]. In
this case, $n = |S|$ and storing each vector $v \in S$ takes $2(k-1)$ $(k-1$ node entries).

---

[1] For large tree databases references easily become 32 bits wide. This is usually an
overestimation of the slot size.

The compression is: $(2(k-1)n)/(nk) = 2 - 2/k$. Occupying more tree entries is impossible, so always strictly less than twice the memory of the plain vectors is used.

Blom et al. [1] also give an example that results in good tree compression: the storage of the cross product of a set of vectors $S = P \times P$, where P consists of m vectors of length $j = \frac{1}{2}k$. The cross product ensures maximum reuse of the left and the right subtree, and results in $n = |S| = |P|^2 = m^2$ entries in only the root node. The left subtree stores $(j-1)|P|$ entries (taking naively the worst case), as does the right, resulting in a total of of $|S| + 2(j-1)|P|$ tree node entries. The size of the tree database for S becomes $2n + 2m(k-2)$. The compression ratio is $2/k + 2/m - 4/(mk)$ (divide by nk), which can be approximated by $2/k$ for sufficiently large n (and hence m). Most vectors can thus be compressed to a size approaching that of one node entry, which is logical since each new vector receives a unique root node entry (Sec. 3.2) and the other node entries are shared.

The optimal case occurs when all the individual tree nodes store cross products of their subtrees. This occurs when the value distribution is equal over all slots: $S = \{\langle s_0, \ldots, s_{k-1}\rangle \mid s_i \in \{1, \ldots, \sqrt[k]{n}\}\}$ and that $k = 2^x$. In this situation, the $\frac{k}{2}$ leaf nodes of the tree each receive $\sqrt[k/2]{n}$ entries: $\{\langle s_i, s_{i+1}\rangle \mid i = 2k\}$. The

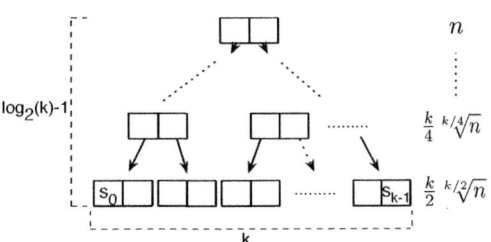

Fig. 6. Optimal entries per tree node level

nodes directly above the leafs, receive each the cross product of that as entries, etc, until the root node which receives n entries (see Fig. 6).

With this insight, we could continue to calculate the total node entries for the optimal case and try to deduce a smaller lower bound, but we can already see that the difference between the optimal case and the previous case is negligible, since: $n + \sqrt{n}(k-2) - (n + 2\sqrt{n} + 4\sqrt[4]{n} + \ldots (\log_2(k) \text{ times}) \ldots + \frac{2}{k}\sqrt[2/k]{n}) \ll n + \sqrt{n}(k-2)$, for any reasonably large n and k. From the comparison between the good and optimal case, we can conclude that only a cross product of entries in the root node is already near-optimal; the only way to get bad compression ratios may be when two related variables are located at different halves of the state vector.

COLLAPSE *compression.* Since the leafs of the process table are directly connected to the root, the compression ratios are easier to calculate. To yield optimal compression for the process table, a more restrictive scenario, than described for the tree above, needs to occur. We require p symmetrical processes with each a local vector of m slots ($k = p \times m$). Related slots may only lay within the bounds of these processes, take $S_m = \{\langle s, \ldots, s\rangle \mid s \in \{1, \ldots, |S_m|\}\}$. Each combination of different local vectors is inserted in the root table (also if $S_m = \{\langle s, 1, \ldots, 1\rangle \mid s \in \{1, \ldots, |S_m|\}\}$), yielding $n = |S_m|^p$ root table entries. The total size of the process table becomes $pn + m\sqrt[p]{n}$. The compression ratio is $(pn + m\sqrt[p]{n})/nk = \frac{p}{k} + m\frac{\sqrt[p]{n}}{nk}$. For large n (hence m), the ratio approaches $\frac{p}{k}$.

Table 1. Theoretical compression ratios of COLLAPSE and tree compression

Structure	Worst case	Best case
Hash table [14]	1	1
Process table	$1 + \frac{p}{k}$	$\frac{p}{k}$
Tree database (Alg. 2, 3)	$2 - \frac{2}{k}$	$\frac{2}{k}$

Comparison. Tab. 1 lists the achieved compression ratio for states, as stored in a normal hash table, a process table and a tree database under the different scenarios that were sketched before. It shows that the worst case of the process table is not as bad as the worst case achieved by the tree. On the other hand, the best case scenario is not as good as that from the tree, which compresses in this case to a fixed constant. We also saw that the tree can reach near-optimal cases easily, placing few constraints on related slots (on the same half). Therefore, we can expect the tree to outperform the compression of process table in more cases, because the latter requires more restrictive conditions. Namely, related slots can only be within the fixed bounds of the state vector (local to one process).

In practice. With a few considerations, the analysis of this section can be applied to both the parallel and the sequential tree databases: (1) the parallel algorithm uses one extra *tag* bit per node entry, causing insignificant overhead, and (2) maximal sharing invalidates the worst-case analysis, but other sets of vectors can be thought up to still cause the same worst-case size. In practice, we can expect little gain from maximal sharing, since the likelihood of similar subvectors decreases rapidly the larger these vectors are, while we saw that the most node entries are likely near the top of the tree (representing larger subvectors). (3) The original sequential version uses an extra reference per node entry of overhead (50%!) to realize stable indexing (Sec. 3.1). Therefore, the proposed concurrent tree implementation even improves the compression ratio by a constant factor.

5   Experiments

We performed experiments on an AMD Opteron 8356 16-core (4×4 cores) server with 64 GB RAM, running a patched Linux 2.6.32 kernel.[2] All tools were compiled using GCC 4.4.3 in 64-bit mode with high compiler optimizations (-O3).

We measured compression ratios and performance characteristics for the models of the BEEM database [19] with three tools: DiVinE 2.2, SPIN 5.2.5 and our own model checker LTSmin [3,15]. LTSmin implements Alg. 3 using a specialized version of the hash table [14] which inlines the *tags* as discussed at the end of Sec. 3.2. Special care was taken to keep all parameters across the different model checkers the same. The size of the hash/node tables was fixed at 2^{28} elements to prevent resizing and model compilation options were optimized on a per tool basis as described in earlier work [3]. We verified state and transition counts

---
[2] https://bugzilla.kernel.org/show_bug.cgi?id=15618, see also [14].

with the BEEM database and DiVinE 2.2. The complete results with over 1500
benchmarks are available online [13].

5.1 Compression Ratios

For a fair comparison of compression ratios between SPIN and LTSmin, we must
take into account the differences between the tools. The BEEM models have been
written in DVE format (DiVinE) and translated to PROMELA. The translated
BEEM models that SPIN uses may have a different state vector length. LTSmin
reads DVE inputs directly, but uses a standardized internal state representation
with one 32-bit integer per *state slot* (state variable) even if a state variable could
be represented by a single byte. Such an approach was chosen in order to reuse
the model checking algorithms for other model inputs (like mCRL, mCRL2 and
DiVinE [2]). Thus, LTSmin can load BEEM models directly, but blows up the
state vector by an average factor of three. Therefore, we compare the average
compressed state vector size instead of compression ratios.

Table 2 shows the uncompressed and compressed vector sizes for COLLAPSE
and tree compression. Tree compression achieves better and almost constant
state compression than COLLAPSE for these selected models, even though original
state vectors are larger in most cases. This confirms the results of our analysis.

We also measured peak memory usage for full state space exploration. The
benefits with respect to hash tables can be staggering for both COLLAPSE and
tree compression: while the hash table column is in the order of gigabytes, the
compressed sizes are in the order of hundreds of megabytes. An extreme case
is `hanoi.3`, where tree compression, although not optimal, is still an order of
magnitude better than COLLAPSE using only 188 MB compared to 1.5 GB with
COLLAPSE and 3 GB with the hash table.

Table 2. Original and compressed state sizes and memory usage for LTSmin with hash
table (*Table*), COLLAPSE (SPIN) and our tree compression (*Tree*) for a representative
selection of all benchmarks

Model	Orig. State [Byte]		Compr. State [Byte]		Memory [MB]		
	SPIN	Tree	SPIN	Tree	Table[a]	SPIN	Tree
at.6	68	56	36.9	8.0	8,576	4,756	1,227
iprotocol.6	164	148	39.8	8.1	5,842	2,511	322
at.5	68	56	37.1	8.0	1,709	1,136	245
bakery.7	48	80	27.4	8.8	2,216	721	245
hanoi.3	116	228	112.1	13.8	3,120	1,533	188
telephony.7	64	96	31.1	8.1	2,011	652	170
anderson.6	68	76	31.7	8.1	1,329	552	140
frogs.4	68	120	73.2	8.2	1,996	1,219	136
phils.6	140	120	58.5	9.3	1,642	780	127
sorter.4	88	104	39.7	8.3	1,308	501	105
elev_plan.2	52	140	67.1	9.2	1,526	732	100
telephony.4	54	80	28.7	8.1	938	350	95
fischer.6	92	72	43.7	8.4	571	348	66

[a] The hash table size is calculated on the base of the LTSmin state sizes.

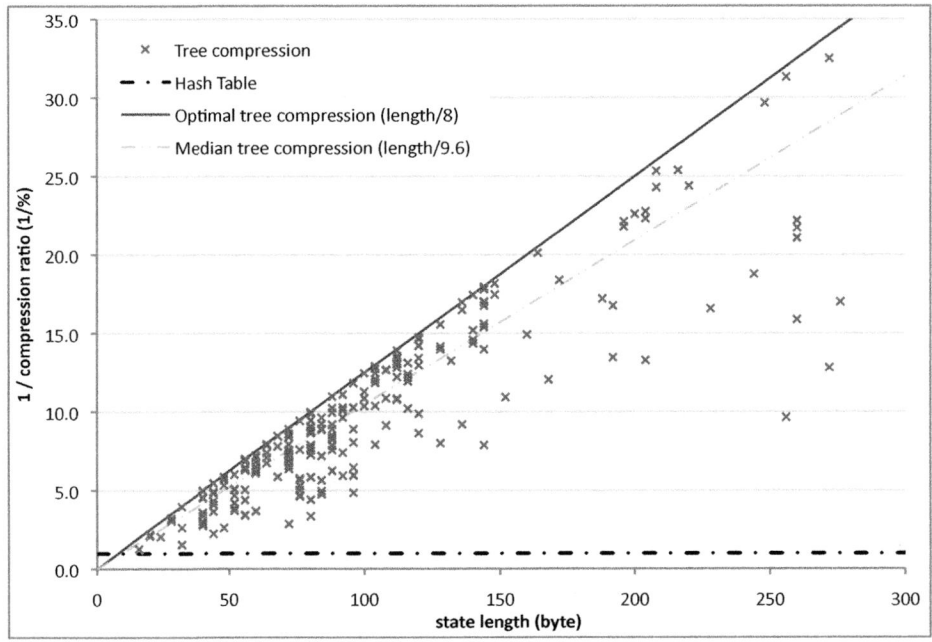

Fig. 7. Compression ratios for 279 models of the BEEM database are close to optimal for tree compression

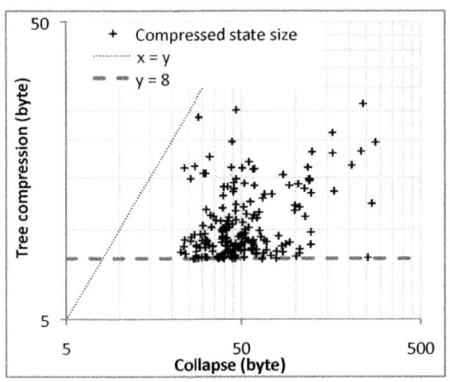

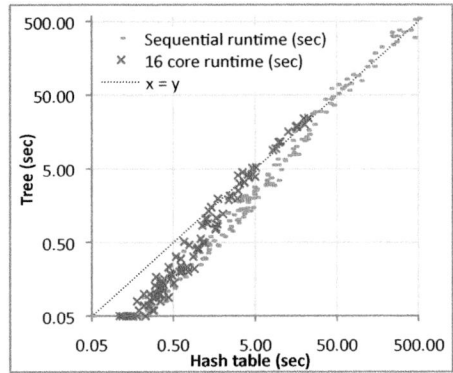

Fig. 8. Log-log scatter plot of COLLAPSE and tree-compressed state sizes (smaller is better): for all tested models, tree compression uses less memory

Fig. 9. Log-log scatter plot of LTSmin run-times for state space exploration with either a hash table or tree compression

To analyze the influence of the model on the compression ratio, we plotted the inverse of the compression ratio against the state length in Fig. 7. The line representing optimal compression is derived from the analysis in Sec. 4 and is linearly dependent on the state size (the average compressed state size is close to 8 bytes: two 32-bit integers for the dominating root node entries in the tree).

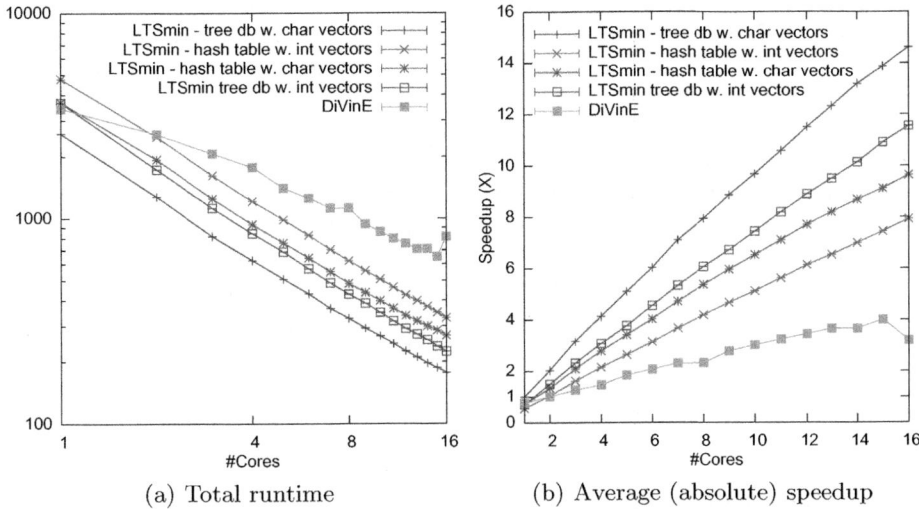

(a) Total runtime   (b) Average (absolute) speedup

Fig. 10. Performance benchmarks for 158 models with DiVinE (hash table) and with LTSmin using tree compression and hash table

With tree compression, a total of 279 BEEM models could each be fully explored using a tree database of pre-configured size, never occupying more than 4 GB memory. Most models exhibit compression ratios close to optimal; the line representing the median compression ratio is merely 17% below the optimal line. The worst cases, with a ratio of three times the optimal, are likely the result of combinatorial growth concentrated around the center of the tree, resulting in equally sized root, left and right sibling tree nodes. Nevertheless, most suboptimal cases lie close too half of the optimal, suggesting only one "full" sibling of the root node. (We verified this to be true for several models.)

Fig. 8 compares compressed state size of COLLAPSE and tree compression. (We could not easily compare compressed state *space* sizes due to differing number of states for some models). Tree compression performs better for all models in our data set. In many cases, the difference is an order of magnitude. While tree compression has an optimal compression ratio that is four times better than COLLAPSE's (empirically established), the median is even five times better for the models of the BEEM database. Finally, as expected (see Sec. 4), we measured insignificant gains from the introduced maximal sharing.

5.2   Performance and Scalability

We compared the performance of the tree database with a hash table in DiVinE and LTSmin. A comparison with SPIN was already provided in earlier work [14]. For a fair comparison, we modified a version of LTSmin[3] to use the (three times) shorter state vectors (*char vectors*) of DiVinE directly. Fig. 10 shows the total

---

[3] This experimental version is distributed separately from LTSmin, because it breaks the language-independent interface.

runtime of 158 BEEM models, which fitted in machine memory using both DiVinE and LTSmin. On average the run-time performance of tree compression is close to a hash table-based search (see Fig. 10(a)). However, the absolute speedup in Fig. 10(b) shows that scalability is better with tree compression, due to a lower memory footprint.

Fig. 9 compares the sequential and multi-core performance of the fastest hash table implementation (LTSmin lockless hash table with char vectors) with the tree database (also with char vectors). The tree matches the performance of the hash table closely.

For both, sequential and multi-core, the performance of the tree database is nearly the same as the fastest hash table implementation, however, with significantly lower memory utilization. For models with fewer states, tree database performance is better than a hash table, undoubtedly due to better cache utilization and lower memory bandwidth.

6   Conclusions

First, this paper presented an analysis and experimental evaluation of the compression ratios of tree compression and COLLAPSE compression, both informed compression techniques that are applicable in on-the-fly model checking. Both analysis and experiments can be considered an implementation-independent comparison of the two techniques. COLLAPSE compression was considered the state-of-the-art compression technique for enumerative model checking. Tree compression was not evaluated as such before. The latter is shown here to perform better than the former, both analytically and in practice. In particular, the median compression ratio of tree compression is five times better than that of COLLAPSE on the BEEM benchmark set. We consider this result representative to real-world usage, due to the varied nature of the BEEM models: the set includes models drawn from extensive case studies on protocols and control systems, and, implementations of planning, scheduling and mutual exclusion algorithms [18].

Furthermore, we presented a solution for parallel tree compression by merging all tree-node tables into a single large table, thereby realizing maximal sharing between entries in these tables. This single hash table design even saves 50% in memory because it exhibits the required stable indexing without any bookkeeping. We proved that the consistency is maintained and use only one bit per entry to parallelize tree insertions. Lastly, we presented an incremental tree compression algorithm that requires a fraction of the table accesses (typically $\mathcal{O}(\log_2(k))$, i.e., logarithmic in the length of a state vector), compared to the original algorithm.

Our experiments show that the incremental and parallel tree database has the same performance as the hash table solutions in both LTSmin and DiVinE (and by implication SPIN [14]). Scalability is also better. All in all, the tree database provides a win-win situation for parallel reachability problems.

Discussion. The absence of resizing could be considered a limitation in certain applications of the tree database. In model checking, however, we may safely dedicate the vast majority of available memory of a system to the state storage. The current implementation of LTSmin [21] supports a maximum of 2^{32} tree nodes, yielding about 4×10^9 states with optimal compression. In the future, we aim to create a more flexible solution that can store more states and automatically scales the number of bits needed per entry, depending on the state vector size. What has hold us back thus far from implementing this are low-level issues, i.e., the ordering of multiple atomic memory accesses across cache line boundaries behave erratically on certain processors.

While this paper discusses tree compression mainly in the context of reachability, it is not limited to this context. For example, on-the-fly algorithms for the verification of liveness properties can also benefit from a space-efficient storage of states as demonstrated by SPIN with its COLLAPSE compression.

Future Work. A few options are still open to improve tree compression. The small tree node entries cover a limited universe of values: $1 + 2 \times \log_2(n)$. This is an ideal case to employ *key quotienting* using *Cleary* [6] or *Very Tight Hashtables* [10]. Neither of the two techniques has been parallelized as far as we can tell.

Static analysis of the dependencies between transitions and state slots could be used to reorder state slots and obtain a better balanced tree, and hence better compression (see Sec. 4). Much like the variable ordering problem of BDDs [5], finding the optimal reordering is an exponential problem (a search through all permutations). While, we are able to improve most of the worse cases by automatic variable reordering, we did not yet find a good heuristic for at least all BEEM models.

Finally, it would be interesting to generalize the tree database by accommodating for the storage of vectors of different sizes.

Acknowledgements

We thank Elwin Pater for taking the time to proofread this work and provide feedback. We thank Stefan Blom for the many useful ideas that he provided.

References

1. Blom, S.C.C., Lisser, B., van de Pol, J.C., Weber, M.: A database approach to distributed state space generation. In: Sixth International Workshop on Parallel and Distributed Methods in Verification, PDMC, pp. 17–32, CTIT, Enschede (2007)
2. Blom, S.C.C., van de Pol, J.C., Weber, M.: Bridging the gap between enumerative and symbolic model checkers. Technical Report TR-CTIT-09-30, University of Twente, Enschede (June 2009)
3. Blom, S., van de Pol, J., Weber, M.: LTSMIN: distributed and symbolic reachability. In: Touili, T., Cook, B., Jackson, P. (eds.) CAV 2010. LNCS, vol. 6174, pp. 354–359. Springer, Heidelberg (2010)

4. Blom, S.C.C., van Langevelde, I., Lisser, B.: Compressed and distributed file formats for labeled transition systems. Electronic Notes in Theoretical Computer Science 89(1), 68–83 (2003) ; PDMC 2003, Parallel and Distributed Model Checking (Satellite Workshop of CAV 2003)
5. Bryant, R.E.: Symbolic boolean manipulation with ordered binary-decision diagrams. ACM Comput. Surv. 24(3), 293–318 (1992)
6. Cleary, J.G.: Compact hash tables using bidirectional linear probing. IEEE Transactions on Computers 33, 828–834 (1984)
7. Cover, T.M., Thomas, J.A.: Elements of Information Theory, 99th edn. Wiley-Interscience, New York (1991)
8. Evangelista, S., Pradat-Peyre, J.-F.: Memory efficient state space storage in explicit software model checking. In: Godefroid, P. (ed.) Model Checking Software. LNCS, vol. 3639, pp. 43–57. Springer, Heidelberg (2005)
9. Geldenhuys, J., de Villiers, P.: Runtime efficient state compaction in SPIN. In: Dams, D.R., Gerth, R., Leue, S., Massink, M. (eds.) SPIN 1999. LNCS, vol. 1680, p. 12. Springer, Heidelberg (1999)
10. Geldenhuys, J., Valmari, A.: A nearly memory-optimal data structure for sets and mappings. In: Ball, T., Rajamani, S.K. (eds.) SPIN 2003. LNCS, vol. 2648, pp. 136–150. Springer, Heidelberg (2003)
11. Holzmann, G.J.: State compression in SPIN: Recursive indexing and compression training runs. In: Proc. of the Third International SPIN Workshop (1997)
12. Holzmann, G.J., Godefroid, P., Pirottin, D.: Coverage preserving reduction strategies for reachability analysis. In: Proceedings of the IFIP TC6/WG6.1 Twelfth International Symposium on Protocol Specification, Testing and Verification XII, pp. 349–363. North-Holland Publishing, Amsterdam (1992)
13. Laarman, A.W.: LTSmin benchmark results (2011) , http://fmt.cs.utwente.nl/tools/ltsmin/spin-2011/ (last accessed: January 24, 2011)
14. Laarman, A.W., van de Pol, J.C., Weber, M.: Boosting multi-core reachability performance with shared hash tables. In: Sharygina, N., Bloem, R. (eds.) Proceedings of the 10th International Conference on Formal Methods in Computer-Aided Design. IEEE Computer Society, USA (2010)
15. Laarman, A., van de Pol, J., Weber, M.: Multi-core lTSMIN: Marrying modularity and scalability. In: Bobaru, M., Havelund, K., Holzmann, G.J., Joshi, R. (eds.) NFM 2011. LNCS, vol. 6617, pp. 506–511. Springer, Heidelberg (2011)
16. Laarman, A.W., van de Pol, J.C., Weber, M.: Parallel recursive state compression for free. In: CoRR, abs/1104.3119 (2011)
17. Larsen, K., Larsson, F., Pettersson, P., Yi, W.: Efficient verification of real-time systems: Compact data structure and state–space reduction. In: Proc. of the 18th IEEE Real-Time Systems Symposium, pp. 14–24. IEEE Computer Society Press, Los Alamitos (1997)
18. Palének, R.: The BEEM website (2011), http://anna.fi.muni.cz/models/cgi/models.cgi (last accessed: January 24,2011)
19. Pelánek, R.: BEEM: Benchmarks for explicit model checkers. In: Bošnački, D., Edelkamp, S. (eds.) SPIN 2007. LNCS, vol. 4595, pp. 263–267. Springer, Heidelberg (2007)
20. Sanders, P.: Lastverteilungsalgorithmen fur parallele tiefensuche. In: Fortschrittsberichte, Reihe 10. VDI, vol. 463. Verlag, Berlin (1997)
21. Weber, M.: The LTSmin website (2011), http://fmt.cs.utwente.nl/tools/ltsmin/ (last accessed:January 24, 2011)

Depth Bounded Explicit-State Model Checking

Abhishek Udupa[1], Ankush Desai[2], and Sriram Rajamani[2]

[1] University of Pennsylvania
[2] Microsoft Research India

Abstract. We present algorithms to efficiently bound the depth of the state spaces explored by explicit-state model checkers. Given a parameter k, our algorithms guarantee finding any violation of an invariant that is witnessed using a counterexample of length k or less from the initial state. Though depth bounding is natural with breadth-first search, explicit-state model checkers are unable to use breadth first search due to prohibitive space requirements, and use depth-first search to explore large state spaces. Thus, we explore efficient ways to perform depth bounding with depth-first search. We prove our algorithms sound (in the sense that they explore exactly all the states reachable within a depth bound), and show their effectiveness on large real-life models from Microsoft's product groups.

1 Introduction

Though several strategies to mitigation the state explosion problem in model checking have been studied extensively (such as symbolic model checking [4],partial order reduction [8,15], symmetry reduction [18], automated abstraction-refinement [6,3,11]), model checkers are still unable to cope with the state spaces of very large models. To cope with very large state spaces, bounding techniques have been proposed to systematically explore a part of the state space. The key idea with bounding based approaches is given by the "small-scope hypothesis"(see, for instance [14]), which states that if a model is buggy then the bug will most likely manifest by exploring all states systematically after bounding a parameter of the model(such as input size, number of processors, number of context switches).

In this paper, we discuss a new algorithm for depth bounding —that is, exploring all states of a model that are reachable within a given depth from the initial states— with iterative deepening of the depth bound. Depth bounding is trivial in symbolic model checking [4], since symbolic model checking is naturally done in a breadth-first manner. If a depth bound d is fixed *a-priori*, then symbolic exploration of all states which are reachable within d steps from the initial states can be reduced to SAT directly, thereby avoiding expensive existential quantification operations during symbolic model checking. This technique is called Bounded Model Checking(BMC) [5], and has been studied widely. In contrast, even though depth bounding has been implemented in popular explicit-state model checkers such as SPIN [12], we find that algorithmic improvements

A. Groce and M. Musuvathi (Eds.): SPIN 2011, LNCS 6823, pp. 57–74, 2011.
© Springer-Verlag Berlin Heidelberg 2011

are still possible to improve efficiency. This paper contains two new techniques:
1) depth threshold, and 2) frontier tree, to improve the efficiency of depth bounding in explicit-state model checking. Before we describe these techniques, we first
motivate why it is nontrivial to bound depth in explicit-state model checking.

Depth bounding in explicit-state model checking. The obvious way to
bound depth in explicit-state model checking is to use breadth-first search (BFS).
However, as we explain below, breadth-first search is infeasible in explicit-state
model checking due to excessive memory consumption. Suppose we have a single
initial state, and each state consumes M bytes of memory. Let F_k be the set of
states whose shortest path from the initial state is of length k. If we perform
breadth-first search, then we first explore all the states in F_1, then all the states
in F_2, F_3, etc in stages. At stage k, storage for the set of states F_k (which are
called the "frontier states") consumes $| F_k | \times M$ bytes. Since $| F_k |$ is exponential
in k, and M is of the order of hundreds of kilobytes, $| F_k | \times M$ explodes for large
k. In contrast with BFS, for depth-first search(DFS), only the states on the DFS
stack need to be stored in full. For visited states that are not on the DFS stack,
only fingerprints or bit-state hashes [13,19] need to be stored to avoid revisiting
states. Even within the DFS stack, only the top most state needs to be stored
in full —each of the remaining states s can be stored in terms of incremental
difference or undo log from the state above s in the DFS stack. Thus, most
explicit-state model checkers use DFS instead of BFS in order to scale to large
models.

In such a setting (DFS based explicit-state model checking), implementing
depth bounding efficiently and correctly is non-trivial. The obvious way to bound
depth is to simply stop exploring a state either if the current depth exceeds the
depth bound, or if the state has been visited earlier. However, as we show in
Section 3, this algorithm is incorrect, since the same state can be visited at
different depths, and can lead to missing states that can be explored within
the given depth bound. Alternatively, we can record the depth of each state
in the state table, and re-explore a state if the current exploration depth is
lesser than the previous exploration depth. This is a correct algorithm, and
is indeed guaranteed to explore all states that are reachable within a depth
bound. However, as our empirical data shows, this results in the same state being
explored several times with different depths and the algorithm is very inefficient.
In this paper, we describe a new algorithm that maintains a *threshold* value for
each state. Intuitively, the threshold value for a state is the maximum depth at
which the state needs to be revisited so that there is a possibility of exploring a
previously unexplored state within the current depth bound. We show how we
can compute thresholds and use thresholds to avoid revisiting states.

Iterative Depth Bounding. Since it is hard to pick a good depth bound *a-
priori*, depth bounding works best if we can iteratively increment the bound and
explore as much depth of the state space as we can, within our time and space
budget. That is, we start with a depth bound d, and first explore all the states
that are reachable using paths of length d or less from the initial state. Then,

we increment the depth bound to $2d$, $3d$, ..., and keep exploring states that are reachable at these larger depths as much as our time and space budgets permit.

Such an iterative depth bounded search combines elements of both DFS and BFS —within each depth bound, we do DFS, and increasing the depth bound essentially amounts to doing BFS at the granularity of the depth increment d. In order to save space for storing the frontier at each of the depth bounds $d, 2d, 3d, \ldots$ in iterative depth bounded search, we represent frontier states using traces (a trace of a state S, is sequence of edge indices along a path from the initial state to S) and a full state is produced on demand by replaying the trace representing the state. Given a trace of length nd producing a full state by replaying takes time $O(nd)$, and the replay overhead becomes large for large values of nd. We propose a data structure called *frontier tree* to reduce the replay overhead to $O(2d)$ during iterative depth bounding.

The main motivation for our work was demand from our users (Microsoft product groups) to explore state spaces of very large models to as large depths as possible. In particular, the Universal Serial Bus (USB) team in the Windows product group found and fixed over 300 design bugs using our model checker, including some bugs that manifest only at very large depths in the state space. Consequently, they wanted to cover every state within as large a depth bound as possible, within a fixed time and memory budget, to get confidence in the correctness of their design. Our algorithms have helped them improve the depth up to which they can cover all states up to 86.8%, and improve the number of states explored up to 1246.8% on one of their large models for a time budget of 5 hours and 30 minutes, and a memory budget of 1200MB. Our efforts have resulted in our model checker being used day-to-day in a production setting. The Windows group uses our depth bounded model checker as key component in design validation.

2 Background

In this section, we give some background about how explicit-state model checkers work.

We assume the existence of the following data-types. A *State* data-type is used to represent states of the system we want to explore. It has the following members: (1) the property fp returns the finger print of the state, (2) the property Depth returns the depth at which the state has been encountered. *Set* is a generic data-type, which supports three methods: (1) the Add method takes an object and adds it to the set, and (2) the Contains method returns true if the object passed as parameter is present in the set, and false otherwise, and (3) the Remove method removes the object passed as parameter if that object is present in the set. We instantiate *Set* with fingerprints of states in this section. In later sections we also instantiate *Set* with states to represent frontier sets.

The fingerprints of states have the property that identical states are guaranteed to have identical fingerprints. That is:

$$\forall S_1, S_2 \in State.S_1 = S_2 \Rightarrow S_1.\mathsf{fp} = S_2.\mathsf{fp}$$

```
 1: Set⟨Fingerprint⟩ DoneStates
 2:
 3: void doDfs(State currentState){
 4: if not DoneStates.Contains(currentState.fp) then
 5:     DoneStates.Add(currentState.fp)
 6:     for all successors S of currentState do
 7:         doDfs(S)
 8:     end for
 9: end if
10: }
11:
12: void DFS(State initialState) {
13: DoneStates= {}
14: doDfs(initialState);
15: }
```

Fig. 1. Simple Explicit-State DFS algorithm

Though the converse of the above implication does not hold, the probability of two different states having the same fingerprint can be made extremely low (see [13,19]).

Figure 1 shows the simple DFS algorithm implemented by most explicit-state model checkers. The fingerprints of all explored states is stored in the set DoneStates. The core of the algorithm is the recursive method doDfs, which is called with the initial state. It works by checking if the current state is already in the set DoneStates, and if not, adds it to DoneStates, and invokes itself on all its successors.

DFS is a space efficient algorithm for explicit-state model checking, since we need to store only fingerprints for explored states. Only states that are on the DFS stack need to be represented in memory as full states. A further optimization is possible— we only need to store the top of the DFS stack as a full state. For every state S that is inside the DFS stack, we can represent S using its difference from the state T that is above S in the DFS stack. This technique is called "state delta" and is routinely used in explicit-state model checkers (see, for instance [2]).

In the next section, we use another generic data-type $Hashtable$, and instantiate it with fingerprints as keys and integers as values. $Hashtable$ supports the following methods: (1) the Add method, which adds a new key-value pair to the table. (2) the Contains method, which returns true if the specified key is in the hash table. (3) the Update method, which takes as input a key-value pair and updates the table with the new value if the key is already present and adds the key-value pair to the table otherwise.

In later sections, we show how to systematically bound the depth of explored states in DFS, without missing any states. For the purposes of soundness proofs of our algorithms, we assume that fingerprints are not lossy. That is,

$$\forall S_1, S_2 \in State.S_1 = S_2 \Leftrightarrow S_1.\mathsf{fp} = S_2.\mathsf{fp}$$

This assumption allows us to separate soundness concerns about our algorithms from soundness concerns about fingerprints.

```
 1: bool IterBoundedDfs(State initialState, int depthCutoff, int inc) {
 2: initialState.Depth= 0
 3: Set⟨State⟩ frontier = {initialState}
 4: Set⟨State⟩ newFrontier= {}
 5: int currentBound  = inc
 6: while currentBound ≤ depthCutoff do
 7:    newFrontier = BoundedDfsFromFrontier(frontier, currentBound)
 8:    if newFrontier = {} then
 9:       return(true)
10:    else
11:       currentBound  = currentBound + inc
12:       frontier = newFrontier
13:    end if
14: end while
15: return(false)
16: }
17:
18: Set⟨State⟩ outFrontier
19: /* outFrontier is a global variable which gets updated inside BoundedDfs*/
20: BoundedDfsFromFrontier(Set⟨State⟩ frontier, int currentBound) {
21: outFrontier= { }
22: for all F ∈ frontier do
23:    BoundedDfs(F, currentBound)
24: end for
25: return(outFrontier)
26:
```

Fig. 2. Iterative Depth Bounded Search Algorithm

3   Depth Bounding: Warmup

The state spaces of real-world systems are too large to be completely explored, and in such circumstances, it is desirable to systematically explore all states within a given depth bound under the small scope hypothesis [14]. To achieve this goal, we modify the simple DFS algorithm given in Section 2 to visit a state *if and only if* it is reachable within d steps from the initial state, and iteratively increasing d. In particular, we perform two attempts —the first one is unsound, and the second one is sound but inefficient. These are intended as warm-up exercises before we present our efficient depth bounding techniques in the next section.

Figure 2 gives the outer loop for iterative depth bounded search. The IterBoundedDfs method takes three arguments: (1) initialState, which is the initial state of the model, (2) depthCutoff, which is the depth cutoff bound for the search and (3) inc, which is the amount by which the depth bound is increased in each iteration. We assume that depthCutoff > 0, inc > 0, and that depthCutoff is divisible by inc.

The method IterBoundedDfs repeatedly calls the BoundedDfsFromFrontier method (line 7) in the while loop from lines 6–14. If all states in the model are reachable within depthCutoff, then IterBoundedDfs returns true, otherwise, it returns false.

The BoundedDfsFromFrontier method takes the current frontier set frontier and a depth bound currentBound as parameters, explores all the states starting from the current frontier set frontier that are reachable within currentBound more steps, and returns a new set of frontiers newFrontier.

```
 1: Set⟨Fingerprint⟩ DoneStates
 2: /* initialized to null-set once in the beginning */
 3:
 4: Set⟨State⟩ outFrontier
 5: /* initialized to null-set in BoundedDfsFromFrontier*/
 6:
 7: void BoundedDfs(State currentState, int depthBound) {
 8: if ¬ DoneStates.Contains(currentState.fp) then
 9:     if currentState.Depth < depthBound then
10:         DoneStates.Add(currentState.fp)
11:         for all successors S of currentState do
12:             S.Depth = currentState.Depth + 1
13:             BoundedDfs(S, depthBound)
14:         end for
15:     else
16:         outFrontier.Add(currentState)
17:     end if
18: end if
19: }
```

Fig. 3. Naïve Unsound Depth Bounded DFS algorithm

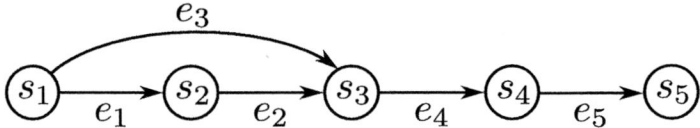

Fig. 4. Example where the algorithm shown in Figure 3 does not cover all reachable states

The implementation of BoundedDfsFromFrontier is shown in lines 20–25. It calls the BoundedDfs function for each state in the frontier set. The BoundedDfs function thus takes a single state and a depth bound and explores all the states that are reachable within the depth bound. States that are reached exactly at the depth bound are added by BoundedDfs to the global set outFrontier to be explored further in the next call to BoundedDfsFromFrontier. The design of BoundedDfs is a deceptively simple problem at the outset, but one that is tricky, if our goal is to be both efficient and correct.

Naïve Unsound Depth Bounded DFS. To give the reader an appreciation for the difficulty in designing BoundedDfs efficiently and correctly, we present our first attempt in Figure 3. We refer to this approach as *Naïve Unsound DBDFS*. Recall that the goal of the BoundedDfs() algorithm is to explore all the states that are reachable within the bound depthBound starting from the input parameter currentState. This algorithm is similar to Figure 1, except that a state is explored only if it is encountered at a depth *less than* the current depth bound (see the conditional at line 9 of Figure 3). If not, then it is added to outFrontier (line 16) to be explored in the next depth bounded iteration.

The algorithm in Figure 3 is incorrect in the sense that it may not explore all the states that are reachable within the given bound depthBound. For instance if a state S is reached initially with a depth of d and later with a depth $d' < d$, the algorithm does not explore the state S, the second time around, which could

```
 1: Hashtable⟨Fingerprint, int⟩ DoneStates
 2: /* initialized to null-set once in the beginning */
 3:
 4: Set⟨State⟩ outFrontier
 5: /* initialized to null-set in BoundedDfsFromFrontier*/
 6:
 7: bool mustExplore(State S) {
 8: if DoneStates.Contains(S.fp) then
 9:     if DoneStates.Lookup(S.fp) ≤ S.Depth then
10:         return(false)
11:     end if
12: end if
13: return(true)
14: }
15:
16: void BoundedDfs(State currentState, int depthBound) {
17: if mustExplore(currentState) then
18:     if currentState.Depth < depthBound then
19:         DoneStates.Update(currentState.fp, currentState.Depth)
20:         outFrontier.Remove(currentState)
21:         for all successors S of currentState do
22:             S.Depth = currentState.Depth + 1
23:             BoundedDfs(S, depthBound)
24:         end for
25:     else
26:         outFrontier.Add(currentState)
27:     end if
28: end if
29: return
```

Fig. 5. Naïve Sound Depth Bounded DFS

lead to not exploring some states, although these states are reachable within the given depth bound. For instance, consider the state space shown in Figure 4. If the algorithm is run with a depth-bound of 3, with s_1 as the initial state, and if e_1, e_2 and e_4 are traversed, adding s_1.fp, s_2.fp and s_3.fp to DoneStates. At this point, the algorithm determines that s_4 is at the depth cut-off and adds it to the frontier set. When the recursion unwinds to the state s_1, it does not explore the state s_3, since s_3.fp ∈ DoneStates already. Thus, the algorithm misses the state s_5, even though s_5 is reachable within three steps (recall that our depth bound is 3) from s_1 via $e_3 - e_4 - e_5$.

Naïve Sound Depth Bounded DFS. Figure 5 shows our second attempt, which we refer to as *Naïve Sound DBDFS*, where we fix the issue of missing states, by tracking the minimum depth at which a state has been reached so far. That is, we use a hash table DoneStates (rather than a set) to store fingerprints of visited states. For each visited state S, the hash table DoneStates maps the fingerprint of S to the minimum depth the state has been reached so far. When a state S is re-visited, the mustExplore method compares the current depth S.Depth with the smallest depth at which S has been encountered so far (which is stored in DoneStates). If the current depth is smaller, then the state is re-explored with the (smaller) depth and the DoneStates hash table is updated to reflect this. All the states that are precisely at the depth bound are added to outFrontier. The declaration of outFrontier, and the body of the BoundedDfsFromFrontier functions are the same as before.

Note that a state that is added to outFrontier at line 26 may indeed later be found to have a shorter path to it. Consequently, in line 20, we invoke outFrontier.Remove for currentState since currentState is currently visited with depth less than the given depth bound, and may have been added to outFrontier earlier.

Below, we state lemmas and a theorem to prove that the algorithm in Figure 5 is correct in the sense that it explores exactly all the states that are reachable from the input frontier set within the depth bound, and that all the states whose shortest distances equal the depth bound are returned in the output frontier.

Lemma 1. *Consider the invocation of the method* BoundedDfs *from the initial state with a depth bound d. Consider any state* S *whose shortest path from the initial state is $\ell < d$, where d is the depth bound. Then, the method* BoundedDfs *in Figure 5 eventually explores* S *through a path of length ℓ from the initial state, and updates the value for key* S.fp *to ℓ in the hash table* DoneStates.

Proof. By induction on ℓ. For $\ell = 0$ the only state is the initial state, and it is easy to check that the fingerprint for the initial state is stored in DoneStates mapped to the value 0. Consider any state S with shortest path ℓ from the initial state. Consider any shortest path P from the initial state to S. Let A be the predecessor of S in P. By induction hypothesis, the algorithm eventually explores A at depth $\ell - 1$ (since P is a shortest path, the shortest distance from the initial state to A is $\ell - 1$). At that instant, either S will be revisited with a depth ℓ, or S has already been visited at depth ℓ through another shortest path P' from the initial state. In either case, the proof is complete.

Lemma 2. *Consider the invocation of the method* BoundedDfs *from the initial state with a depth bound d. For any state* S, *we have that* S $\in$ outFrontier *on completion of the call to* BoundedDfs *if and only if the shortest path from the initial state to* S *is d.*

The Proof of Lemma 2 follows from Lemma 1. Note that a state S with shortest path $\ell < d$ may be initially added to outFrontier if it is first visited through a path of length d. However, when it is later revisited through a path of length $\ell < d$, it will be removed from outFrontier.

Theorem 1. *The algorithm shown in Figure 5, in conjunction with the algorithm in Figure 2, run with a depth increment of i and a depth bound d, explores a state if and only if it is reachable from the initial state via at least one path of length less than or equal to the depth bound d.*

Proof. As mentioned earlier, we assume that $i > 0$, $d > 0$ and d divides i. The Theorem follows by repeated application of Lemma 1 and Lemma 2 for each level of the iterated depth bounded DFS.

4   Efficient Depth Bounding

Though the algorithm in Figure 5 is correct, it has two main inefficiencies. First, it ends up revisiting the same state several times (see Section 5 for empirical

```
1:  Hashtable⟨Fingerprint, int⟩ Threshold
2:
3:  ⟨bool, int⟩ mustExplore(State S) {
4:  if Threshold.Contains(S.fp) then
5:      if S.Depth < Threshold.Lookup(S.fp) then
6:          return(⟨true, Threshold.Lookup(S.fp)⟩)
7:      else
8:          return(⟨false, Threshold.Lookup(S.fp)⟩)
9:      end if
10: else
11:     return(⟨true, S.Depth⟩)
12: end if
13: }
14:
15: int BoundedDfs(State currentState, int depthBound) {
16: int currThreshold = ⊥
17: int myThreshold = −1
18: bool needsexploration = false
19: ⟨needsexploration, currThreshold⟩ = mustExplore(currentState)
20: if ¬needsexploration then
21:     return(currThreshold)
22: end if
23: if currentState.Depth < depthBound then
24:     Threshold.Update(currentState, currentState.Depth)
25:     outFrontier.Remove(currentState)
26:     for all Successors S of currentState do
27:         S.Depth = currentState.Depth + 1
28:         currThreshold= BoundedDfs(S, depthBound)
29:         myThreshold = max(myThreshold, currThreshold − 1)
30:     end for
31:     Threshold.Update(currentState, myThreshold)
32: else
33:     outFrontier.Add(currentState)
34:     myThreshold = currentState.Depth
35: end if
36: return(myThreshold)
37: }
```

Fig. 6. Efficient Depth Bounded DFS with Thresholding

validation). Second, the storage requirement for frontier states for large depths is prohibitive. In this section, we propose optimizations for both these problems. The first optimization is a thresholding technique to reduce the number of revisits, and the second is a technique to represent frontier states efficiently using traces rather than full states and exploiting the tree-structure among these traces to reduce replay overhead.

4.1 Efficient Depth Bounded DFS with Thresholding

Figure 6 presents an improved algorithm for depth bounded DFS. The key idea in this algorithm is to *propagate* the reason why a state need not be explored upwards in the call stack (which represents the depth bounded DFS stack) by maintaining a threshold value for each visited state. Intuitively, the threshold value for a state S corresponds to the maximum depth at which the S needs to be revisited so that there is a possibility of exploring a previously unexplored state within the current depth bound.

The example in Figure 7 motivates the use of threshold. In the example, we suppose that the state S is explored at a depth of 50. Further, suppose (for

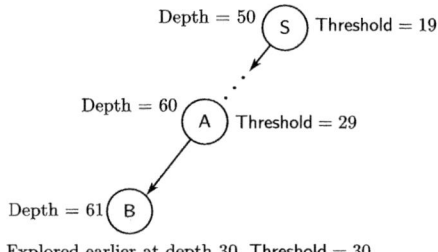

Fig. 7. Example to motivate use of threshold

simplicity) S has only one successor, and each transitive successor of S also has only one successor. After 10 more steps, suppose state A is explored, at a depth of 60. Finally, suppose the successor B of A has been explored before at a lower depth 30. In this case, the algorithm in Figure 5 merely stops exploring state B, since it has been encountered at a lower depth 30 before. However, in the hash table DoneStates, the minimum depth at which A has been encountered is still set to 60, and the minimum depth at which S has been encountered is still set to 50. Suppose S is now revisited with a depth of 45. Then, the algorithm in Figure 5 revisits all the states from S to A, since they are now revisited at lower depths. In particular, A is now revisited at a lower depth 55. However, all the revisits of the states along the path S to A are wasteful, since B is encountered at a depth 56, which is still higher than 30. The idea behind thresholds is to propagate the lower bound 30 for revisiting B back along the path from S to A. In particular, since B is the only successor of A, the threshold for revisiting A is 29, which is one less than 30. By repeating this propagation along the path from S to A, the threshold for S is calculated as 19. This means, that even though the minimum depth at which S has been encountered so far is 50, a revisit of S is needed only at depths lesser than 19, since revisits at depths larger than 19 will not lead to any new states being explored. In this example, S and its successors had only one successor. We can easily generalize to the case where S has multiple successors by calculating the threshold of S to be maximum among the thresholds propagated from all the successors of S.

The algorithm in Figure 6 maintains thresholds instead of minimum depths for each state S in the hash table Threshold. The threshold of a state represents the depth at which the state needs to be revisited. It is guaranteed that exploring the state at a depth greater than the threshold will never result in exploring new states within the current depth bound. Whenever the mustExplore function returns **false**, indicating that a state need not be explored, it also returns a threshold value for the state. The BoundedDfs function then calculates and updates the threshold value for a state S as the maximum of the thresholds of all its successors minus one, thus propagating the threshold values up the call stack.

We use the expression Threshold(S), where S is a state to represent the threshold value for S as stored in Threshold. Also, we use the expression minDepth(S) to represent the length of the shortest path from the initial state to S. At any point in the execution of the algorithm S.Depth is the current depth at which S has been reached. One invariant (which holds at all times during the algorithm) is that minDepth(S) $\leq$ S.Depth for all states S. For any state S $\in$ Threshold, we also maintain the invariant that Threshold(S) $\leq$ S.Depth. Further, the threshold for a given state is non-increasing over the course of the algorithm execution.

We define a *frontier state* as a state which is reachable by a shortest path of length exactly d from the initial state, and an *internal state* as a state which is reachable by a shortest path of length strictly less than d, where d is the current depth bound.

The main technical difficulty in establishing the correctness of Algorithm 6 is that Lemma 1 does not hold. Specifically, during the execution of Algorithm 6, suppose for a state S, we have that Threshold(S) < minDepth(S). Consequently, mustExplore returns `false` for any attempt to revisit S, and the shortest path to S is not explored by the algorithm. Thus, Lemma 1 does not hold, and the correctness of Algorithm 6 is nontrivial. Interestingly, when Threshold(S) < minDepth(S), even though we may miss exploring the shortest path to S, this does not affect the frontier states that can be reached from S. Below, we formalize this intuition and establish the correctness of Algorithm 6.

Lemma 3. *For a given state* S *if* Threshold(S) < minDepth(S) *at some point in the execution of the algorithm shown in Figure 6, then* S *is not along any shortest path from the initial state to some frontier state.*

Proof. Suppose that a S was along the shortest path from the initial state to a frontier state F and that Threshold(S) < minDepth(S). Consider the point of time during the execution of the algorithm that the update to Threshold(S) making it less than minDepth(S) occurred. Since the updates occur *after* all the recursive calls have completed, it must be the case that S was explored during the call at which the update occurred. Since S is along the shortest path to some frontier state F either the frontier itself was reached and the recursive returns along this path effectively propagated the depth at which S was encountered back to S, in which case Threshold(S) = S.Depth, a contradiction! The other case is that the frontier was not explored along this path due to S not being encountered at its minimum depth. In this case as well, some other state F' will be added to the frontier and Threshold(S) will again be set to S.Depth. But S.Depth $\geq$ minDepth(S) $\implies$ Threshold(S) $\geq$ minDepth(S), which is again a contradiction, completing the proof.

Lemma 4. *Exploring a state* S *when encountered at a depth greater than the* Threshold(S) *will not result in any new states being discovered in the current depth bounded iteration.*

Proof. For all the states S where Threshold(S) $\geq$ minDepth(S), the proof holds from Theorem 1, since in this case, the optimized algorithm is equivalent to the naïve algorithm. For the cases where Threshold(S) < minDepth(S), we have from Lemma 3 that these states are not along the shortest path to any frontier state. This implies that *all* states S' that are reachable from S are also reachable at a lower depth via some other state. The threshold calculations in this case effectively propagate the depth at which this S must be revisited in order to have any possibility of exploring new states.

Theorem 2. *The algorithm shown in Figure 6 in conjunction with the algorithm shown in Figure 2, when run with a depth bound d, explores all states that are reachable within d states from the initial state.*

Proof. We can conclude this result from Lemma 4 and Theorem 1; Since the algorithm in Figure 6 is essentially the same as the algorithm in Figure 5, except for the decision to revisit or not which is based on the Threshold instead of the depth of the state.

Section 5 gives empirical data with shows that the Optimized Depth Bounded DFS algorithm greatly reduces the number of revisits to states without compromising on correctness.

4.2   Traces and Frontier Trees

Though the optimized depth bounded DFS algorithm in Figure 6 greatly reduces the number of revisits for a state, we still have the issue that the space required to store the frontier states at each iteration of the depth bounded search explodes with increasing depth. In particular, the amount of storage required to store the set outFrontier in Figure 2 becomes prohibitively expensive for large depths. Thus, we end up storing in lieu of each state s in outFrontier a *trace t*, which is a path from the initial state to s. If the length of the path is d, the storage requirement for t is $O(kd)$ bits for some small k, since at each level we only need to store a unique identifier for each outgoing edge from each state. In contrast, the storage requirement for a state s is on the order of hundreds of kilobytes for the large models we have. However, the price paid for storing t instead of s is that we finally need s in order to explore successors of s, and generating s from t takes time $O(d)$, which becomes expensive for large d.

```
 1: class FrontierNode {
 2: FrontierNode p
 3: Trace t
 4: }
 5:
 6: State getState( FrontierNode f, State sf, FrontierNode g) {
 7: FrontierNode a = LowestCommonAncestor(f,g)
 8: t = TraceFrom(g, a)
 9: State sa = sf.UnwindTo(a)
10: State sg= sa.ExecuteTrace(t)
11: return (sg)
12: }
```

Fig. 8. Using frontier trees to optimize replay overhead

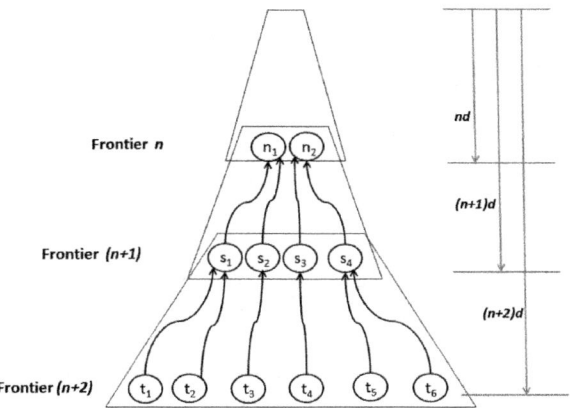

Fig. 9. Frontier tree

To optimize the trade-off between space and time, we introduce a data structure called frontier tree. Instead of storing states at the frontier, we store a FrontierNode for each state (see Figure 8) with two fields: (1) a pointer p to the parent node, and (2) a trace t from the parent node p to this node. Figure 9 shows a pictorial description of the frontier tree that is formed using the frontier nodes at levels nd, $(n+1)d$, and $(n+2)d$. Suppose we have just finished exploring all the successors of frontier node t_1 in Figure 9. Next, we need to explore the successors of t_2. To get the state corresponding to t_2, if we replay the trace associated with t_2 all the way from the initial state, the replay would take $O((n+2)d)$ time. Instead, we can find the least common ancestor of t_1 and t_2 in the frontier tree, which is s_1, and do the following: (1) first construct the state corresponding to s_1 by executing the undo logs from s_1 to t_1 using "state-delta" (See Section 2), and (2) replay only the trace from s_1 to t_2 to get the state corresponding to t_2. This can be done in $O(2d)$ time, since it takes $O(d)$ time to execute undo logs from t_1 to s_1 and another $O(d)$ time to execute the trace from s_1 to t_2. Procedure getState in Figure 8 shows that given a frontier node f with corresponding state sf, we can construct the state corresponding to frontier node g by unwinding to the least common ancestor a of f and g, and replaying only the trace from a to g.

As shown by our empirical results in Section 5, this greatly reduces the overhead of replay, and hence the overall execution time of the iterative depth bounded search.

5   Empirical Results

We have implemented both the optimized iterative depth bounding DFS algorithm (Figure 6, Section 4) as well as the frontier tree optimization (Section 4) in the ZING model checker [1,2]. We evaluate the effectiveness of these optimizations below.

Table 1. States explored and peak memory usage for a fixed time budget (depth increment = 1000)

Model	Time budget (hh:mm)	Distinct States Explored			Maximum Depth Explored			Peak Memory Usage	
		Unopt	Opt	Increase (%)	Unopt	Opt	Increase (%)	Unopt (MB)	Opt (MB)
ISM	2:30	5.933M	7.499M	26.4%	975	1025	5.1%	1644	1712
PSM30	3:30	499.1K	1.462M	192.9%	2750	3400	23.6%	1201	1341
PSM20	5:30	859.0K	2.233M	159.9%	2500	2800	12%	767	872
DSM	5:30	92.31K	1.243M	1246.8%	2650	4950	86.8%	1108	1127

The primary motivation for the algorithms described in this paper was to help with the design of the USB stack in the Windows operating system. Our models of the USB stack have very large state spaces with very large depths, and we have not been able to explore all the states of these models. Thus, we do not even know the total number of states or depth of the state space of these models. However, even by exploring all states within fixed depth bounds, we have been able to find and fix over 300 bugs in the design of the USB stack. Several of the bugs were only discovered at depths greater than 1000. Every time the USB designers run the model checker, they fix a time budget(say a few hours or a few days), and they want to explore all states of these models for as large a depth bound as possible within this time budget, to get high confidence in their design.

We evaluate the efficacy of our optimizations on models from the USB team. Table 1 shows this data for 4 different models: ISM, PSM30, PSM20 and DSM. In this table "Unopt"refers to the unoptimized algorithm in Figure 5, but with traces used to represent frontier states (if we store frontier states in full, we run out of memory for these models), and "Opt" refers to the optimized algorithm in Figure 6, with frontier trees. Thus, the data in Table 1 measures the combined gains due to the depth thresholding and frontier tree optimizations.

The second column in Table 1 shows the amount of time budget given to the optimized and unoptimized algorithms, and the remaining columns compare the number of distinct states and the maximum depth that was completely explored within that time budget. We note that the optimizations enable the model checker to explore more states, and also enable the model checker to explore all the states up to larger depths. Most notably, in the DSM model the optimizations enable the model checker to explore all states up to a depth of 4950, which is an 86.8% improvement in the depth of states explored, and 1246.8% improvement in the number of states explored. We also note that the optimizations add only a very small memory overhead, as evidenced by the data in the last two columns.

We note that we know of no other method that can explore all reachable states of these models for as large a depth bound as possible within a fixed time and memory budget. Breadth-first search simply runs out of memory for these models since each state in the frontier occupies hundreds of kilobytes.

Table 2. Reduction in number of revisits due to thresholding

Model	Depth	Distinct States Explored	Depth Increment = 1000			Depth Increment = 50		
			Revisits Without Threshold	Revisits With Threshold	Reduction in revisits	Revisits Without Threshold	Revisits With Threshold	Reduction in revisits
TMComplet-ionEventFixed	1000	231.1K	52.32K	24.49K	53.2%	15.6K	15.3K	1.9%
TMHash-TableFixed	1000	3.000M	1.902M	113.2K	1581%	272.47K	268.25K	1.52%
ISM	1000	4.924M	2.404M	2.317M	3.6%	1.41M	1.39M	1.4%
PSM20	2700	649.9K	3.834M	2.205M	42.5%	785.5K	690.49K	12.09%
PSM30	3000	145.3K	3.233M	1.968M	39.1%	284.69K	249.9K	12.22%
DSM	6000	423.3K	3.133M	1.822M	42%	1.36M	1.34M	1.47%
HSM	16000	186.9K	438.9K	287.8K	34.3%	50.54K	48.49K	4.05%

Table 3. Time to explore a fixed depth with and without frontier tree

Model	Depth	Depth Increment = 50				
		Without Frontier-Tree		With Frontier-Tree		Reduction in
		Execution Time(sec.)	getState() Time(sec.)	Execution Time(sec.)	getState() Time(sec.)	execution time (%)
ISM	1000	3006	621	2430	64	19.1%
PSM20	2700	7411	4183	3033	284	59.1%
PSM30	2700	1674	951	704	115	57.9%
DSM	6000	15023	9695	4391	536	70.8%
HSM	16000	6530	4579	1114	365	82.9%

Next, we measure the effect of the thresholding and frontier tree optimizations separately. First, we measure the reduction in the number of revisits of states due to thresholding. Table 2 compares the number of revisits of states with and without the use of thresholds. The first two models, TMCompletionEventFixed and TMHashTableFixed are models of a distributed transaction manager. The remaining models ISM, PSM20, PSM30, DSM and HSM are all various state machine components of the USB stack. As the results show, thresholding reduces revisits, without compromising on the soundness. The reduction in the number of revisits is dependent on both the model and the depth increment. With a large depth increment (such as 1000), each state is reachable through a large number of paths within each iteration of BoundedDfs, and thresholding is able to greatly reduce the number of revisits. With a small depth increment (such as 50), the number of revisits is relatively small even without the use of thresholding, and thresholding is relatively less effective.

Finally, we measure the gains due to frontier trees. We fix a large depth bound for these models and measure how long it takes to explore all the states within the depth bound with and without frontier trees. We do these measurements

Table 4. Time to explore a fixed depth with and without frontier tree

Model	Depth	Depth Increment = 1000				
		Without Frontier-Tree		With Frontier-Tree		Reduction in
		Execution Time(sec.)	getState() Time(sec.)	Execution Time(sec.)	getState() Time(sec.)	execution time (%)
ISM	1000	9198	3	9197	4	0.01%
PSM20	2700	24420	15621	18123	11284	25.78%
PSM30	2700	11523	7819	8136	1693	29.39%
DSM	6000	38623	28133	24929	14455	35.45%
HSM	16000	16860	16080	3355	2498	80.1%

both for a depth increment of 50 (see Table 3) and a depth increment of 1000 (see Table 4). The results show substantial reduction in execution times due to the frontier trees. The reduction is larger with depth increment 50 than depth increment 1000, since at depth increment 50, there are several more frontiers, and several more replays done, and the scope for savings in replay is more. The results both establish that (1) the time required to replay traces to generate full states for the frontier is a significant fraction of the total execution time, and (2) the frontier tree optimization greatly reduces the replay overhead.

The results show that thresholding is more effective at large depth increments, and frontier trees are more effective at small depth increments. The combination of the two optimizations improves the effectiveness of the model checker for all depth increments.

6   Related Work

The use of fingerprints to save storage in model checkers was first introduced by Holzmann who called it "bit-state hashing" [13]. Holzmann's SPIN model checker also supports bounded depth first search, but it does not attempt to optimize the number of revisits or the replay overhead, which are the main contributions of our work.

The use of traces instead of states to space has been observed before in software model checking. In particular, Verisoft [9] is a stateless model checker, which only remembers traces of states to save space, and works essentially by replaying traces from the initial state. The use of "state delta" or undo logs to store only differences between states on the DFS stack has been explored before in several model checkers such as CMC [17], JPF [10] and ZING [2]. Frontier trees combine the use of traces and undo logs to greatly reduce the replay overhead during iterative depth bounded DFS.

While at first glance, our approach to depth-bounding looks similar to the iterative deepening algorithms such as IDA* [16], there are significant differences. The approach presented in [16] and other related work primarily aims to reduce the number of states visited while arriving at an optimal solution. In contrast, the work presented in this paper aims to reduced the number of *revisits* to a given state, while ensuring that *every* state which is reachable, given the depth bound, is indeed explored. Also, the algorithms along the lines of the algorithm presented in [16] require the use of a heuristic *cost-function* f with some characteristics: specifically, that f never overestimate the true cost of exploring a given path and that f have some monotonicity properties. In our context, since a bug can manifest anywhere, the use of such monotonic cost metrics is not feasible.

7 Conclusion

We presented algorithms to systematically bound the depth of the state spaces explored by explicit-state model checkers. Since explicit-state space model checkers use DFS for space efficiency, depth bounding is non-trivial to do correctly and efficiently. In particular, we presented a bounding algorithm to greatly avoid the number of revisits of states, and a new data structure called Frontier Tree to optimize the replay overhead during iterative depth bounding. Our depth-bounded model checker has been used by product groups inside Microsoft to successfully find several hundred bugs in large real-world models, and the use of depth bounding was crucial in these applications.

Though we focus on checking safety properties, our techniques can be adapted to check liveness properties as well. Let Θ be the set of all states of a model that are reachable from the initial state. Let $\Theta_d \subseteq \Theta$ be the set of all states that can be reached from the initial state at a depth of d or less. Let $\Gamma \subseteq \Theta$ be a set of Büchi states. Our algorithms can be adapted to look for all lassos which consist of a "stem" from an initial state to a state $S \in \Gamma$ and a cycle back to S such that all states in the lasso are reachable within a distance d from the initial state. In particular, consider the nested depth-first algorithm of Corcoubetis, Vardi, Wolper and Yannakakis [7]. Given a depth bound d, we can first compute Θ_d using the techniques given in Section 3 and Section 4. Then, we can restrict the search in both phases of the nested DFS algorithm to remain within Θ_d. This can be proved to search for all lassos such that all states in the lasso are reachable within a distance d from the initial state.

Currently, we are working on parallelizing the depth bounded model checker in both multi-cores and clusters of workstations. We plan to present these results in a future paper.

Acknowledgment. We thank Randy Aull, Tom Ball, Vivek Gupta, Vlad Levin, Madan Musuvathi, Aditya Nori and Shaz Qadeer for helpful discussions.

References

1. Andrews, T., Qadeer, S., Rajamani, S.K., Rehof, J., Xie, Y.: Zing: A model checker for concurrent software. In: Alur, R., Peled, D.A. (eds.) CAV 2004. LNCS, vol. 3114, pp. 484–487. Springer, Heidelberg (2004)
2. Andrews, T., Qadeer, S., Rajamani, S.K., Rehof, J., Xie, Y.: Zing: Exploiting program structure for model checking concurrent software. In: Gardner, P., Yoshida, N. (eds.) CONCUR 2004. LNCS, vol. 3170, pp. 1–15. Springer, Heidelberg (2004)

3. Ball, T., Rajamani, S.K.: The SLAM Project: Debugging system software via static analysis. In: POPL 2002: Principles of Programming Languages, pp. 1–3. ACM, New York (2002)
4. Burch, J.R., Clarke, E.M., McMillan, K.L., Dill, D.L., Hwang, L.J.: Symbolic model checking: 10^{20} states and beyond. In: LICS 1990: Logic in Computer Science, pp. 428–439 (1990)
5. Clarke, E.M., Biere, A., Raimi, R., Zhu, Y.: Bounded model checking using satisfiability solving. Formal Methods in System Design 19(1), 7–34 (2001)
6. Clarke, E.M., Grumberg, O., Jha, S., Lu, Y., Veith, H.: Counterexample-guided abstraction refinement. In: Emerson, E.A., Sistla, A.P. (eds.) CAV 2000. LNCS, vol. 1855, pp. 154–169. Springer, Heidelberg (2000)
7. Courcoubetis, C., Vardi, M.Y., Wolper, P., Yannakakis, M.: Memory efficient algorithms for the verification of temporal properties. In: Clarke, E., Kurshan, R.P. (eds.) CAV 1990. LNCS, vol. 531, pp. 58–328. Springer, Heidelberg (1991)
8. Godefroid, P.: Partial-Order Methods for the Verification of Concurrent Systems: An Approach to the State-Explosion Problem. Springer, Heidelberg (1996)
9. Godefroid, P.: Software Model Checking: The Verisoft Approach. Formal Methods in System Design 26, 77–101 (2005)
10. Havelund, K., Pressburger, T.: Model checking Java programs using Java PathFinder. International Journal on Software Tools for Technology Transfer (STTT) 2, 366–381 (2000)
11. Henzinger, T.A., Jhala, R., Majumdar, R., Sutre, G.: Lazy abstraction. In: POPL 2002: Principles of Programming Languages, pp. 58–70. ACM, New York (2002)
12. Holzmann, G.: The model checker SPIN. IEEE Transactions on Software Engineering 23(5), 279–295 (May 1997)
13. Holzmann, G.J.: An analysis of bitstate hashing. Form. Methods Syst. Des. 13, 289–307 (1998)
14. Jackson, D.: Software Abstractions: Logic, Language, and Analysis. MIT Press, Cambridge (2006)
15. Katz, S., Peled, D.: Verification of distributed programs using representative interleaving sequences, vol. 6, pp. 107–120 (1992)
16. Korf, R.E.: Depth-first Iterative-deepening: An Optimal Admissible Tree Search. In the Journal of Artificial Intelligence 27, 97–109 (1985)
17. Musuvathi, M., Park, D.Y.W., Chou, A., Engler, D.R., Dill, D.L.: CMC: a pragmatic approach to model checking real code. SIGOPS Oper. Syst. Rev. 36, 75–88 (2002)
18. Sistla, A.P., Godefroid, P.: Symmetry and reduced symmetry in model checking. ACM Trans. Program. Lang. Syst. 26, 702–734 (2004)
19. Stern, U., Dill, D.L.: Improved probabilistic verification by hash compaction. In: Camurati, P.E., Eveking, H. (eds.) CHARME 1995. LNCS, vol. 987, pp. 206–224. Springer, Heidelberg (1995)

Randomized Backtracking in State Space Traversal

Pavel Parízek and Ondřej Lhoták

David R. Cheriton School of Computer Science, University of Waterloo

Abstract. While exhaustive state space traversal is not feasible in reasonable time for complex concurrent programs, many techniques for efficient detection of concurrency errors and testing of concurrent programs have been introduced in recent years, such as directed search and context-bounded model checking.

We propose to use depth-first traversal with randomized backtracking, where it is possible to backtrack from a state before all outgoing transitions have been explored, and the whole process is driven by random number choices. Experiments with a prototype implementation in JPF on several Java programs show that, in most cases, fewer states must be explored to find an error with our approach than using the existing techniques.

1 Introduction

Exhaustive state space traversal is a means of software verification that is suitable especially for concurrent systems and detection of concurrency errors like deadlocks and race conditions. It is, however, not feasible for large and complex software systems with many threads, because the number of possible thread interleavings that must be explored is too high. A common practice is to employ state space traversal for testing of concurrent programs and detection of concurrency errors. Many techniques that aim to find errors in a reasonable time have recently been proposed. Techniques in one group are based on directed (guided) search that uses heuristics for navigation of the search towards the error state [7,5,11,21,6], so that the part of the state space that is more likely to contain error states is explored first and the rest is explored afterwards, thus making it possible to discover errors in less time. Some other techniques use randomization or parallel state space traversal with the goal of finding errors in less time [2,3,9,11,18]. Approaches from another category perform incomplete search with the assumption that many important errors can be found in a particular small part of the system's state space and searching for the other errors is not tractable because of state explosion. This category includes bounding of the number of thread context switches [16] in explicit-state model checking [13] and SAT-based model checking [17], and a random partial order sampling algorithm [20].

In this paper we propose to use *randomized backtracking* in explicit state depth-first traversal for the purpose of efficient detection of concurrency errors. The key ideas are (1) to allow backtracking also from states that still have some unexplored outgoing transitions and (2) to use the results of random number choice in the decision whether to backtrack from such a state (and thus prune a part of the state space) or continue forward along some unexplored transition.

A. Groce and M. Musuvathi (Eds.): SPIN 2011, LNCS 6823, pp. 75–89, 2011.

We implemented our approach in Java PathFinder [10] and evaluated it on seven multi-threaded Java programs that contain various concurrency errors. State space traversal with randomized backtracking has better performance than existing techniques supported by JPF on six of the seven benchmark programs, i.e. fewer states are explored by JPF before it detects an error. For the last benchmark, our approach has comparable performance with the best existing technique. On the other hand, a consequence of randomized backtracking is that an incomplete search is performed, because parts of the state space are pruned by backtracking from a state with unexplored transitions, so it cannot be guaranteed that all errors will be discovered.

2 Background and Related Work

We consider only explicit state space traversal, where each state is a snapshot of program variables and threads at one point on one execution path and each transition is a sequence of instructions executed by one thread — each transition is associated with a specific thread. We further assume that each transition in the state space is bounded by non-deterministic choices (e.g., thread scheduling choices). Figure 1 shows the basic algorithm for depth-first state space traversal in this context. The function enabled returns a set of transitions enabled in the state s that must be explored.

```
DFS ( ) :                          procedure explore ( s )
    visited = {}                       if error ( s ) then
    stack = [ ]                            counterexample = stack
    push ( stack , s_0 )                   terminate
    explore ( s_0 )                    end if
                                       transitions = order ( enabled ( s ) )
                                       for tr ∈ transitions do
                                           s' = execute ( tr )
                                           if s' ∉ visited then
                                               visited = visited ∪ s'
                                               push ( stack , s' )
                                               explore ( s' )
                                               pop ( stack )
                                           end if
                                       end for
                                   end proc
```

Fig. 1. Algorithm for depth-first state space traversal

An important parameter of the algorithm for depth-first traversal is the *search order* that determines the sequence in which the transitions leading from a state are explored. The search order is implemented by the function order, which creates a list of transitions with a specific ordering from the given set.

In the rest of this section, we describe in more detail selected existing approaches to more efficient detection of concurrency errors that are based on state space traversal.

Each tool for state space traversal of concurrent programs uses a specific default search order. The basic implementation of the function enabled in most of the tools returns a set that contains one transition for each thread runnable in the given state s. Many optimizations aiming at efficient detection of errors can be expressed through different implementations of the functions enabled and order.

Techniques based on directed (guided) search typically use custom implementations of the order function, which sort transitions according to some heuristic function over the end states of the transitions or over the transitions themselves. A useful heuristic for detection of concurrency errors is to prefer thread context switches (thread interleavings) [7] — when the state s being processed was reached by execution of thread t, the function order puts transitions associated with threads other than t at the beginning of the list. Another useful heuristic gives preference to transitions that may interfere with some of the previous transitions on the current state space path [22]. Two transitions can interfere, for example, if they are associated with different threads and contain instructions that access the same shared variables.

It is also possible to use a random search order, in which the transitions leading from a state s are explored in a random order and the order is selected separately for each state (i.e., there is no common random order for all states). The technique described in [18] combines guided search with a random order such that transitions with the same value of the heuristic function are ordered randomly. Another possible use of randomization, which was proposed in [2], is to explore the complete execution paths in a random order during stateless search.

All techniques that use a custom implementation only for the order function still explore the whole state space if they detect no error during traversal. For an incomplete state space traversal, it is necessary to use a custom implementation of the enabled function that prunes the state space according to some criteria. A very popular approach is to bound the number of thread preemptions (context switches) on each explored state space path [16], where preemption means that the thread associated with a previous transition is still runnable but a transition associated with some other thread is selected. The set returned by the customized function enabled does not contain a transition if its selection would exceed the number of allowed preemptions. The value of the bound determines how many errors are found and the time cost of the search, i.e. a higher bound means that more errors are found and the search takes more time, but it was shown that many errors are found with only two context switches [13].

3   Randomized Backtracking

We alter the standard algorithm for depth-first state space traversal with the following two modifications.

- Rather than backtracking only from fully processed states (whose outgoing transitions have all been explored) and already visited states, the modified algorithm may also backtrack from states still containing unexplored outgoing transitions.
- When the state s that is currently being processed has some unexplored outgoing transitions, random number choice is used to decide whether (a) to move forward

and explore one of the outgoing transitions or (b) backtrack already and ignore the remaining unexplored transitions.

The process of state space traversal with randomized backtracking is controlled by three parameters, which will be explained next: (1) *threshold* to enable the randomized backtracking at some search depth, (2) *strategy* to determine the length of backtrack jumps, and (3) *ratio* to decide between going forward and backtracking from a state with unexplored transitions. The parameters are used together to decide whether to backtrack from a state with unexplored transitions and how the results of random number choices are used. Specific values of the parameters make a *configuration* of randomized backtracking.

Algorithm. Figure 2 shows the algorithm for depth-first state space traversal with randomized backtracking. Differences from the basic algorithm in Figure 1 are highlighted by underlining. For each unexplored transition tr from the state s, the algorithm decides whether to execute the transition or backtrack to some earlier state on the current path. The function call rnd(0,1) returns a random number from the interval $\langle 0, 1 \rangle$. After each backtracking step, i.e. after the recursive call to explore returns, the backtrackAgain procedure is used to determine whether, according to the selected strategy, the algorithm should backtrack further. Note that randomized backtracking does not involve custom implementations of the functions order and enabled, and therefore our algorithm can be combined with any existing technique that uses special versions of these functions.

Threshold. Backtracking from a state with some unexplored outgoing transitions is enabled only if the current search depth (i.e., the number of transitions between the initial state and the current state) is greater than the value of the threshold parameter. The algorithm will not backtrack from the state s whose depth is smaller than the threshold until all transitions outgoing from s are explored. Setting this parameter to a specific non-zero value is useful, for example, when the prefix of each state space path represents an initialization phase and the algorithm should not backtrack too early, pruning the state space, before it reaches the interesting part of the state space with respect to the presence of concurrency errors.

Strategy. When the traversal algorithm decides to backtrack from the state s, either because it is fully processed or using the results of random choice, it uses the given strategy to determine the number of transitions that it backtracks over (the length of the backtrack jump). If the strategy defines a backtrack jump of a length greater than the current search depth, the algorithm backtracks through all transitions on the current path and the state space traversal finishes. We consider the following three strategies: fixed, random, and Luby.

The *fixed strategy* corresponds to the behavior of the standard algorithm for depth-first traversal. It means that the algorithm backtracks over a single transition and then decides whether to go forward along some unexplored transition or backtrack again.

When the *random strategy* is used, the algorithm backtracks over a random number of transitions at each occasion, i.e. each backtrack jump has a random length. This strategy imposes no bound on the length of the backtrack jumps.

```
DFS_RB ( threshold, strategy, ratio ) :          procedure  explore ( s )
    visited = { }                                    if  error ( s )  then
    stack = [ ]                                          counterexample = stack
    push ( stack , s₀ )                                  terminate
    explore ( s₀ )                                   end if
                                                     transitions = order ( enabled ( s ) )
                                                     for  tr ∈ transitions  do
                                                         depth = size ( stack )
                                                         if depth >= threshold then
                                                             if rnd(0, 1) > ratio( depth ) return
                                                         end if
                                                         s' = execute ( tr )
                                                         if  s' ∉ visited  then
                                                             visited = visited ∪ s'
                                                             push ( stack , s' )
                                                             explore ( s' )
                                                             pop ( stack )
                                                             if backtrackAgain( strategy ) return
                                                         end if
                                                     end for
                                                 end proc
```

Fig. 2. Algorithm for depth-first state space traversal with randomized backtracking

Usage of the *Luby strategy* [12] requires the algorithm to record the total count of backtracking jumps already performed from the start of the state space traversal. The length of a backtrack jump N is equal to the number at the corresponding position in the Luby sequence $l_1, l_2, \ldots$, which is defined by the following expression:

$$l_i = 2^{n-1}, \text{ if } i = 2^n - 1$$
$$l_i = l_{i-2^{n-1}+1} \text{ if } 2^{n-1} \leq i < 2^n - 1$$

The first few elements of the sequence are: 1, 1, 2, 1, 1, 2, 4, 1, 1, 2, 1, 1, 2, 4, 8. For example, the third backtrack jump will step over two transitions. For any integer $n > 0$, there are exactly 2^i elements with the value 2^{n-i} between any pair of elements with the value 2^n, and the element with the value 2^n occurs for the first time at the position $2^{n+1} - 1$. Therefore, the maximal possible length of a backtrack jump is bounded by the number of already performed backtrack jumps.

Ratio. The ratio parameter allows to express the degree of general preference for going forward along some unexplored transition over backtracking for decisions based on random number choice. Assuming that the value of this parameter is R, when the state s that is currently being processed has some unexplored transitions, then the algorithm backtracks from s (instead of exploring some outgoing transition) only if the randomly selected number from the interval $\langle 0, 1 \rangle$ is greater than R. The ratio can be defined as a

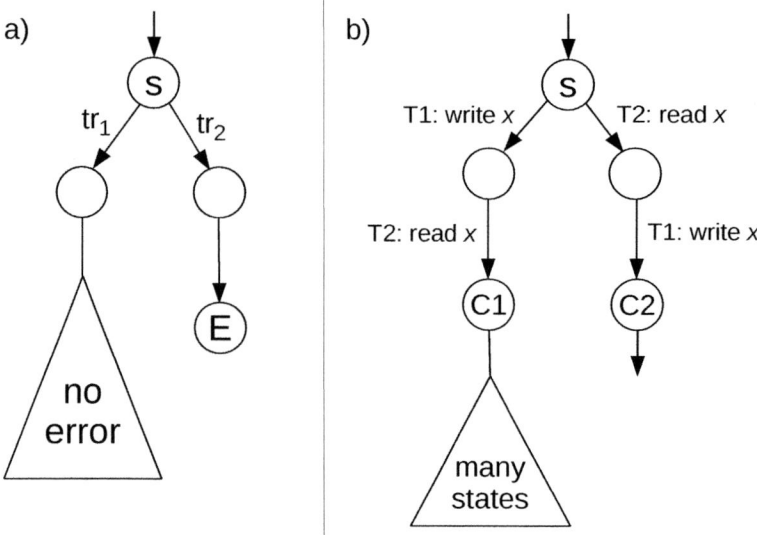

Fig. 3. State space fragments that illustrate pruning by randomized backtracking

constant number or as a function of the search depth that is represented by an expression $R = 1 - d/c$, where d is the current search depth and c is an integer constant. In the latter case, backtracking becomes more likely from states with a greater depth.

State space pruning. A consequence of the use of randomized backtracking is that an incomplete traversal is performed, because parts of the state space are pruned by backtracking from a state with some unexplored transitions, and therefore errors may be discovered in less time than with existing techniques (e.g., with the exhaustive search). On the other hand, it is not guaranteed that an error state is reached when the randomized backtracking is used, and therefore no error may be detected for some configurations and randomly chosen numbers.

Consider the state space fragment in Figure 3a. Assuming that the transition tr_1 from the state s is explored first, randomized backtracking may prune the possibly large part of the state space that does not contain any error state and thus avoid spending a lot of time in traversing the error-free part. The standard algorithm would exhaustively traverse the whole error-free part before exploring the transition tr_2.

Figure 3b shows how randomized backtracking can reduce the time needed to discover a race condition, which involves a pair of unsynchronized accesses to the same variable x in two threads $T1$ and $T2$ such that at least one of the accesses is a write and the accesses are performed in different orders in different thread schedules. After exploring the state c_1 on the state space path that corresponds to the schedule $T1; T2$, in which the first sequence of conflicting accesses is detected, the large subtree below c_1 may be pruned and a different state space path that corresponds to the schedule $T2; T1$ may be explored instead. In this case, the race condition is recognized when the state c_2 is reached and the second sequence of conflicting accesses with reverse order is detected.

For each state s, the algorithm decides whether to backtrack (based on random number choice) separately for each transition outgoing from s. A consequence of this behavior is that each outgoing transition from s has a different probability (chance) that it will be explored and not pruned — for the first transition in the list returned by the order function, the probability that it will be explored is equal to the ratio R, while a transition with the index i in the list has the probability R^i that it will be explored.

4 Evaluation

We implemented the proposed algorithm for depth-first state space traversal with randomized backtracking in Java PathFinder (JPF) [10] and evaluated its performance on seven multi-threaded Java programs: the Daisy file system [15], the Elevator benchmark from the PJBench suite [14], and five small programs used in a recent comparison of tools for detection of concurrency errors [19] that are publicly available in the CTC repository [1] — the programs are Alarm Clock, Linked List, Producer Consumer, RAX Extended, and Replicated Workers.

Basic characteristics of the programs are provided in Table 1 — total number of source code lines and maximal number of concurrently running threads.

Our implementation and the complete set of experimental results are available at the web site http://plg.uwaterloo.ca/~pparizek/jpf/spin11/. The benchmark programs can be downloaded from web sites listed in the references.

Table 1. Information about benchmark programs

Program	Source code lines	Number of threads
Daisy file system	1150	2
Elevator	320	4
Alarm Clock	180	3
Linked List	185	2
Producer Consumer	135	7
RAX Extended	150	5
Replicated Workers	430	6

We designed experiments on the seven benchmark programs to answer the following three questions about the performance of the state space traversal with randomized backtracking. In the context of this paper, performance corresponds to the number of states processed before an error is found — a lower number of processed states implies better performance.

Q1) For each benchmark, which configuration of randomized backtracking has the best performance (i.e., processes the least number of states before finding an error), and does it have better performance than existing techniques?

Q2) How much different is the performance of different configurations of randomized backtracking for each individual benchmark, i.e. what is the variability of performance over all configurations?

Q3) Is there a configuration that has reasonably good performance (better than existing techniques) for all programs?

The rest of this section contains a description of the experimental setup and then answers to the three questions. In the experimental setup and presentation of results, we followed the general recommendations for evaluating path-sensitive error detection techniques that are described in [4]. We provide values of system-independent metrics, like the number of processed states and depth of the error state.

Experimental setup. For the purpose of the experiments, we manually injected concurrency errors into those benchmark programs that did not already contain any — we created race conditions in all benchmarks except Linked List and Daisy by modifying the scope of synchronized blocks, and we inserted assertions into Daisy that are violated as a consequence of complex race conditions that already existed in the code but JPF cannot detect them directly. The Linked List benchmark already contained a race condition that JPF can detect. We tried to inject such errors as to get benchmarks with low density of error paths (as recommended in [4]), i.e., to inject hard-to-find errors, but this was not possible in some cases without changing the benchmark design and code very significantly. The following benchmarks have a low number of error paths: Daisy file system (0.03 % of paths lead to the error state), Elevator (0.006 %), and RAX Extended (3 %). Other benchmarks contain easy-to-find bugs, for which a large percentage of state space paths lead to the error.

We consider the following existing techniques that are implemented in JPF: exhaustive traversal with default search order, traversal with random search order, directed search with a heuristic that prefers thread interleavings, and context-bounded search. The default search order of JPF means that transitions in the list are ordered by the indices of the associated threads. For the context-bounded search, we considered the following bounds on the number of thread preemptions: 2, 5, 10.

With randomized backtracking, we performed experiments with configurations that correspond to all combinations of threshold values from the set $\{5, 10, 20, 50, 100\}$, values of the ratio parameter from the set $\{0.5, 0.75, 0.9, 0.99, 1 - d/20, 1 - d/50, 1 - d/100, 1 - d/1000\}$, where d is the current search depth, and all three strategies for the length of backtrack jump (fixed, random, and Luby). Names of configurations have the form of tuples (threshold, strategy, ratio).

For experiments that involve randomization, we repeated JPF runs with the same configuration until either 10 runs found an error or 100 runs were performed. The context-bounded traversal is not complete, but it does not involve any randomization, and thus the percentage of JPF runs that find an error is always either 100% or 0%.

Answer to question Q1 (best configuration for each benchmark). Table 2 provides for each benchmark program the experimental results for: (1) traversal with the default search order, (2) the existing technique with the best performance, and (3) the configuration of randomized backtracking with the best average performance from those where 100% of JPF runs found an error. For some benchmarks (Daisy file system, Alarm Clock, Linked List, and RAX Extended), better performance can be achieved by requiring only 50% of JPF runs to find an error. For these benchmarks, the table contains a fourth row showing the best performing such configuration. Note that for the Elevator benchmark, there was no configuration for which the number of JPF runs that found an error is in the interval $[50, 100)$. Each row contains values of the following metrics: the number of states processed before an error was found (mean μ, minimum, maximum,

Table 2. Configurations with the best average performance

Configuration	Processed states				Error found
	μ	min	max	σ	
Daisy file system					
default search order	282			0	100 %
thread interleavings	139			0	100 %
$(10, random, 1 - d/1000)$	108	102	116	5	100 %
$(5, fixed, 0.75)$	51	22	88	19	56 %
Elevator					
default search order	143373			0	100 %
random search order	2399	1062	3833	787	100 %
$(50, random, 1 - d/100)$	270	255	293	12	100 %
Alarm Clock					
default search order	188			0	100 %
random search order	192	12	380	111	100 %
$(10, Luby, 1 - d/1000)$	44	20	165	41	100 %
$(5, fixed, 1 - d/20)$	37	15	93	22	91 %
Linked List					
default search order	328			0	100 %
random search order	186	15	234	70	100 %
$(10, fixed, 1 - d/50)$	112	51	215	59	100 %
$(10, Luby, 0.99)$	58	50	71	7	59 %
Producer Consumer					
default search order	9299			0	100 %
random search order	48	25	73	13	100 %
$(10, fixed, 1 - d/100)$	57	23	157	41	100 %
RAX Extended					
default search order	1617			0	100 %
thread interleavings	104			0	100 %
$(10, Luby, 0.99)$	97	86	113	8	100 %
$(5, Luby, 0.9)$	8	8	9	0	59 %
Replicated Workers					
default search order	9881			0	100 %
context bound (10)	6585			0	100 %
$(50, fixed, 0.9)$	148	95	278	55	100 %

and standard deviation σ), and the percentage of JPF runs for the given configuration that found an error. The running times of JPF are less than one minute for Elevator and Replicated Workers, and a few seconds for all other benchmarks.

The results show that state space traversal with randomized backtracking has much better performance than all of the existing techniques for six of the seven benchmarks. For each of these benchmarks, there is a configuration of randomized backtracking with which 100% of JPF runs find an error, yet the number of explored states is a factor of 1.1 to 44 times lower than for the best existing technique. The exception is the Producer Consumer benchmark, for which both complete search with random search order and randomized backtracking have similar performance; they both explore fewer states than the JPF default search order by a factor of over 160. Although the state space traversal with random search order yields a lower minimal number of explored states than randomized backtracking for the Alarm Clock and Linked List benchmarks, randomized backtracking yields a lower average and maximum than random search order, and therefore we claim that randomized backtracking has better performance for these two benchmarks. Usage of randomized backtracking has significantly better performance than existing techniques in particular for benchmark programs with deep errors (such that a large number of states must be explored to find the error), like the Elevator and Replicated Workers benchmarks, for which the mean number of states explored is reduced by a factor of 8.9 and 44, respectively.

For some benchmark programs, significantly better performance can be achieved by the appropriate configurations when it is not required that all JPF runs find an error — see data for Daisy file system and RAX Extended, which show improvement by a factor of 2.1 and 12, respectively, over the best configuration where 100% of JPF runs found an error. If the percentage of JPF runs that find an error is greater than 50% and each run finishes quickly, then an error would be found with a very high probability (close to 100%) by performing a sequence of JPF runs with the given configuration. The total running time of this sequence of JPF runs might be smaller than the running time of some existing technique and also than the running time of a single JPF run with a different configuration (for which every JPF run that we performed found an error).

Answer to question Q2 (variability of performance by configuration). Table 3 provides for each benchmark program the experimental results for configurations of randomized backtracking that yield the following extremes over the set of all JPF runs for all configurations: minimal number of states processed by some JPF run and maximal number of states processed by some JPF run. We consider only configurations where 50% or more of JPF runs detected some error. Moreover, the table provides also the configuration for which the lowest percentage of JPF runs discovered an error.

Each row of the table contains values of the following metrics: number of states processed before an error was found (mean μ, minimum, maximum, and standard deviation σ), and percentage of JPF runs for the given configuration that found some error. If no error was found by any JPF run for some configuration, then columns for all metrics related to the number of processed states and search depth in the table contain the character "-".

The results show that there is great variability in performance yielded by different configurations and different outcomes of random number choices on each benchmark program. In particular, the minimal and maximal numbers of states processed by a JPF run that were recorded over all configurations and JPF runs differ by an order of magnitude for some benchmarks (e.g., for the Producer Consumer and Replicated Workers benchmarks). Note that the worst configurations of randomized backtracking (that yield maximum numbers) still have better or the same performance as the default search order, but they have worse performance than other existing techniques, such as the random search order for Producer Consumer, Linked List and RAX Extended.

The numbers of states processed before an error is found also differ significantly among JPF runs with a single configuration for some benchmarks. Consider for example the Replicated Workers benchmark and the configuration $(50, \text{Luby}, 1 - d/20)$, in which

Table 3. Configurations that yield performance extremes

Configuration	Processed states				Error found
	μ	min	max	σ	
Daisy file system					
(5, fixed, 0.9)	135	19	467	165	67 %
(20, fixed, 0.5)	282	282	282	0	100 %
(5, random, $1 - d/20$)	-	-	-	-	0 %
Elevator					
(50, fixed, 0.99)	358	253	424	49	100 %
(100, fixed, $1 - d/50$)	2263	2227	2338	38	100 %
(5, fixed, 0.5)	-	-	-	-	0 %
Alarm Clock					
(5, fixed, 0.5)	85	13	251	74	100 %
(5, fixed, 0.9)	94	13	447	120	100 %
(5, random, $1 - d/100$)	57	19	112	30	19 %
Linked List					
(5, fixed, $1 - d/50$)	74	38	133	27	56 %
(20, fixed, 0.9)	235	170	408	66	100 %
(5, Luby, 0.5)	-	-	-	-	0 %
Producer Consumer					
(10, fixed, $1 - d/50$)	196	18	1251	355	100 %
(50, fixed, 0.5)	9299	9299	9299	0	100 %
(5, Luby, $1 - d/1000$)	242	242	242	0	1 %
RAX Extended					
(5, fixed, 0.5)	60	8	313	88	67 %
(50, fixed, 0.5)	1617	1617	1617	0	100 %
(5, random, $1 - d/50$)	10	8	15	2	26 %
Replicated Workers					
(50, fixed, 0.5)	339	71	1282	385	100 %
(50, Luby, $1 - d/20$)	6258	139	19190	5673	100 %
(5, random, 0.5)	-	-	-	-	0 %

case (i) the standard deviation of the number of processed states is approximately equal to the mean value and (ii) the maximum number of states processed by some JPF run with that configuration is 138 times bigger than the minimum number of processed states. Also the percentage of JPF runs that find an error varies to a great degree among different configurations. For some benchmark programs and configurations, a small percentage of JPF runs (or none at all) found an error (e.g. Linked List).

Answer to question Q3 (a generally good configuration). Although different configurations yield the best performance for each benchmark program, reasonably good performance for all of them is achieved by configurations with the ratio 0.9 and the random strategy. Table 4 shows for each benchmark program the results for: (1) the existing technique with the best performance, (2) the configuration of randomized backtracking with the best average performance, and (3) the configuration (H, random, 0.9) with the benchmark-specific threshold value H that achieves the best performance (for the ratio 0.9 and random strategy).

Table 4. Configuration with good performance for all benchmarks

Configuration	Processed states				Error found
	μ	min	max	σ	
Daisy file system					
thread interleavings	139			0	100 %
$(10, random, 1 - d/1000)$	108	102	116	5	100 %
$(10, random, 0.9)$	110	103	119	5.4	100 %
Elevator					
random search order	2399	1062	3833	787	100 %
$(50, random, 1 - d/100)$	270	255	293	12	100 %
$(50, random, 0.9)$	290	261	312	15	100 %
Alarm Clock					
random search order	192	12	380	111	100 %
$(5, fixed, 1 - d/20)$	37	15	93	22	91 %
$(10, random, 0.9)$	90	23	220	64	100 %
Linked List					
random search order	186	15	234	70	100 %
$(10, Luby, 0.99)$	58	50	71	7	59 %
$(20, random, 0.9)$	197	171	266	29	100 %
Producer Consumer					
random search order	48	25	73	13	100 %
$(10, fixed, 1 - d/100)$	57	23	157	41	100 %
$(10, random, 0.9)$	189	22	435	133	100 %
RAX Extended					
thread interleavings	104			0	100 %
$(5, Luby, 0.9)$	8	8	9	0	59 %
$(10, random, 0.9)$	100	79	119	11	100 %
Replicated Workers					
context bound (10)	6585			0	100 %
$(50, fixed, 0.9)$	148	95	278	55	100 %
$(100, random, 0.9)$	522	263	905	203	100 %

The configuration $(H, random, 0.9)$ yields better or the same performance as the best existing technique for all benchmarks except Producer Consumer, for which the random search order has better performance. Note also that for some benchmarks, such as the Daisy file system and Elevator, the performance of randomized backtracking with the configuration $(H, random, 0.9)$ is very close to the performance of the best configuration for the given benchmark.

The threshold value H must be selected with regard to the given benchmark program, since it influences (i) the chance that a JPF run will find an error and (ii) whether randomized backtracking will have any effect on the number of states traversed. If the threshold is too low, the error will not be found by most of the JPF runs. If the threshold is too high, randomized backtracking will never occur and therefore exhaustive state space traversal with the default search order will be performed by JPF.

Table 5. Performance of the configuration (H, random, 0.9) for different threshold values

Threshold:		5	10	20	50	100
Daisy file system						
States	μ	30	110	282	282	282
Depth	μ	6	7	7	7	7
	σ	0	0	0	0	0
Error found		1 %	100 %	100 %	100 %	100 %
Elevator						
States	μ	-	-	-	290	2185
Depth	μ	-	-	-	45	45
	σ	-	-	-	0	0
Error found		0 %	0 %	0 %	100 %	100 %
Alarm Clock						
States	μ	59	90	188	188	188
Depth	μ	13	13	13	13	13
	σ	1.7	4.5	0	0	0
Error found		25.6 %	100 %	100 %	100 %	100 %
Linked List						
States	μ	-	75	197	276	328
Depth	μ	-	12	19	48	48
	σ	-	1	1.4	0	0
Error found		0 %	40 %	100 %	100 %	100 %
Producer Consumer						
States	μ	127	189	204	9299	9299
Depth	μ	29	19	25	23	23
	σ	6.4	3.6	0	0	0
Error found		10.3 %	100 %	100 %	100 %	100 %
RAX Extended						
States	μ	12	100	441	1617	1617
Depth	μ	6	6	20	38	38
	σ	0	0	1	0	0
Error found		35.7 %	100 %	100 %	100 %	100 %
Replicated Workers						
States	μ	-	-	-	1774	522
Depth	μ	-	-	-	62	106
	σ	-	-	-	3.2	6.2
Error found		0 %	0 %	0 %	100 %	100 %

Table 5 illustrates how the threshold value H influences the performance of randomized backtracking with the configuration (H, random, 0.9) and the percentage of JPF runs that detect an error. For each benchmark and threshold value, the table provides values of the following metrics: the search depth at which the error was detected (mean μ and standard deviation σ) and the percentage of JPF runs that found some error.

Different values of the threshold parameter work for different benchmarks in general. However, the results imply the following three general properties of the performance of randomized backtracking based on the threshold value:

- very few JPF runs may find an error in a given program if the threshold value is too small (significantly smaller than the depth of the error state), because JPF may often backtrack too early before reaching the error state;
- even though the usage of randomized backtracking does not guarantee that an error is discovered, the results show that an error is discovered by all JPF runs for a given threshold (or by a very high percentage of JPF runs), as long as the threshold value is not too small (compared to the depth of the error state);
- if the threshold is too big, randomized backtracking does not have any effect (i.e., it does not have better performance than the existing techniques), because JPF finds an error at a search depth lower than the threshold value and therefore it never backtracks from a state with unexplored outgoing transitions.

For example, the threshold value 5 is too small for Daisy file system and the threshold value 10 is too small for the Elevator benchmark. On the other hand, threshold values 50 or higher are too big for the RAX Extended benchmark.

5   Conclusion

We introduced the idea of using randomized backtracking in state space traversal for the purpose of fast error detection. Experiments with our implementation in JPF on several multi-threaded Java programs show that randomized backtracking has better performance than existing techniques in most cases.

In particular, randomized backtracking has better performance than existing techniques in search for hard-to-find errors that are triggered only by a few paths (e.g., Elevator) and also in search for easy-to-find errors (e.g., Replicated Workers).

There is no single best configuration of randomized backtracking that would have the best performance for any benchmark program. However, we recommend to use the configuration $(H, \text{random}, 0.9)$ with a specific threshold H, because it performs reasonably well for all benchmarks and, in particular, has significantly better performance than existing techniques in most cases. Since the optimal threshold value is specific to the benchmark program, a viable approach is to run several instances of JPF with the configuration $(H, \text{random}, 0.9)$ and different threshold values in parallel, and stop all of them when one finds an error. The "embarrassingly parallel" approach to search for errors, proposed in [8, 9], could be used.

In the future, we would like to evaluate randomized backtracking on more complex Java programs and to investigate possible approaches to determining reasonable threshold values (e.g., using heuristics). There might be some relation between good threshold values and bounds on the number of preemptions in context-bounded model checking. Another possible application of randomized backtracking is the search for errors in programs with infinite state spaces or infinite paths (e.g., programs that involve some ever increasing counter).

Acknowledgements. This research was supported by the Natural Sciences and Engineering Research Council of Canada.

References

1. Concurrency Tool Comparison repository, https://facwiki.cs.byu.edu/vv-lab/index.php/Concurrency_Tool_Comparison
2. Coons, K.E., Burckhardt, S., Musuvathi, M.: GAMBIT: Effective Unit Testing for Concurrency Libraries. In: PPoPP 2010, ACM, New York (2010)
3. Dwyer, M.B., Elbaum, S.G., Person, S., Purandare, R.: Parallel Randomized State-Space Search. In: ICSE. IEEE CS, Los Alamitos (2007)
4. Dwyer, M.B., Person, S., Elbaum, S.G.: Controlling Factors in Evaluating Path-Sensitive Error Detection Techniques. In: FSE 2006. ACM, New York (2006)
5. Edelkamp, S., Leue, S., Lluch-Lafuente, A.: Directed Explicit-State Model Checking in the Validation of Communication Protocols. International Journal on Software Tools for Technology Transfer 5(2-3) (2004)
6. Edelkamp, S., Schuppan, V., Bosnacki, D., Wijs, A., Fehnker, A., Aljazzar, H.: Survey on Directed Model Checking. In: Peled, D.A., Wooldridge, M.J. (eds.) MoChArt 2008. LNCS, vol. 5348, pp. 65–89. Springer, Heidelberg (2009)
7. Groce, A., Visser, W.: Heuristics for Model Checking Java Programs. International Journal on Software Tools for Technology Transfer 6(4) (2004)
8. Holzmann, G.J., Joshi, R., Groce, A.: Tackling Large Verification Problems with the Swarm Tool. In: Havelund, K., Majumdar, R. (eds.) SPIN 2008. LNCS, vol. 5156, pp. 134–143. Springer, Heidelberg (2008)
9. Holzmann, G.J., Joshi, R., Groce, A.: Swarm Verification. In: ASE 2008. IEEE CS, Los Alamitos (2008)
10. Java PathFinder, http://babelfish.arc.nasa.gov/trac/jpf/
11. Jones, M., Mercer, E.G.: Explicit State Model Checking with Hopper. In: Graf, S., Mounier, L. (eds.) SPIN 2004. LNCS, vol. 2989, pp. 146–150. Springer, Heidelberg (2004)
12. Luby, M., Sinclair, A., Zuckerman, D.: Optimal Speedup of Las Vegas Algorithms. Information Processing Letters 47(4) (1993)
13. Musuvathi, M., Qadeer, S.: Iterative Context Bounding for Systematic Testing of Multithreaded Programs. In: PLDI. ACM, New York (2007)
14. Parallel Java Benchmarks, http://code.google.com/p/pjbench
15. Qadeer, S.: Daisy File System. Joint CAV/ISSTA special event on specification, verification and testing of concurrent software (2004)
16. Qadeer, S., Rehof, J.: Context-Bounded Model Checking of Concurrent Software. In: Halbwachs, N., Zuck, L.D. (eds.) TACAS 2005. LNCS, vol. 3440, pp. 93–107. Springer, Heidelberg (2005)
17. Rabinovitz, I., Grumberg, O.: Bounded Model Checking of Concurrent Programs. In: Etessami, K., Rajamani, S.K. (eds.) CAV 2005. LNCS, vol. 3576, pp. 82–97. Springer, Heidelberg (2005)
18. Rungta, N., Mercer, E.G.: Generating Counter-Examples Through Randomized Guided Search. In: Bošnački, D., Edelkamp, S. (eds.) SPIN 2007. LNCS, vol. 4595, pp. 39–57. Springer, Heidelberg (2007)
19. Rungta, N., Mercer, E.: Clash of the Titans: Tools and Techniques for Hunting Bugs in Concurrent Programs. In: PADTAD. ACM, New York (2009)
20. Sen, K.: Effective Random Testing of Concurrent Programs. In: ASE. ACM, New York (2007)
21. Seppi, K., Jones, M., Lamborn, P.: Guided Model Checking with a Bayesian Meta-Heuristic. Fundamenta Informaticae 70(1-2) (2006)
22. Wehrle, M., Kupferschmid, S.: Context-Enhanced Directed Model Checking. In: van de Pol, J., Weber, M. (eds.) Model Checking Software. LNCS, vol. 6349, pp. 88–105. Springer, Heidelberg (2010)

An Analytic Evaluation of SystemC Encodings in Promela

Daniele Campana, Alessandro Cimatti, Iman Narasamdya, and Marco Roveri

Fondazione Bruno Kessler — Irst
{campana, cimatti, narasamdya, roveri}@fbk.eu

Abstract. SystemC is a de-facto standard language for high-level modeling of systems on chip. We investigate the feasibility of explicit state model checking of SystemC programs, proposing several ways to convert SystemC into Promela. We analyze the expressiveness of the various encoding styles, and we experimentally evaluate their impact on the search carried out by SPIN on a significant set of benchmarks. We also compare the results with recent approaches to symbolic verification of SystemC. Our approach never returns false positives, detects assertion violations much faster than recent formal approaches, and has the novel feature of pinpointing non-progressing delta cycles.

1 Introduction

SystemC is a de-facto standard language for writing high-level executable system designs of System-on-Chips (SoCs). SystemC allows for high-speed simulations before synthesizing the RTL hardware description. A SystemC design can be viewed as a multi-threaded program with a specific scheduling policy [19].

Verification of SystemC is crucial in order to pinpoint errors in the design (or in the specification), and to prevent their propagation down to the hardware. Despite the efficiency of simulations, simulation-based verification is not always effective in finding bugs, due to inherently complex behaviors caused by concurrency and thread interleavings. Since each simulation only explores one possible sequence of thread interleavings, simulations can miss bugs that are caused by unexplored thread interleavings.

Formal verification of SystemC has recently gained significant interests with the use of software model checking [5,6,14] and bounded model checking [8,9] techniques, or by reduction to model checking for finite state [17,21] and timed [11] systems.

In this paper, we present and evaluate a family of encodings of SystemC designs in Promela [12]. All the proposed encodings accurately model the full semantics of SystemC. Yet, they feature different characteristics in terms of the properties that can be verified and in terms of the efficiency of the search carried out by SPIN [12]. All the proposed encodings are obtained by combining a generic encoding of the SystemC scheduler, and an encoding of each thread in the SystemC design, and they all allow for checking program assertions. They differ in the way the scheduler-threads synchronization is modeled, and in the use of Promela constructs to control atomicity. As a result, the various encodings can allow for observations of the SystemC design at different granularities. In fact, the simulation of a SystemC design is divided into one or more

A. Groce and M. Musuvathi (Eds.): SPIN 2011, LNCS 6823, pp. 90–107, 2011.

delta cycles, which in turn are composed of several phases, during which each thread can be activated multiple times. Depending on the specific features of the encoding, there may be significant variations in the number of stored states and explored transitions during the search. The work in [21] also proposes a Promela encoding of SystemC designs, but the encoding covers only a subset of SystemC semantics.

Detection of the presence of non-progressing delta cycles is very important. Indeed, if a design shows a non-progressing delta cycle, then the design is not synthesizeable. Clearly it is impossible to verify that the SystemC design will eventually exit from every delta cycle using simulation. Our approach is also unique in the ability to check for the absence of non-progressing delta cycles in the SystemC design. This is made possible by the accurate encoding of the scheduler, and is carried out by reduction to checking the absence of non-progress cycles with SPIN.

We carry out a thorough investigation of the features of the various encodings, first analytically, and then experimentally. We have implemented the encodings in a tool called SC2PROMELA. The SPIN model checker is called with different modalities, to check for assertion violations and for the presence of non-progressing delta cycles. We conduct experiments with the encodings on a significant set of benchmarks taken and adapted from [6]. The results of experiments support the analytical conjectures in terms of the features of the search. Moreover, our techniques allow us to discover that some of the benchmarks used in [6] have non-progressing delta cycles.

The proposed approach is oriented to bug finding. In fact, all the encodings proposed in this paper exhibit under-approximations of SystemC designs. That is, we restrict the input values that can be read from the environment. In other words, we perform the verification of the SystemC designs under certain assumptions about the input values.

We also compared the different encodings with ESST [5], a recent and promising technique for SystemC verification. ESST is based on the combination of explicit state model checking techniques to handle the SystemC scheduler with the symbolic lazy abstraction [10] technique to handle the threads. This comparison clearly shows that our Promela encodings are complementary to ESST in that they appear to be very effective in finding bugs that are nested deeply inside a thread. ESST often requires many refinement steps, and turns out to be surprisingly inefficient.

This paper is organized in the following way. Section 2 introduces SystemC and shows a running example that will be used throughout the paper. Section 3 shows our Promela encodings. Section 4 describes analytical comparisons of the encodings. Section 5 describes the experimental evaluation. Section 6 discusses some related work. Finally, Section 7 concludes this paper and outlines some future work.

2   Structure of SystemC Design

SystemC is a C++ library that provides a core language for specifying components of a system design and their interconnections by means of, respectively, modules and channels. The core language also provides threads for modeling the parallel behavior of the design and events for synchronizing the threads. In addition to the core language, SystemC includes a scheduler that runs the threads during a simulation. Thus, a SystemC design can be viewed as a multi-threaded program with a specific scheduler. An

```
1  SC_MODULE( Producer ) {              27  SC_MODULE( Consumer ) {
2    sc_event e;                        28  public:
3  public:                              29    sc_in<int> port_in;
4    sc_in<int> port_in;                30    sc_out<int> port_out;
5    sc_out<int> port_out;              31    SC_CTOR( Consumer ) {
6    SC_CTOR( Producer ) {              32      SC_METHOD( read_and_ack );
7      SC_THREAD( write );              33      sensitive << port_in;
8      SC_METHOD( read_ack );           34      dont_initialize();
9      sensitive << port_in; dont_initialize();  35    }
10   }                                  36    void read_and_ack() {
11   void write() {                     37      int ack = process ( port_in.read() );
12     wait(SC_ZERO_TIME);              38      port_out.write(ack);
13     while (1) {                      39    }
14       port_out.write( input() );     40  };
15       wait(e);                       41  int sc_main() {
16     }                                42    sc_signal<int> p_to_c, c_to_p;
17   }                                  43    Producer *p = new Producer(''P'');
18   void read_ack() {                  44    Consumer *c = new Consumer(''C'');
19     output( port_in.read() );        45    p->port_out(p_to_c); c->port_in(p_to_c);
20     e.notify();                      46    p->port_in(c_to_p); c->port_out(c_to_p);
21   }                                  47    sc_start();
22  };                                  48  }
```

Fig. 1. Example of SystemC design

example of a SystemC design is depicted in Figure 1. In the example we have two components, `Producer` and `Consumer`. The constructor of the `Producer` specifies two threads: `write` for writing value to the `Consumer` through the channel bound to its output port `port_out`, and `read_ack` for reading the acknowledgment value sent by the `Consumer`. For simplicity, we treat a process declared by `SC_METHOD` as a thread that suspends itself only if its execution terminates. The constructor also says that the thread `read_ack` is sensitive to the value update of the channel bound to the input port `port_in`, and that it is not runnable at the beginning of the simulation (see call to `dont_initialize()`).

SystemC simulation can be divided into so-called delta cycles. The transition from one delta-cycle into the next one occurs when there are no more runnable threads. In our example the thread `write` first waits until the next delta cycle, by `wait(SC_ZERO_TIME)`, before entering the loop that feeds value for the `Consumer`. Every time it writes a value to the `Consumer`, it suspends itself and waits for the notification of the event e by `wait(e)`. The structure and behavior of `Consumer` can be described similarly to that of the `Producer`. The main function `sc_main` instantiates one `Producer` and one `Consumer`, binds their ports to the appropriate signal channels, and then starts the simulation by `sc_start()`.

The SystemC scheduler has several phases[1], as shown in Figure 2(a). In the initialization phase all channels are updated according to their first initialization, and a delta notification is performed to signify the start of a delta cycle. The scheduler then enters the evaluation phase. In this phase the scheduler runs all runnable threads, one at a time, until there are no more runnable threads, while postponing the materializations of channel updates. This phase constitutes one delta cycle.

Having no more runnable threads, the scheduler enters the channel-update phase where it materializes all channel updates. These updates could make some threads runnable, and so the scheduler goes back to the evaluation phase to run these threads. Otherwise, the scheduler accelerates the simulation time to the nearest time point where there exists an event to be notified. This event notification in turn could make some

---

[1] For further details and discussions about the SystemC scheduler we refer the reader to [19].

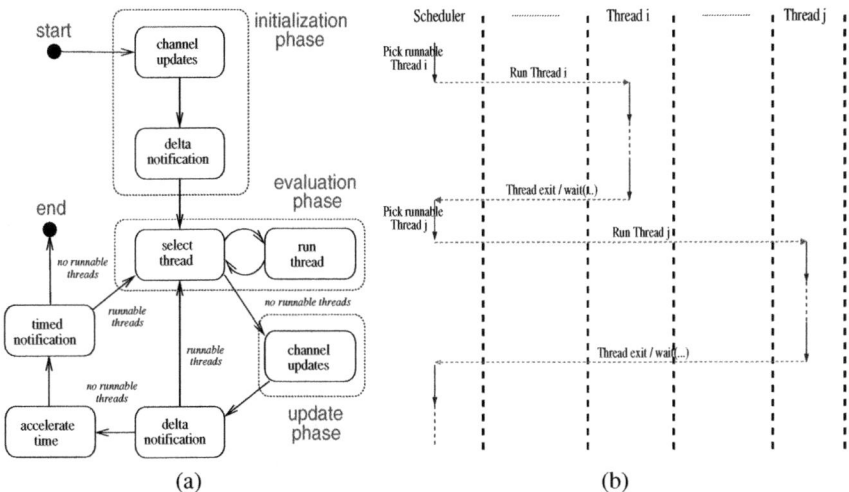

Fig. 2. (a) The SystemC scheduler. (b) The dynamic view of a SystemC design

threads runnable, and so the scheduler goes back to the evaluation phase again. Otherwise, the scheduler ends the simulation.

The evaluation phase of the scheduler employs a cooperative scheduling with an exclusive run of each thread. That is, as shown in Figure 2(b), when the scheduler gives the control to a thread to run, it never preempts the control from the running thread, but waits until the thread suspends itself and gives the control back to the scheduler.

3   Encoding SystemC in Promela

In this work we consider three different Promela encodings of SystemC designs. In all of these encodings we capture the full semantics of SystemC. These encodings differ in the number of Promela processes, the modeling of communication between the threads and the scheduler, and the granularity of atomicity in simulations. These differences can affect the search behavior of the protocol analyzer generated from the resulting Promela models as well as kinds of property that can be verified.

In developing the encodings, we rely on several assumptions. First, we assume that the number of threads and events are known a priori. Thus, we do not handle SystemC designs that contain dynamic creations of objects or threads. Second, we assume that all function calls can statically be inlined. These limitations, however, do not affect the applicability of the proposed techniques since, to the best of our knowledge, most real SystemC design satisfy these assumptions.

For presenting our encodings, we will use the example introduced in the previous section. Although the example only uses a small subset of SystemC features, the example is sufficient to describe our encodings. We believe that other SystemC features that are not used in the example can be encoded in a similar way to those here presented.

```
1  inline write() {
2
3    // Entry procedure.
4    thread_entry(write_ID);
5
6    // Jump table.
7    if
8      :: write_PC == wait_1 -> goto wait_1_loc;
9      :: write_PC == wait_2 -> goto wait_2_loc;
10     :: else              -> skip;
11   fi;
12
13   // Thread body.
14   wait_time(write_ID,0);
15   thread_suspend(write_ID,write_PC,wait_1,write_exit);
16
17   wait_1_loc:
18   while_start:
19     p_to_s_new = input();
20     wait_event(write_ID,e_ID);
21     thread_suspend(write_ID,write_PC,wait_2,write_exit);
22   wait_2_loc:
23     goto while_start;
24
25     // Exit procedure.
26     thread_exit(write_ID);
27
28 }
```

(a)

```
1  inline wait_event(thread_ID, event_ID) {
2    ThreadEvents[thread_ID] = event_ID;
3    ThreadStates[thread_ID] = SLEEP;
4  }
5
6  inline wait_time(thread_ID, time) {
7    NotifyTimes[thread_ID] = time;
8    ThreadEvents[thread_ID] = thread_ID;
9    ThreadStates[thread_ID] = SLEEP;
10 }
```

(b)

```
1  proctype Scheduler() {
2    bool runnable_t;
3    start_DeltaCycle:
4    exists_runnable_thread(runnable_t);
5    if
6      :: !runnable_t -> goto TimedNotification;
7      :: else -> skip;
8    fi;
9    evaluation_phase();
10   progress_DeltaCycle:
11   update_phase();
12   delta_notification_phase();
13   goto start_DeltaCycle;
14   TimedNotification:
15   timed_notification_phase();
16   exists_runnable_thread(runnable_t);
17   if
18     :: !runnable_t -> goto SchedulerExit;
19     :: else -> goto start_DeltaCycle;
20   fi;
21   SchedulerExit:
22 }
```

(c)

Fig. 3. Encodings of (a) thread, (b) synchronization primitive, and (c) scheduler

3.1 Basic Building Blocks

The three encodings we propose in this paper are built on some basic building blocks that represent the imperative constructs of the body of the SystemC threads and channels, the synchronization primitives, and the scheduler.

Encoding threads. We first associate each SystemC thread t with a unique id t_ID. Figure 3(a) shows the encoding of the thread write in the previous example. Each thread t is encoded as inline code that starts with an entry procedure encoded in the inline code thread_entry(t_ID) and ends with an exit procedure encoded in the inline code thread_exit(t_ID).

The entry procedure thread_entry(t_ID) describes the passing of control from the scheduler to the thread. Because the synchronization between the scheduler and the threads are modeled differently in our encodings, so are the expansions of thread_entry in the encodings.

The entry procedure is then followed by a "jump table" that determines where the execution of the thread body has to start or, in case of thread suspension, to resume. To be able to resume the thread execution from the middle of the thread body, we have to keep track the program counter. To this end, we associate each thread t with a variable t_PC whose values correspond to code labels.

The translation of the thread body into Promela code is straight-forward due to the large similarities of the imperative constructs between SystemC and Promela. For example, the while loop can be translated into Promela if-fi and goto constructs.

When its execution is suspended, by for example calling wait functions, the thread t has to (1) update $t\_$PC with the location where it will resume its execution, (2) go to the suspension location, which is the exit label $t\_$exit, and (3) return the control back to the scheduler. These three steps are encoded in thread_suspend($t\_$ID, $t\_$PC, r1, s1), where r1 is a value that corresponds to the resume location, and s1 is the suspension location. We will show later that the exit label $t\_$exit is placed immediately following the inline code that encodes the thread.

On exiting the execution, the thread t has to establish its sensitivity that could dynamically change during its execution, and then it has to give the control back to the scheduler. We encode this exiting procedure in thread_exit($t\_$ID). Similar to thread_entry, the expansions of thread_suspend and thread_exit can be different in our encodings.

Encoding channels. Figure 3(a) also provides a glimpse of how SystemC channels can be encoded into Promela. For example, a SystemC signal s or a port bound to that signal is modeled by a pair ($s\_$new, $s\_$old) of variables such that every write to s is a write to $s\_$new and every read from s is a read from $s\_$old. We also associate an event for each signal, and use it to wake up the threads sensitive to that signal.

For each signal, we have the encoding of its update function as an inline Promela code. This code is executed in the channel update phase and accounts for updating the content of $s\_$old with the value of $s\_$new when they are not equal. When the content of $s\_$old gets updated, the inline code will notify the event associated with the signal s. Other kinds of channel can be encoded in a similar way.

Encoding synchronization primitives. Similar to the threads we associate each event e with a unique id $e\_$ID. To encode synchronization primitives, the encoding of the scheduler maintains three different arrays: ThreadStates indexed by thread id's, ThreadEvents indexed by thread id's, and NotifyTimes indexed by event id's. ThreadStates contains the states of threads. A thread state is either RUNNABLE or SLEEP. ThreadEvents contains the id's of the events whose notifications are waited by the threads. While, NotifyTimes indicates the notification times of events.

We encode the call to wait(e), for an event e, into inline code wait_event($t\_$ID, $e\_$ID), as shown in Figure 3(b), such that t is the calling thread. We note in ThreadEvents that the calling thread t is now waiting for an event e, and update the thread's state in ThreadStates to SLEEP.

To encode wait_time, we associate each thread t with an event. We reuse the id of the thread as id for the event associated with it. Then, using the array NotifyTimes, we note that the event associated with the thread should be woken up at some time.

The encoding of notify_event(e) is as follows: we iterate over the array ThreadStates to check if a thread t is sleeping or not. If t is sleeping and is waiting for the notification of e, then we update the state of t to RUNNABLE and we update the arrays ThreadEvents and NotifyTimes at index $e\_$ID with -1.

Encoding scheduler. The encoding of the scheduler, shown in Figure 3(c), follows the description shown in Figure 2(a). The inline code evaluation_phase simply non-deterministically selects a thread whose status is RUNNABLE and executes the thread. The inline code update_phase updates every channel that needs to be updated by executing the corresponding update function. The inline code delta_notification_phase changes the status of a thread from SLEEP to RUNNABLE if the thread is sensitive to the channel that has just been updated or is waiting for the notification of an event that should be notified at the delta-cycle boundary. The inline code timed_notification_phase encodes the time acceleration and time notification. The time acceleration is modeled by substracting the notification times in the array NotifyTimes by the distance to the nearest time point where an event can be notified. To support the under-approximations, we can set the limit of simulation time.

In our Promela encodings, the schedulers differ only in the inline code evaluation_phase, while other parts remain the same.

Encoding non-deterministic inputs. We encode input reading as inline code that selects non-deterministically values from a finite set of random values. This can be thought as verifying the design under certain assumptions about the input values.

3.2 Thread-To-Process Encoding

Our first encoding treats the scheduler and the threads as separate Promela processes, as shown in Figure 4. In particular the encoding of each thread can optionally be enclosed within a Promela atomic block. We call our first encoding *thread-to-process*.

In this encoding the synchronization between threads and the scheduler is modeled by passing a CONTROL_TOKEN through the Promela rendezvous channels that connect the threads with the scheduler. We maintain the array ControlChannel of Promela rendezvous channels such that each rendezvous channel is associated with a thread by means of thread_ID. Recall that passing control from the scheduler to a thread is encoded in the inline code thread_entry. Such a control passing is modeled as sending (operator !) and receiving (operator ?) the CONTROL_TOKEN through the designated rendezvous channel, as shown in Figure 5. Follow-

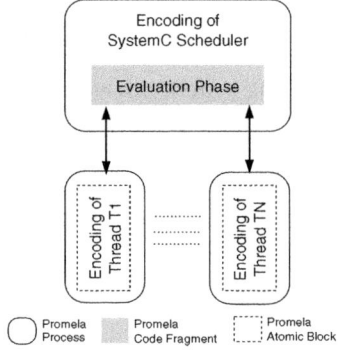

Fig. 4. Thread-to-process encoding

ing the semantics of Promela, the receive statement is executable only if the associated rendezvous channel receives the CONTROL_TOKEN.

Exiting and suspending the thread execution in thread-to-process encoding are modeled as sending the CONTROL_TOKEN back to the scheduler, as shown in Figure 5 by the inline code thread_exit and thread_suspend, respectively. On exiting the thread execution, we set the state of the thread to SLEEP and establish the event sensitivity of the thread. Note that, for presentation only, we assume that each thread is sensitive to at most one event. However, in our implementation the elements of the arrays ThreadEvents and ThreadSensitivity are of composite type that can handle threads with more than one sensitive events.

Similar to exiting the thread execution, on suspending the thread we set the state of the thread to SLEEP. Unlike exiting the thread execution, before handing over the

```
1  inline thread_entry(t_ID) {
2     ControlChannel[t_ID] ? CONTROL_TOKEN;
3  }
4
5  inline thread_exit(t_ID) {
6     ThreadState[t_ID] = SLEEP;
7     ThreadEvents[t_ID] = ThreadSensitivity[t_ID];
8     ControlChannel[t_ID] ! CONTROL_TOKEN;
9  }
10
11 inline thread_suspend(t_ID, t_PC, res_loc, susp_loc) {
12    thread_PC = res_loc;
13    ThreadState[t_ID] = SLEEP;
14    ControlChannel[t_ID] ! CONTROL_TOKEN;
15    goto susp_loc;
16 }
17
18 inline thread_suspend_optimize(t_ID) {
19    ThreadState[t_ID] = SLEEP;
20    ControlChannel[t_ID] ! CONTROL_TOKEN;
21    ControlChannel[t_ID] ? CONTROL_TOKEN;
22 }
```

```
1  proctype write_thread() {
2     write_entry:
3        atomic { write(); }
4     write_exit:
5        goto write_entry;
6  }
7
8  inline evaluation_phase() {
9     do
10       :: ThreadStates[write_ID] == RUNNABLE
11          -> ControlChannel[thread_ID] ! CONTROL_TOKEN;
12             ControlChannel[thread_ID] ? CONTROL_TOKEN;
13       :: ThreadStates[read_ack_ID] == RUNNABLE
14          -> ControlChannel[read_ack_ID] ! CONTROL_TOKEN;
15             ControlChannel[read_ack_ID] ? CONTROL_TOKEN;
16       :: else -> break;
17    od;
18 }
```

Fig. 5. Thread-to-process encoding: Promela code

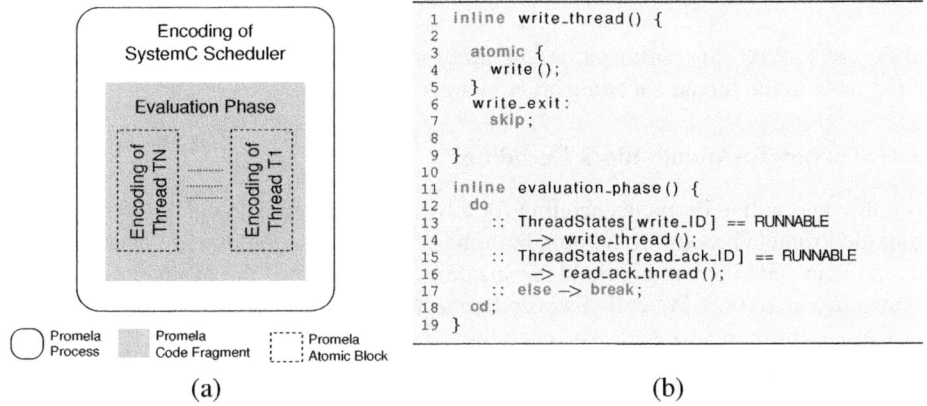

```
1  inline write_thread() {
2
3     atomic {
4        write();
5     }
6     write_exit:
7        skip;
8
9  }
10
11 inline evaluation_phase() {
12    do
13       :: ThreadStates[write_ID] == RUNNABLE
14          -> write_thread();
15       :: ThreadStates[read_ack_ID] == RUNNABLE
16          -> read_ack_thread();
17       :: else -> break;
18    od;
19 }
```

Encoding of SystemC Scheduler

Evaluation Phase

Encoding of Thread TN

Encoding of Thread T1

○ Promela Process   ▨ Promela Code Fragment   ⌐ Promela Atomic Block

(a)   (b)

Fig. 6. (a) Thread-to-atomic-block encoding, and (b) threads and scheduler encoding

control to the scheduler, we first have to set the program counter of the thread, which is thread_PC, to point to the location where the thread will resume its execution, which is represented by resume_loc. Having passed the control to the scheduler, the thread then waits for the control at the suspension location represented by suspend_loc.

Using the example of thread write, Figure 5 shows that the thread itself is encoded as a non-terminating process write_thread, such that its body, which is encoded as the inline code write, can be enclosed within an atomic block. Note that the body of the thread can only be executed if the thread gets the CONTROL_TOKEN from the scheduler.

Figure 5 also shows the encoding of the evaluation phase. To model the cooperativeness of this phase and to allows the exploration of all possible thread interleavings, the scheduler non-deterministically picks a runnable thread and sends the CONTROL_TOKEN to the thread. It then waits for the thread to give back the CONTROL_TOKEN.

We can optimize the thread-to-process encoding by using the message passing on the rendezvous channels to keep track of the program counter implicitly. This optimization amounts to replacing thread_suspend by thread_suspend_optimize shown

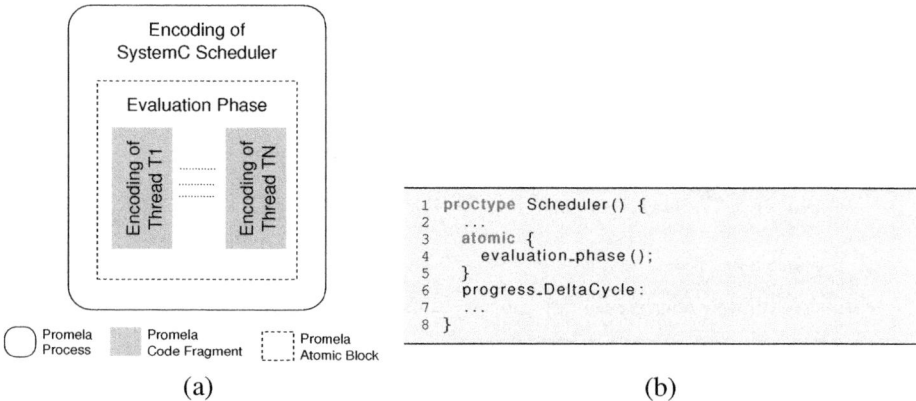

Fig. 7. (a) One-atomic-block encoding. (b) Encoding of the scheduler.

in Figure 5. With this optimization, the program counter t_PC for the thread t and the jump table in the thread encoding are no longer needed.

3.3 Thread-To-Atomic-Block Encoding

Another alternative Promela encoding for a SystemC design is to encode the design as a single Promela process containing both the scheduler and the threads, such that each thread is encoded as an atomic block inside the encoding of the evaluation phase, as shown in Figure 6(a). We call this encoding *thread-to-atomic-block*.

Unlike the thread-to-process encoding, in this encoding we no longer need the rendezvous channels and the control token. The encodings of `thread_entry`, `thread_exit`, and `thread_suspend` in thread-to-atomic-block encoding can be obtained from that of the thread-to-process encoding by replacing the sending and receiving statements with the `skip` statement.

The thread itself is now encoded as inline code instead of a process. The body of the thread encoding is surrounded by an atomic block. Passing control to the thread in the evaluation phase is modeled by executing the inline code of the thread encoding, while giving back control to the scheduler is modeled by simply finishing the execution of the inline code. The encodings of the thread and the scheduler for this thread-to-atomic-block encoding are shown in Figure 6(b).

3.4 One-Atomic-Block Encoding

Yet another alternative encoding can be derived from the thread-to-atomic-block encoding, that is, by enclosing the whole evaluation phase in an atomic block. We call such encoding *one-atomic-block* encoding and depicts its structure in Figure 7(a). Although the modification from the thread-to-atomic-block encoding is small, as we will discuss in the next section, it can change the search behavior dramatically and affect the property that can be verified.

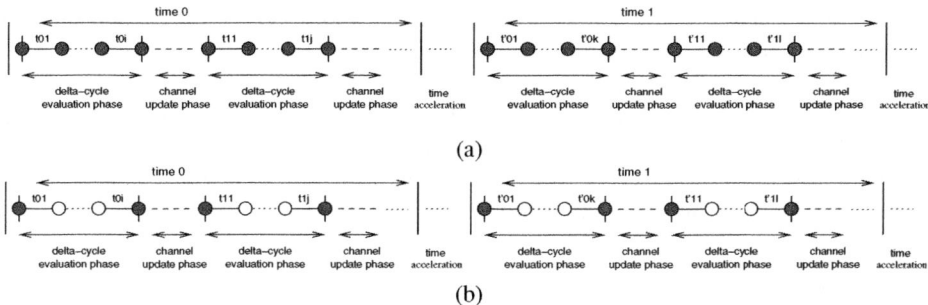

Fig. 8. Sampling rates of (a) thread-to-process and thread-to-atomic-block encodings, and (b) one-atomic-block encoding

4   Analytical Comparison of Encodings

The Promela encodings of SystemC designs proposed in this paper capture the full semantics of SystemC by modeling all the phases of the SystemC scheduler. However, they differ in terms of (1) the kinds of property that can be verified, and (2) the search behavior during the verification.

4.1   Properties to Verify

A general approach for defining temporal languages for SystemC has been described in [19]. The approach allows for greater flexibility in the temporal resolution granularity of the specification through the definition of finer grained execution traces following the state machine of SystemC scheduler described in Figure 2(a).

Similar to [19], the encodings presented here define the sampling rates of stored states in the execution traces. In the thread-to-process and the thread-to-atomic-block encodings the states before and after the execution of a thread in the evaluation phase are sampled (see the dark circles in Figure 8(a)). In addition to checking for assertion violations, this kind of sampling allows us to check for consistency properties that should hold before and after the execution of each thread in the evaluation phase.

The one-atomic-block encoding only samples states before and after the evaluation phase itself (see Figure 8(b)). Thus, it can only check for consistency properties at the delta-cycle boundary or at a timed-cycle boundary. But, as well as the thread-to-process and thread-to-atomic-block encodings are capable of, this encoding can be used to check for assertion violations.

To be synthesizable, the SystemC design under verification must not contain non-progressing delta cycles. To this end, in the encoding of the scheduler shown in Figure 3 we place the progress label `progress_DeltaCycle`. In SPIN, during the state space exploration, a label prefixed by `progress` has to be visited infinitely often in an infinite execution; violation of this property yields a non-progressing cycle.

To check for non-progressing delta cycles, the states before and after the execution of each thread in the evaluation phase must be sampled (or stored). Otherwise, a cycle of states in the state space that occurs during the exploration of the evaluation phase might go undetected, and can cause non-termination. Because the one-atomic-block encoding only samples states before and after the evaluation phase, one cannot use the encoding to check for non-progressing delta cycles.

As we have mentioned before, the atomic block surrounding the encoding of the thread body in the thread-to-process and the thread-to-atomic-block encodings is optional. By omitting the `atomic` keyword, these encodings also sample intermediate states during the thread executions. This sampling will allow us to verify temporal properties that speak about states and transitions in the thread body.

4.2 Search Behavior

The Promela encodings that we propose yield different search behavior. The differences are concerned with the number of transitions and states that need to be explored, the size of states, and the optimal applicability of optimizations that SPIN provides.

In the thread-to-process encoding each of the SystemC threads and scheduler is encoded as a separate process. The processes that encode the threads interact with the process that encodes the scheduler by means of rendezvous channels. The more SystemC threads in the design, the more processes and rendezvous channels we need, and thus the larger the size of the states is.

On the other hand, in the thread-to-atomic-block and the one-atomic-block encodings any SystemC design is encoded as a single process and use no channels for synchronizations. So the size of the state should be smaller than that of the thread-to-process encoding.

When there are only small variations of the values of global variables or of the local variables of processes, one can apply the collapse compression method [12] provided by SPIN to reduce the size of state in the thread-to-process encoding. That is, instead of replicating the complete description of all objects that are local to a process in each state, SPIN stores smaller state components separately and assigns small unique index to each of the components. The unique indices are then combined to form the global state. The division of state components usually consists of a descriptor for global data objects and a descriptor for each process. The collapse compression method has some run time overhead, but it should significantly reduce the memory consumed to store the state space. However, although the method is also applicable to the thread-to-atomic-block and one-atomic-block encodings, the reductions of memory consumption will not be as significant as its application to the thread-to-process encoding.

Comparing the thread-to-atomic-block and the one-atomic-block encoding, it is obvious that the one-atomic-block encoding will explore a smaller number of states than that of the thread-to-atomic-block encoding. However, the one-atomic-block encoding can explore more transitions than the thread-to-atomic-block encoding. Consider three threads t_1, t_2, and t_3 such that they are runnable in the evaluation phase and each thread only accesses variables local to the thread. Suppose that the first exploration in the evaluation phase goes with the sequence t_1, t_2, t_3. Now, if in the second exploration we end up with the prefix t_2, t_1, then with the thread-to-atomic-block encoding we can detect that we are visiting the state that we have visited before. That is, the resulting state of performing t_1, t_2 is the same as that of t_2, t_1. Thus, during the second exploration the search does not try to explore t_3. However, since the intermediate states between thread executions are not stored in the one-atomic-block encoding, the encoding has to explore t_3 during the second exploration.

SPIN implements a partial-order reduction (POR) [13] method that allows the verification search to explore only representative subsets of transition interleavings. POR in turn can reduce the number of visited states. However, the application of the POR method provided by SPIN to the proposed Promela encodings is suboptimal (or might not reduce the number of explored transitions at all) because the POR method loses the intrinsic structure of the SystemC designs. A non-interleaved transition in a SystemC design is a code fragment between two synchronization primitives that can make threads suspend themselves, and the static analysis implemented in the POR of SPIN does not recognize such a non-interleaved transition. Thus, the dependence relation between transitions computed by SPIN is rather coarse.

One can think of adding Promela code into the encodings such that the code contains static dependence relation between the SystemC non-interleaved transitions. However, this is not sufficient for checking safety properties because to check such properties we have to make sure that the reduction proviso condition described in [13] is satisfied at the level of SystemC non-interleaved transitions. This condition disallows the existence of a cycle of states in the state space such that there is a transition enabled in one of the state in the cycle, but that transition is never taken into the representative subsets of the explored transitions in any states in the cycle. To satisfy the reduction proviso condition, one needs to be able to access the states stored by the protocol analyzer generated by SPIN from the Promela encodings.

4.3 Other Existing Encodings

There have been several work on translating SystemC designs into Promela code; see [16, 21]. Similar to our thread-to-process encoding, these translations encode each SystemC thread as a Promela process, but, unlike ours, they embed the SystemC scheduler into the encoding of the synchronization primitives. Thus, there is no separate process for the SystemC scheduler.

The focus of these encodings is to verify SystemC designs at the high level of transaction level modeling (TLM). At that level of TLM, the delta cycles are typically not visible and communication between threads are usually through shared global variables instead of SystemC channels. Thus, unlike our encodings where we capture the full semantics of the SystemC scheduler, the existing encodings only considers the evaluation and the timed update phases of the scheduler. Moreover, since the evaluation phase of these encodings is encoded implicitly in the encoding of the synchronization primitives, these encodings cannot be used to detect non-progress delta cycles.

The work in [21] translates each SystemC thread into an automaton, which in turn is translated into a Promela process. The automaton itself is essentially the control-flow graph of the resulting Promela process. The translation from the automaton to the Promela process is not efficient because the resulting Promela process has to keep track of the program counter of the control-flow graph instead of the program counter of suspension points. Moreover, the encodings in [21] assume that time is discrete.

The Promela encoding presented in [16] is considered an improvement of the one in [21]. The aims of the encoding are twofold: (1) to reduce the number of interactions between the encodings of the threads, and (2) to make the application of SPIN optimizations optimal. The encoding manages to achieve (1) by exploiting the blocking statements of Promela, but is unclear about (2).

All the existing work mentioned above does not address the notion of under-approximation due to the restriction of input values.

5   Experimental Evaluation

We have developed a translator, called SC2PROMELA, that takes a SystemC design as an input and performs the Promela encodings proposed in this paper. The translator is a back-end extension of PINAPA [18] that extracts from a SystemC design information that is useful for performing the encodings. Such information includes structures of module instances, their interconnections, and the abstract syntax tree of the threads.

Recall that the verification against the resulting Promela models are under-approximations, and so are the protocol analyzers (or pan) generated by SPIN from the Promela models. If the SystemC design reads inputs from the environment and the corresponding pan terminates gracefully (no time-out and no memory-out), and an assertion violation or a non-progressing cycle is detected, then we have found a real bug. Otherwise, if neither assertion violations nor non-progressing cycles are detected, and the search does not exceed the depth limit, then the design is safe under the assumption about the input values. In the experiments, we model input reading by selecting non-deterministically a value from a set of ten random values. For the unsafe benchmarks in our experiments, this assumption turns out to be sufficient to find the bugs.

Experimental evaluation setup. We compare the search behavior of our Promela encodings in terms of the number of stored states and the number of transitions, as well as the effectiveness of optimizations provided by SPIN. In the experiments we focus on checking for assertion violations and non-progressing delta cycles. We also compare the Promela encodings against ESST [6] that has been implemented in KRATOS [4]. ESST is not capable of identifying non-progressing delta cycles, and so the comparison with ESST is only about checking for assertion violations.

We run our experiments on a Linux box with Intel-Xeon DC 3GHz processor and 4GB of RAM. We set the time limit to 1000s, the memory limit to 2GB, and the search depth limit to 1,000,000.

Test cases. We use the benchmarks provided in [6] and derive new benchmarks pipeline_bug, token_ring_bug and mem_slave_tlm_bug from the respective safe benchmarks by introducing new assertions that can be violated. The mem_slave_tlm_bug family have been modified by introducing a memory overflow, that can only be reached by going through a long iteration in the model.

Results. Table 1 reports for the three encodings the following information: the number of stored states (# States stored), the number of explored transitions (# Transitions), the size of state in byte (# State size), and the run time in second (Time). We mark experiment results with TO and MO, for, respectively, out of time and out of memory. In the Time column we mark the time with * to indicate that the corresponding experiment reaches the search depth limit. For the checks for assertion violations (V), we use U and S for, respectively, unsafe (an assertion is violated) and safe (no assertion violations). For the checks for non-progressing cycles (NP), we considered only the thread-to-process and the thread-to-atomic-block encodings since the one-atomic-block

Table 1. Results for the experimental evaluation of the different Promela encodings

File	V	NP	ESST	thread-to-process						thread-to-atomic-block						one-atomic-block					
				# States stored	# Transitions	State size (byte)	Time (sec)	Compression (%)	# Transition No POR	# States stored	# Transitions	State size (byte)	Time (sec)	Compression (%)	# Transition No POR	States stored	# Transitions	State size (byte)	Time (sec)	Compression (%)	# Transition No POR
best_cell	S	(?)	0.50	8	17	204	0.00	—	15	8	17	188	0.00	—	15	6	15	188	0.00	—	15
kundu	S	(?)	1.10	1386	3175	268	0.03	—	3175	1386	3175	188	0.02	—	3175	405	2806	220	0.02	—	2806
kundu-bug_1	U	(?)	0.39	18	18	196	0.00	—	18	18	18	164	0.00	—	18	111	11	164	0.00	—	11
kundu-bug_2	U	(?)	1.10	121	181	268	0.00	—	181	121	181	220	0.01	—	181	36	105	220	0.00	—	105
mem_slave_tlm_1	S	(?)	2.79	93	93	310	0.00	—	310	93	93	324	0.01	—	310	6	2014	334	0.09	—	2014
mem_slave_tlm_2	S	(?)	13.60	137	137	363	0.00	—	363	137	137	332	0.00	—	363	6	20014	332	0.90	—	2014
mem_slave_tlm_3	S	(?)	152.19	181	181	372	0.01	—	416	181	181	332	0.01	—	416	6	20014	332	9.25	—	20014
mem_slave_tlm_4	S	(?)	42.80	225	225	372	0.01	—	469	225	225	340	0.00	—	469	6	200014	340	93.90	—	200014
mem_slave_tlm_5	S	(?)	773.14	269	269	372	0.01	—	522	269	269	340	0.01	—	522	6	20000014	340	967.00	—	20000014
mem_slave_tlm_bug_1	U	(?)	3.80	16	16	364	0.00	—	16	16	16	324	0.00	—	16	3	3	324	0.00	—	3
mem_slave_tlm_bug_2	U	(?)	20.80	24	24	364	0.00	—	24	24	24	332	0.00	—	24	3	3	332	0.01	—	3
mem_slave_tlm_bug_3	U	(?)	100.99	32	32	372	0.01	—	32	32	32	332	0.00	—	32	3	3	332	0.01	—	3
mem_slave_tlm_bug_4	U	(?)	347.87	40	40	372	0.01	—	40	40	40	340	0.00	—	40	3	3	340	0.01	—	3
mem_slave_tlm_bug_5	U	(?)	TO	48	48	380	0.01	—	48	48	48	340	0.00	—	48	3	3	340	0.01	—	3
pc-sfifo_1	S	(?)	0.30	5640647	7948186	180	*72.50	51.85	7948186	7090367	9999436	152	*66.50	55.04	9999436	TO	TO	1000.99	—	3
pc-sfifo_2	S	(?)	0.30	10376427	12074486	196	*91.50	44.51	12074486	12221427	14221346	160	*85.20	46.89	14221346	7020793	8935572	160	*63.70	66.93	8935572
pipeline	S	(?)	77.09	MO	MO	MO	222.49	MO	MO	616	616	151.88	—	TO	616	TO	TO	1000.03	—	DL
pipeline-bug	U	(?)	132.99	76	76	700	0.00	—	76	76	76	616	0.00	—	76	26	26	616	0.01	—	26
token_ring_1	S	(?)	0.10	107	107	156	0.00	—	216	107	107	128	0.00	—	216	TO	TO	1000.03	—	TO
token_ring_2	S	NP	0.10	274	274	228	0.00	—	414	274	274	184	0.01	—	414	TO	TO	1000.37	—	TO
token_ring_3	S	NP	0.20	640	640	316	0.00	—	904	640	640	184	0.01	—	904	TO	TO	1000.02	—	TO
token_ring_4	S	NP	0.20	1466	1466	420	0.02	—	2102	1466	1466	248	0.02	—	2102	TO	TO	1000.09	—	TO
token_ring_5	S	NP	0.30	3336	3336	532	0.06	80.07	4964	3336	3336	336	0.03	96.11	4964	TO	TO	1000.05	—	TO
token_ring_6	S	NP	0.40	7542	7542	668	0.15	35.76	11650	7542	11650	440	0.10	43.08	11650	TO	TO	1000.08	—	TO
token_ring_7	S	NP	0.70	16916	16916	820	0.40	24.30	26976	16916	26976	552	0.25	28.86	26976	TO	TO	1000.01	—	TO
token_ring_8	S	NP	0.70	37618	37618	988	1.02	19.75	61566	37618	61566	688	0.66	20.64	61566	TO	TO	1000.08	—	TO
token_ring_9	S	NP	1.99	82960	82960	1164	2.60	16.71	138652	82960	138652	840	1.67	17.00	138652	TO	TO	1000.01	—	TO
token_ring_10	S	NP	2.40	181550	181550	1364	6.52	14.80	308666	181550	308666	1000	4.17	14.95	308666	TO	TO	1000.99	—	TO
token_ring_11	S	NP	4.50	394572	394572	1580	16.60	13.38	680408	394572	680408	1184	10.59	13.48	680408	TO	TO	1000.99	—	TO
token_ring_12	S	NP	4.10	852330	852330	1812	39.20	12.66	1487350	852330	1487350	1376	26.00	12.30	1487350	TO	TO	1000.04	—	TO
token_ring_13	S	NP	7.50	1831304	1831304	2052	94.80	11.69	3228180	1831304	3228180	1592	63.30	11.36	3228180	TO	TO	1000.02	—	TO
toy	S	(?)	0.00	322250	355609	156	*3.94	40.02	355609	414332	457217	128	*3.52	49.70	457217	22908	45835	128	*1.43	—	45835
toy-bug_1	U	(?)	1.60	142869	142870	412	*5.21	48.50	142870	183119	183123	332	*5.12	64.12	183123	11418	11422	332	*4.08	—	11422
toy-bug_2	U	(?)	0.69	144460	144460	412	*5.46	45.44	144460	185738	185742	332	*5.34	64.29	185742	11457	11459	332	*4.15	—	11459
transmitter_1	U	(?)	0.00	8	8	140	0.00	—	10	8	8	100	0.00	—	10	3	3	128	0.00	—	3
transmitter_2	U	(?)	0.10	12	12	204	0.00	—	14	12	12	156	0.00	—	14	3	3	184	0.01	—	3
transmitter_3	U	(?)	0.10	16	16	284	0.00	—	18	16	16	220	0.00	—	18	3	3	248	0.00	—	3
transmitter_4	U	(?)	0.10	20	20	380	0.00	—	20	20	20	300	0.00	—	20	3	3	336	0.00	—	3
transmitter_5	U	(?)	0.30	24	24	500	0.00	—	28	24	24	396	0.00	—	28	3	3	440	0.01	—	3
transmitter_6	U	(?)	0.10	28	28	628	0.00	—	28	28	28	508	0.00	—	28	3	3	552	0.00	—	3
transmitter_7	U	(?)	0.20	32	32	772	0.01	—	32	32	32	636	0.00	—	32	3	3	688	0.02	—	3
transmitter_8	U	(?)	0.09	36	36	932	0.00	—	36	36	36	780	0.00	—	36	3	3	840	0.00	—	3
transmitter_9	U	(?)	0.10	40	40	1116	0.00	—	40	40	40	940	0.00	—	40	3	3	1000	0.00	—	3
transmitter_10	U	(?)	0.10	56	57	1308	0.01	—	57	56	57	1124	0.00	—	57	6	6	1184	0.00	—	6
transmitter_11	U	(?)	0.20	66	69	1364	0.00	—	69	66	69	1376	0.00	—	69	10	10	1376	0.01	—	10
transmitter_12	U	(?)	0.39	83	91	1740	0.01	—	91	83	91	1524	0.00	—	91	12	12	1524	0.01	—	12
transmitter_13	U	(?)	0.20	116	137	1988	0.00	—	137	116	137	1748	0.01	—	137	42	42	1748	0.02	—	42

encoding is not suitable for this check. We use NP and (?) to indicate the detection of a non-progressing cycle and an inconclusive results, respectively. We report neither the time needed to translate SystemC designs into Promela models nor the time needed to compile the resulting protocol analyzer since they are negligible.

Table 1 also reports the results of enabling and disabling some SPIN optimizations. In particular it reports the amount of collapse compression in percentage (Compression) and the number of explored transitions when the partial-order reduction is disabled (# Transitions No POR). In the Compression column we use − to denote the case when the collapse compression is unsuccessful.

As shown on Table 1, our Promela encodings outperforms ESST in verifying the unsafe benchmarks. ESST performs over-approximations that involve expensive symbolic computations. These over-approximations often require many refinements. This comparison has shown that the Promela encodings are efficient for formal bug finding, and thus they can fruitfully complement ESST in the verification of SystemC designs.

Comparisons on the safe benchmarks are irrelevant because ESST performs over-approximations, while the Promela encodings perform under-approximation. One interesting fact is shown by the experiment on the `pipeline` benchmark. On this benchmark our Promela encodings yield either out of memory or out of time. In this benchmark there are a huge number of possible thread interleavings that need to be explored to check for assertion violations. The size of input values also affect the number of thread interleavings. ESST, on the other hand, has been equipped with a partial-order reduction technique that works at the transition atomicity level of SystemC designs [6]. Thus, ESST explores a less number of thread interleavings. Moreover, due to its over-approximations, ESST is not affected by the size of input values.

Table 1 shows that on most of the benchmarks the thread-to-process and the thread-to-atomic-block encodings store the same number of states and explore the same number of transitions. This fact shows that the synchronization mechanism using token passing through rendezvous channels does not interact negatively with the search behavior. However, in accordance with our analysis, the size of state for the thread-to-process encoding is larger than that of the thread-to-atomic-block encoding.

Regarding the one-atomic-block encoding, Table 1 shows that, for the safe benchmarks, the thread-to-atomic-block encoding stores more states but less transitions than the one-atomic-block encoding. These results are in accordance with our analysis in the previous section. For the unsafe benchmarks, like the family of `token_ring_bug`, the one-atomic-block encoding outperforms the thread-to-atomic-block encoding in terms of the number of stored states and the number of explored transitions. In these benchmarks the assertion violation is found in the first delta cycle. In principle, when the assertion violation occurs after several delta cycles, and there is no guarantee that the delta cycles are progressing, then the one-atomic-block encoding might go out of time.

For the `token_ring` safe family, although we restrict the number of input values, the one-atomic-block encoding goes out of time since the delta cycle does not progress. Hence, because there are no intermediate states sampled in the evaluation phase, the protocol analyzer does not know how to stop the search.

The application of the collapse compression on most of the benchmarks is unsuccessful. That is, due to the overhead incurred by the collapse compression, the actual memory usage for the states is larger than if the collapse compression is disabled. Upon close inspection, it turns out that the threads in most of the benchmarks do not have variables that are local to the threads, but use heavily global variables in their computations. These global variables encode the channels and other global data that are used by the threads to communicate with each other. As mentioned in the previous section, the global data object constitutes one portion in the state component. Moreover, in those benchmarks there is a large number of different variations of the global data objects. Consequently, (1) the collapse compression is not effective for the benchmarks, and (2) when the collapse compression is successful, the differences of compression between the thread-to-process and the thread-to-atomic-block are not significant.

In the family of toy-bug benchmarks the application of the collapse compression is effective to reduce the memory consumption. In fact in this family of benchmarks the threads use variables that are local to them in their computations, and in particular, in the thread-to-process encoding, there are only small variations of process states. Thus, with the thread-to-process encoding the actual memory usage can be compressed to less than 49% of the original memory usage, while with the thread-to-atomic-block and one-atomic-block encodings the compression is larger than 64%.

Our experiments confirm the analysis in the previous section that the partial-order reduction provided by SPIN is not effective to reduce the number of explored transitions. In fact, for all encodings and for each benchmark, whether or not the reduction is enabled, the numbers of explored transitions are the same.

We have not been able to empirically compare our Promela encodings with the existing ones described in the previous section. There seems to be a regression that breaks the tool used to generate the encodings.[2] The benchmarks used in [16] are essentially the same as the family of transmitter benchmarks used in our work. For transmitter of size 13, the encoding in [16] explored 8306 states, while our encodings store no more than 116 states and explore no more than 137 transitions.

On Table 1, column NP, the thread-to-process and the thread-to-atomic-block encodings find non-progressing delta cycles in some benchmarks, in particular in the families of token_ring_bug benchmarks. Such bugs were not known beforehand and were not addressed in [5].

Experiments on some of the benchmarks reach the search depth limit. In those benchmarks there are counters that range over integer values and are independent of the input values. It turns out that we can perform more under-approximation on those benchmarks by making the counters range over byte values. In so doing, we are able to verify that the benchmark pc_sfifo_1 has a non-progressing cycle.

All the benchmarks and the scripts for reproducing the performed experiments can be downloaded at: http://es.fbk.eu/people/roveri/tests/spin2011.

6   Related Work

There have been several work on to the formal verification of SystemC designs [5, 6, 8, 9, 11, 14, 17, 21]. We have already discussed in Section 4.3 the work in [16, 21], that are the most closely related to our work.

SystemC verification via translation to other languages have been reported in a number of papers. In [5, 9] SystemC designs are translated into sequential C programs that can be checked by existing software-model checkers. It is also shown in [5] that complete verification of such sequential C programs is ineffective due to the size of the encoded scheduler and the need for precise information on the scheduler states.

Bounded model checking (BMC) have been applied for bug hunting in SystemC designs, as described in [9]. Unlike our work, the work in [9] only addresses untimed SystemC designs, and needs to determine the unwinding depth even though all loops in the input SystemC design are bounded. Similar to our work, the use of BMC is another kinds of under-approximation. In addition to bug hunting, the work in [9] also proposes a complete technique based on induction.

---

[2] Personal communication with Matthieu Moy.

An encoding of SystemC designs into networks of timed automata is presented in [11]. The resulting timed automata are then verified with UPPAAL [1]. The Lussy tool chain described in [17] translates SystemC designs into sets of parallel automata. The automata themselves are in turn translated into different models, like SMV models and Lustre model. The experimental results in [11,17] demonstrate limited scalability of the proposed techniques, related to the symbolic techniques used to check the automata.

The work in [14] translates SystemC designs into labeled Kripke structures. However, the translation abstracts away the scheduler, that is, the scheduler is encoded implicitly in each of the threads, and the encoding only considers the evaluation phase.

In [5] we have proposed a technique, called ESST, for the verification of SystemC designs. The technique combines explicit model checking technique to deal with the scheduler and symbolic technique, based on the lazy predicate abstraction [10], to deal with the threads. In [6] we apply a partial-order reduction method to ESST. Although ESST shows promising results, the bottleneck caused by slow refinements make it inefficient for a quick bug finding, as confirmed by our experimental evaluation.

Recent work on monitoring SystemC properties is discussed in [20]. The work needs to modify the SystemC scheduler and instrument the design to observe desirable properties during simulations. However, SystemC simulations do not explore all possible schedules, and so the monitoring process can miss some bugs.

Weakly related to our work is the tool Scoot described in [3]. Scoot extracts from a SystemC design a flat C++ model that can be analyzed by SATABS [7]. The SystemC scheduler itself is included in the flat model. Scoot has been used to synthesize a SystemC scheduler that can speed up simulations by performing race analysis [2]. Scoot has also been used to perform run-time verification. Other work on scalable testing of SystemC designs by using partial-order reduction is described in [15].

7   Conclusions and Future Work

We have proposed three Promela encodings of SystemC designs, and have provided a thorough analysis of them in terms of the kinds of property they allow to verify, and in terms of the search behaviors during the verification. The empirical results obtained from our experiments on these encodings support the analytical comparison between the encodings. The results of experimental evaluation also show that our technique is effective and efficient in finding bugs, can detect non-progressing delta cycles, and can complement existing symbolic verification techniques based on lazy abstraction.

As future work, we will investigate the applicability of test generation to relieve the problem of range restrictions. We will address the problem of redundant thread interleavings. In fact, the POR techniques implemented in SPIN turn out to be largely ineffective in this setting.

Input values can also play a role in causing non-progressing delta cycles. As we restrict the range of input values, our technique can miss such non-progressing cycles. We would like to investigate the applicability of automatic techniques for checking non-termination.

Another direction of future work is to combine under-approximation and over-approximation techniques for full verification of SystemC designs. Finally, we would like to support more SystemC (and C++ in general) features, to allow our proposed technique to be tested on a larger set of benchmarks.

References

1. Behrmann, G., David, A., Larsen, K.G., Håkansson, J., Pettersson, P., Yi, W., Hendriks, M.: UPPAAL 4.0. In: QEST, pp. 125–126. IEEE, New York (2006)
2. Blanc, N., Kroening, D.: Race Analysis for SystemC using Model Checking. In: ICCAD, pp. 356–363. IEEE, New York (2008)
3. Blanc, N., Kroening, D., Sharygina, N.: SCOOT: A Tool for the Analysis of SystemC Models. In: Ramakrishnan, C.R., Rehof, J. (eds.) TACAS 2008. LNCS, vol. 4963, pp. 467–470. Springer, Heidelberg (2008)
4. Cimatti, A., Griggio, A., Micheli, A., Narasamdya, I., Roveri, M.: Kratos: A Software Model Checker for SystemC. In: CAV (to appear, 2011)
5. Cimatti, A., Micheli, A., Narasamdya, I., Roveri, M.: Verifying SystemC: a Software Model Checking Approach. In: FMCAD, pp. 51–59 (2010)
6. Cimatti, A., Narasamdya, I., Roveri, M.: Boosting lazy abstraction for systemc with partial order reduction. In: Abdulla, P.A., Leino, K.R.M. (eds.) TACAS 2011. LNCS, vol. 6605, pp. 341–356. Springer, Heidelberg (2011)
7. Clarke, E., Kröning, D., Sharygina, N., Yorav, K.: SATABS: SAT-Based Predicate Abstraction for ANSI-C. In: Halbwachs, N., Zuck, L.D. (eds.) TACAS 2005. LNCS, vol. 3440, pp. 570–574. Springer, Heidelberg (2005)
8. Große, D., Drechsler, R.: CheckSyC: An Efficient Property Checker for RTL SystemC Designs. In: ISCAS, vol. 4, pp. 4167–4170. IEEE, New York (2005)
9. Grosse, D., Le, H., Drechsler, R.: Proving Transaction and System-level Properties of Untimed SystemC TLM Designs. In: MEMOCODE, pp. 113–122 (2010)
10. Henzinger, T.A., Jhala, R., Majumdar, R., Sutre, G.: Lazy Abstraction. In: POPL, pp. 58–70 (2002)
11. Herber, P., Fellmuth, J., Glesner, S.: Model Checking SystemC Designs using Timed Automata. In: CODES+ISSS, pp. 131–136. ACM, New York (2008)
12. Holzmann, G.J.: Software Model Checking with SPIN. Adv. in Comp. 65, 78–109 (2005)
13. Holzmann, G.J., Peled, D.: An improvement in formal verification. In: Proceedings of the 7th IFIP WG6.1 International Conference on Formal Description Techniques VII, pp. 197–211. Chapman & Hall, Ltd, London (1995)
14. Kroening, D., Sharygina, N.: Formal Verification of SystemC by Automatic Hardware/Software Partitioning. In: MEMOCODE, pp. 101–110. IEEE, New York (2005)
15. Kundu, S., Ganai, M.K., Gupta, R.: Partial Order Reduction for Scalable Testing of SystemC TLM Designs. In: DAC, pp. 936–941. ACM, New York (2008)
16. Marquet, K., Jeannet, B., Moy, M.: Efficient Encoding of SystemC/TLM in Promela. Technical report, Verimag, Verimag Research Report no TR-2010-7 (2010)
17. Moy, M., Maraninchi, F., Maillet-Contoz, L.: LusSy: A Toolbox for the Analysis of Systems-on-a-Chip at the Transactional Level. In: ACSD, pp. 26–35. IEEE, New York (2005)
18. Moy, M., Maraninchi, F., Maillet-Contoz, L.: Pinapa: An Extraction Tool for SystemC Descriptions of Systems-on-a-Chip. In: EMSOFT, pp. 317–324. ACM, New York (2005)
19. Tabakov, D., Kamhi, G., Vardi, M.Y., Singerman, E.: A Temporal Language for SystemC. In: FMCAD, pp. 1–9. IEEE, New York (2008)
20. Tabakov, D., Vardi, M.: Monitoring Temporal SystemC Properties. In: MEMOCODE, pp. 123–132 (2010)
21. Traulsen, C., Cornet, J., Moy, M., Maraninchi, F.: A SystemC/TLM Semantics in PROMELA and Its Possible Applications. In: Bošnački, D., Edelkamp, S. (eds.) SPIN 2007. LNCS, vol. 4595, pp. 204–222. Springer, Heidelberg (2007)

Building Extensible Specifications and Implementations of Promela with AbleP

Yogesh Mali and Eric Van Wyk[*]

Department of Computer Science and Engineering
University of Minnesota, Minneapolis, MN 55455, USA
{yomali,evw}@cs.umn.edu

Abstract. This paper describes how new language features can be seamlessly added to an extensible specification of Promela to provide new (domain-specific) notations and analyses to the engineer. This is accomplished using ABLEP, an extensible specification and implementation of Promela, the modeling language used by the SPIN model checker. Language extensions described here include an enhanced select-statement, a convenient tabular notation for boolean expressions, a notion of discrete time, and extended type checking. ABLEP and the extensions are developed using the SILVER attribute grammar system and the COPPER parser and scanner generator. These tools support the modular development and composition of language extensions so that independently developed extensions can be imported into ABLEP by an engineer with little knowledge of language design and implementation issues.

1 Introduction and Motivation

Modeling languages such as Promela, Lustre, Esterel, and others, allow engineers to specify problem solutions in an abstract high-level declarative language that more closely matches the problem domain than low-level programming languages such as C. These languages are typically designed to enable some sort of analysis of the specifications written in them. The Promela model checker SPIN [10,9] takes advantage of the high-level constructs, such as processes and guarded-statements, and the restrictions in Promela, such as the absence of floating point numbers, to efficiently analyze and verify properties on Promela programs.

Yet, modeling languages often lack linguistic support for some commonly-used general purpose and less commonly-used domain-specific concepts; this leaves the engineer to encode them as idioms, a time-consuming and error-prone process. This is not necessarily the fault of the language designers. It is a problem for them as well as they must try to strike a balance in determining which features to include in the language, weighing the benefits of the feature against the cost of implementing, maintaining, and documenting a larger language.

[*] This material is based on work partially supported by NSF Awards No. 0905581 and No. 1047961 and DARPA and the United States Air Force (Air Force Research Lab) under Contract No. FA8650-10-C-7076.

A. Groce and M. Musuvathi (Eds.): SPIN 2011, LNCS 6823, pp. 108–125, 2011.

A few examples may illustrate these points. Consider the `select` statement added to Promela in SPIN version 6 that non-deterministically assigns a value within a specified range to a variable. For example, `select (v : 1..10)` will assign a value between 1 and 10 to the variable v. In previous versions of Promela, engineers had to "code this up" using an idiom of several (non-guarded) assignments as options in an `if` statement. Presumably the perceived need of this features outweighed the costs of adding it to the language. This feature and the new `for` loop are added in the Promela parser and expanded into Promela do-loops a the idioms engineers have typically used previously to express them.

As an *domain-specific* example, consider the discrete-time features introduced in DTSPIN [1]. A new `timer` datatype and operations on values of this type are provided. These features can be implemented as simple C pre-processor macros, a very lightweight approach to language extension. Another approach modifies the SPIN source code to provide a more efficient implementation of an underlying clock-tick operation, a rather heavyweight solution. Domain-specific extensions like this are often very useful, but to a smaller group of users than may justify their direct inclusion in the language.

A third example is the type analysis provided by ETCH [4]. This tool provides a constraint based type inference system to detect type errors in Promela specifications that have not always been detected by SPIN. Finding such errors statically saves engineers time. This tool implements its own scanner and parser for Promela, using SableCC [7], to build an abstract specification on which type checking is performed. Developing a new scanner and parser for Promela is a non-trivial task that detracts from the developer's main aim of type checking.

This paper describes a *middle-weight* solution to these language evolution and extensions problems. ABLEP (Attribute grammar-Based Language Extensions for Promela) is an extensible language framework that lies between the lightweight solution of simple macros and the heavyweight solutions of modifying the SPIN code base or building an entirely separate system for parsing and analysing Promela specifications. ABLEP allows new language features to be specified in a highly modular manner so that engineers can easily select the language extensions that they desire for a particular problem and seamlessly import them into ABLEP. These features may be new language constructs that add new syntax to the *host language* Promela. They may also be new semantic analyses of these new constructs or new semantic analyses to the Promela constructs. For frameworks such as ABLEP to be useful to a wide audience we believe that new features, packaged as *language extensions*, must be easily imported by an engineer or programmer without requiring significant knowledge of language design and implementation techniques. Thus, while extension *developers* need this sort of knowledge, extension *users* need not; users simply direct the framework to *import* the desired set of extensions. This is not unlike importing libraries in traditional programming languages. In such frameworks, the engineer imports a set of extensions to create a customized language, and its supporting analysis and translation tools, that address the specific programming or modeling task at hand.

Section 2 of this paper describes several language extensions in ABLEP and shows how an engineer uses ABLEP and imports extensions into it. These extensions include aspects of those described above as well an extension that provides a tabular representation for complex boolean expressions. Section 3 shows how ABLEP and these modular extensions are implemented using the SILVER attribute grammar system [14] and the COPPER parser and context-aware scanner generator [16]. It also describes how these tools support the seamless and automatic composition of extensions designed by independent parties. Section 3.3 describes how these tools handle some challenging aspects of the Promela language including inlining and embedded C code. Section 4 describes related work and section 5 discusses the challenges faced by, and merits of, ABLEP.

2   Use of AbleP and Its Language Extensions

In Section 2.1 we describe some sample language extensions to Promela and show how they are used in the ABLEP extensible language framework in which Promela plays the role as the host language. In Section 2.2 we show how an engineer can import a chosen set of extensions into ABLEP and generate a processor for the custom language with the features that suit his or her specific needs.

2.1   Using an AbleP Extended Language Framework

In this section we describe a set of ABLEP extensions that add an enhanced `select` statement, tabular boolean expressions, type-checking analysis in the spirit of ETCH, and features for discrete time based on DTSPIN. A model that uses these features is shown in Fig. 1. This extended language model is based on a sample altitude switch for an aircraft that computes an altitude status value of *Unknown*, *Above*, or *Below* from a simulated altitude reading, an indication of confidence in the altitude readings, an altitude threshold, and a hysteresis value.

An *instantiation* of ABLEP, the framework extended with a specific set of extensions, is used by the engineer to analyze a model and translate it down to its semantically equivalent model in pure Promela to be used by the SPIN model checker. Thus, ABLEP instantiations are essentially sophisticated pre-processors that go beyond the capabilities of simple macro pre-processors by performing syntactic and semantic analysis on the model to detect certain (domain-specific) errors and direct the translation down to pure Promela. ABLEP processors are generated by the SILVER [14] and COPPER [16] tools from the specifications of the host language and chosen extensions. These tools are Java-based and the generated instantiation is realized as a Java `.jar` file. In Section 2.2 we show how the engineer creates these, but here we assume that this has been done, resulting in a instantiation stored in `ableJ.aviation.jar`. The engineer need only provide the name of extended-language model to the processor, in this case `AltSwitch.xpml`, which checks for semantic errors and generates the translation down to pure Promela stored in a file with a `.pml` extension, here `AltSwitch.pml`. This can be processed by SPIN as the engineer would normally.

```
mtype = {Unknown, Above, Below } ;      /* altitude status values */
mtype = {High, Med, Low} ;              /* quality of instrument readings */

chan startup = [0] of {int, int} ;
chan monitor = [0] of {mtype, mtype} ;

timer trouble_t, above_t ;              /* expands to "int trouble_t = -1;" */

active proctype determineStatus ()
{
 int altitude, threshold, hyst ;
 mtype altQuality, altStatus = Unknown ;

 startup ? threshold, hyst;   /* receive threshold and hysteresis values */
 run monitorStatus ( );       /* start monitoring process */

 check:
  /* select, non-deterministically, values for altitude and altQuality */
  select (altitude: 1000 .. 10000 step 100) ;
  select (altQuality: High, Med, Low) ;

  /* use condition tables to assign a value to altStatus */
  if :: tbl altStatus == Unknown        : T *
            altQuality == High          : T T
            altitude > threshold        : T T
            altitude > threshold + hyst : * T
        lbt -> altStatus = Above ;
     :: tbl altQuality == High   : T
            altitude > threshold : F
        lbt -> altStatus = Below ;
     :: else; altStatus = (altQuality == High -> Unknown : altStatus) ;
  fi ;

  if :: altStatus == Above -> goto above;
     :: altStatus == Below || altStatus == Unknown -> goto trouble;
  fi ;

 above:
   delay(above_t,1);                     /* delay until next "tick" */
   goto check ;

 trouble:
   monitor!altStatus,altitude ;          /* send msg to monitor     */
   trouble_t = 1; expire(trouble_t);     /* what delay expands to    */
   goto check ;
}
```

Fig. 1. The extended-Promela program `AltSwitch.xpml` processed by ABLEP

The primary goal of the model in Fig. 1 is to compute a value for the altStatus variable and assign to it a value from the mtype values of Unknown, Above, and Below specified on the first line. The quality of the instrument readings is represented by the second mtype declaration of the values High, Med, and Low. Next, a startup channel is declared and used to receive the integer threshold and hysteresis values. A monitor channel is declared; it is used to send the status and altitude values to a monitoring process monitorStatus (whose definition is not shown here). Skipping for now the declarations of variables of type timer, the determineStatus process declares its local variables altitude, threshold, hyst, altQuality (which takes values of High, Med, and Low), and altStatus (which takes values of Unknown, Above, and Below). The process determineStatus first receives values for the threshold and hysteresis variables and starts the monitorStatus process.

Enhanced select statements: The first use of a language extension follows the check label. This enhanced select statement is an extended version of the one introduced to Promela in SPIN version 6. Here, we've added a step value of 100. This statement non-deterministically selects an altitude value in the range beginning at 1000, increasing by values of 100, and ending at 10000. The second example non-deterministically picks a value for altitude quality from one of the three valid mtype values of High, Med, or Low.

ABLEP supports language extensions that have the same look-and-feel as built-in constructs. Thus, their syntax should be natural and they should report error messages based on analysis of the extension, not on its translation to pure Promela. While at least the first extended-select could easily be specified as a CPP macro, as is commonly done in Promela models, we choose not to do this in order to support this semantic analysis. Consider changing the second expression Med in the second select statement to startup, which has type chan. The language extension will report the following error message:

```
Error: select statement requires all possible choices to have the
  same type as variable assigned to, which is "mtype":  line 17.
```

This ABLEP extension translates this second select statement to a semantically equivalent construct in pure Promela; in this case that phrase is

```
if ::altQuality=High; ::altQuality=Med; ::altQuality=Low; fi;
```

The first select statement can be translated to a do loop in which the variable altitude is initially set to the lower bound of 1000 and is incremented by the step value of 100 until the upper bound is reached or the loop non-deterministically exits, which is shown in Fig. 2(a). The extension, however, inspects the lower bound, upper bound, and step expressions. If they are all constants (known statically), then a (possibly large) non-deterministic if statement can be generated instead. Part of the translation that is generated for the first select statement is shown in Fig. 2(b). An advantage of this translation is that during interactive simulation with SPIN of the generated Promela model,

```
altitude = 1000 ;                    |    if :: altitude = 1000 ;
do  :: goto 130 ;                    |       :: altitude = 1100 ;
    :: (altitude < 10000) ;          |       :: altitude = 1200 ;
       altitude = (altitude + 100) ; |       :: altitude = 1300 ;
od ;                                 |       ...
130: skip ;                          |    fi ;
        (a)                          |            (b)
```

Fig. 2. Two translations of `select` to pure Promela

the user is asked to pick a transition that will select the desired value without having to step through the loop the appropriate number of times.

These extensions are straightforward and primarily introduced as an initial example. The first could be specified as a do-loop-generating CPP macro, but the second requires a bit more processing. We see how this is done in Section 3.

Boolean Table Expressions: In Fig. 1, after values for `altitude` and `altQuality` have been selected a guarded `if` statement assigns a value to `altStatus`. The guards on the first two options are boolean expressions represented in a tabular form. Due to the complexity of these conditions, the engineer may decide to use *condition tables*, such as those found in RSML^{-e}. These are sometimes useful when reviewing the models with domain experts. These tables, indicated with keywords `tbl` and `lbt`, consist of rows with leading boolean expressions followed by a list of "truth values": T for true, F for false, and * for "don't care". These specify the required truthfulness of the expression at the beginning of the row. All rows must have the same number of truth values. The value of a table is determined by taking the disjunction of the boolean value computed for each column. This column value is the conjunction of checking that each expression has the required truth value. For example, the first column in the table is true if all expression are true except for the last one, which can take any value. The first table is translated to the following pure Promela expression.

```
(((altStatus == Unknown) && ((altQuality == High) &&
 ((altitude > threshold) && true))) ||
(true && ((altQuality == High) &&
 ((altitude > threshold) && (altitude > (threshold + hyst))))))
```

Besides generating this translation, the extension also checks that each expression has an appropriate boolean type and that the rows have the same number of truth values, something not easily done on the generated expression. This extension is based on an extension that we originally developed for Lustre [8].

Extended Type Checking: Donaldson and Gay created a tool to perform extended type checking of Promela models called ETCH [4]. It adds no syntactic constructs to Promela but adds a sophisticated typing analysis. If we modify the `run monitorStatus()` statement in the `determineStatus` process to pass in some number of arguments we would create a semantic error that SPIN would detect. If we made additional use of channels, specifically passing them as parameters to processes, their types become more difficult to check. This is because channel types are specified simply as chan which does not indicate the types of values to be passed along it. SPIN does not detect these types of errors statically, only at simulation or verification time. ETCH, however, includes an static type inference and checking analysis to find type errors such as those that SPIN does not. When ETCH was developed it detected the simple typing errors, such as incorrect number of arguments, that SPIN has now been extended to detect.

ETCH implements its own scanner and parser for Promela, using the SableCC compiler toolkit, in order to generate the representation on which its typing analysis can be performed. This effort of implementing the scanner and parser can be avoided in ABLEP. Instead one can specify the typing analysis as a *semantic* extension to ABLEP that works over the abstract syntax tree of the Promela model that is generated by the scanner and parser in ABLEP. Such an extension can then contribute messages describing any errors that it detects to the error-reporting facility in ABLEP. In Section 3 we will show this is done.

The language extension described here is also, in a sense, separate from the host language implementation of Promela in ABLEP, and it illustrates how analysis of this sort can be done as a composable language extension. It does not, however, implement the sophisticated type inference and checking algorithms of ETCH, but instead provides a simpler type checking facility.

Discrete Time in SPIN*:* With DTSPIN, Bosnacki and Dams introduce the notion of discrete time into Promela [1]. Discrete time occurs in many domains and the correctness of the system may include timing aspects. This is often the case in communication protocols. DTSPIN introduces a timer type and operations on values of this type. These include a set(t,v) operation to set timer t to integer value v, an expire(t) operation that waits until timer t counts down to 0, and a delay(t,v) operation that is syntactic sugar for set(t,v); expire(t). Bosnacki and Dams define these using simple macros as follows:

```
#define timer int
#define set(tmr,val) (tmr=val)
#define expire(tmr) (tmr==0)
#define delay(tmr,val) set(tmr,val); expire(tmr)
#define tick(tmr) if :: tmr>=0 -> tmr=tmr-1 :: else fi
proctype Timers() {do ::timeout -> atomic{tick(t1); tick(t2)} od}
```

Note that the Timers process must be modified in each model to apply the tick operation to all timers on a timeout.

We've implemented similar constructs as a modular language extension to ABLEP to address some of the shortcoming of simple macros. Fig. 1 makes use of a few of these. The model declares two timers, above_t and trouble_t, and uses them after the above and trouble labels respectively. In the first, delay is used to wait for the timer to proceed one tick of the clock and in the second the set/expire pair is used instead, but set is done using a type-safe assignment.

The extension overloads assignment to allow for the case of a timer variable on the left and an integer value on the right. Otherwise the extension treats timers as separate types from numeric ones and does not allow coercions between them. The timer values are represented by integers in the generated pure Promela model, but only after this type checking has been done to prevent timers from mistakenly being used as integers.

The extension also initializes timer values to -1 (as done in DTSPIN). Global declarations and local declarations in the initial declaration section of a process are translated into initializing integer declarations (*e.g.* `int trouble_t = -1` in Fig. 1). Local declarations after this section are translated to declaration/assignment statement pairs (*e.g.* `int t; t = -1`).

It is straightforward for the extension to generate the `Timers` process to "tick" the globally-declared timers; note that it is not present in Fig. 1. For locally declared timers it is not so simple and the current extension assumes that engineers will handle them explicitly. A possible solution, however, is to represent local timers differently, essentially lifting them a global array of timers and overloading references to them to access this global array. We are currently investigating this possibility.

Our extension does not, however, address the efficiency issues that are solved by modifying the SPIN source code to implement the clock *tick* operator directly. But as it stands the extension does provide some benefits over a plain macro based implementation and may be sufficient for some purposes. Extensions of the type possible in ABLEP may provide a good "proving grounds" for ideas before taking on the larger effort of moving them into the host language. For discrete time, the best solution may be to do what DTSPIN has done and modify the SPIN source code.

Extension utility: Note that we are not making claims about the utility of these specific extensions. The papers that introduced these features do a fine job at that. Our goal here is to demonstrate that such features can be specified in a modular and composable manner in ABLEP and then easily imported and used by the engineer.

2.2   Extending AbleP with Independently Developed Extensions

A distinguishing feature of extensible language frameworks such as ABLEP is that it is quite straightforward to create new language processors and translators by combining the host language specifications with those of the chosen language extensions. The underlying tools, SILVER and COPPER, have a number of features which enable this high degree of modularity and ensure that compositions will be well-defined. Fig. 3 shows the complete specification that an engineer would need to write to compose the host language with the four extensions described above and used in the example in Fig. 1.

The first line of this specification names the grammar and indicates that this instantiation is in the `artifacts` directory in ABLEP and has the name `aviation`, to indicate, perhaps, that this combination of features is suitable for avionics applications. Below this `import` statements indicate the host language

```
grammar edu:umn:cs:melt:ableP:artifacts:aviation ;

import edu:umn:cs:melt:ableP:host ;
import edu:umn:cs:melt:ableP:extensions:tables ;
import edu:umn:cs:melt:ableP:extensions:enhancedSelect ;
import edu:umn:cs:melt:ableP:extensions:typeChecking ;
import edu:umn:cs:melt:ableP:extensions:discreteTime ;

parser aviationParser :: Program_c {
  edu:umn:cs:melt:ableP:host ;
  edu:umn:cs:melt:ableP:extensions:tables ;
  edu:umn:cs:melt:ableP:extensions:enhancedSelect ;
  edu:umn:cs:melt:ableP:extensions:discreteTime ;          }

function main  IOVal<Integer> ::= args::[String] mainIO::IO
{ return driver (args, aviationParser, mainIO) ;  }
```

Fig. 3. SILVER specification of the avionics-inspired ABLEP instantiation

and the set of extensions that are to be combined by SILVER to form the semantic analysis and translation of the extended language. Below this, a parser (aviationParser) is defined and includes the host grammar and extensions that add new language constructs (new concrete syntax) to the extended language. Since the type-checking extension does not add new constructs it need not be listed, though doing so causes no problems. Finally, a main function is provided that calls the driver function that controls the ABLEP translation process. To generate the ableP.aviation.jar file used above the engineer needs to run the following on the command line.

```
% silver -o ableP.aviation.jar     \
        edu:umn:cs:melt:ableP:artifacts:aviation
```

Similar files for other instantiations have the same simple, boiler-plate format. There is little here except the naming of the host language and the desired language extensions. We have considered extensions to SILVER that would simplify this so that the start nonterminal in the grammar (Program_c), the parser name, and the main function need not be specified but can easily be generated. We choose not to use them here in order to show, in a plain SILVER specification, that there is no needed glue code or other specifications that require any language processing skills on the part of the engineer.

3   Implementing AbleP and Its Language Extensions

In our approach to extensible language frameworks, the instantiations are generated by composing the specifications of the host language (Promela) and the the user-chosen language extension specifications. The two primary challenges are composing concrete syntax specifications in order to generate a scanner and parser for the extended language, and composing semantic specifications to generate the part of the instantiation the performs semantics analysis of the model and that generates the translation of the extended model down to pure Promela. To address these challenges we developed COPPER [16], a parser and context-aware scanner generator, and SILVER [14], an extensible attribute grammar system.[1] As we saw above, SILVER reads a file containing a specification, follows the import statements to collect all the grammars that are to be included, and generates the files needed by COPPER to create the scanner and parser.

3.1 Specification and Composition of Syntax

COPPER specifications are context free grammars in which the terminal symbols have associated regular expressions; from these the parser and scanner are generated. The generated parser is slightly modified LALR(1) parser that uses the *context-aware scanner* [16] that is generated from the regular expressions. These specifications, in essence, contain the same information as found in specifications to popular parser generators such as Yacc or Bison and scanner generators such as Lex — though the information is processed in a slightly different manner to address challenges in parsing extensible languages.

Consider first the concrete syntax specification for the select-from construct used to assign to altQuality in Fig. 1:

```
s::Special_c ::= sl::'select' '(' v::Varref_c ':' es::Exprs_c ')'
{ s.ast = selectFrom (sl, v.ast, es.ast) ; }
```

This production's left-hand-side nonterminal, Special_c, is a type of statement. On the right are the select keyword, some punctuation, and the variable reference and expression list from which the value is chosen. In SILVER productions the symbols are named; the names precede the :: operator (read "has type") which precedes the type assigned to the name. The types are the terminal and nonterminal symbols found in the grammar. The name sl is used for the *select* keyword terminal defined in the ABLEP host language grammar and es is used for the comma-separated list of expressions that are derived from the host language nonterminal Exprs_c. This production is defined in the extension grammar edu:umn:cs:melt:ableP:extensions:enhancedSelect but uses only terminals and nonterminals defined in the host language grammar.

The semantics associated with the production build the abstract syntax tree (AST) for the construct using the extension-introduced abstract production selectFrom and attribute ast. The selectFrom parameters are the select-keyword terminal and the ASTs taken from the variable reference v and the list of expressions es. Below we will see how this abstract production detects errors on the construct and translates it down to a pure Promela guarded-if statement.

---

[1] Both are licensed under the LGPL open source license and distributed in both source and executable formats (as Java .jar files). See http://melt.cs.umn.edu.

To see where context-aware scanning has an impact consider the following terminal declarations and concrete productions for the `for` loop defined in the host language grammar (the semantics are elided).

```
terminal IN  'in' ;
terminal FOR 'for' lexer classes {promela_kwd} ;
fp::ForPre_c ::= f::FOR '(' v::Varref_c   { ... }
fp::ForPost_c ::= '{' s::Sequence_c os::OS_c '}'  { ... }
s::Special_c ::= fpre::ForPre_c ':' low::Expr_c '..'upp::Expr_c')'
                fpost::ForPost_c  { ... }
s::Special_c ::= fpre::ForPre_c in::IN v::Varref_c ')'
                fpost::ForPost_c  { ... }
```

These productions are the same as the ones that appear in the Yacc grammar spin.y in the SPIN distribution. Of special interest is the reserved keyword in shown in the last production above. As of SPIN version 6, in may not be allowed as an identifier. This is because the (hand-coded) SPIN scanner does not take context into account when processing the string "in ..." and thus simply always treats in as a keyword. Context-aware scanning lets us specify a scanner and parser in which the phrase in can be treated as the keyword in the context of a for-loop and as an identifier in other contexts. (Since ABLEP generates Promela we need to rename identifiers named in for SPIN to properly handle them.)

In COPPER this notion of context comes from the LR parser state. Each state associates an action (*shift*, *reduce*, *accept*, or *error*) with each terminal symbol of the (composed) grammar. When the context-aware scanner is called to retrieve the next token it is passed the set of terminals which are valid in the current state (those with action *shift*, *reduce*, or *accept*, but not *error*). The scanner will only return tokens for terminals in this set. If the parser is in a state where it has so far matched input derivable from the nonterminal ForPre_c then, as seen from the last production above, the terminal IN is valid. Since the identifier terminal (ID) is not valid in this state the scanner will return the keyword IN token and not the identifier ID token. On the other hand, the terminal FOR is specified as being a keyword and thus has lexical precedence (in the usual sense) over identifiers. Since both identifiers and the keyword FOR are valid at the beginning of a statement we must reserve FOR as a keyword to prevent lexical ambiguities.

This use of context in the scanner means that there are fewer lexical conflicts and we can use different terminals for overlapping regular expressions. In our experience this makes it easier to write a grammar that stays within the class of LALR(1). This leads to the modular determinism analysis [11] that allows extension developers to "certify" the concrete syntax of their extensions against the host language grammar to determine if the extension can be safely combined with any other "certified" extensions (those that also pass this analysis). Thus, when the engineer selects only extensions whose concrete syntax passes this analysis he or she has a guarantee that the composed grammar containing the host language grammar and the extension grammar fragments will have no conflicts (so that an LALR(1) parser can be generated from it) and no lexical ambiguities (so that a deterministic scanner can be generated from it).

The concrete syntax for the enhanced select statement and the discrete time extensions are syntactically quite simple. The boolean tables example provides a more interesting example. The productions themselves are straightforward, and thus not shown, but it shows how non-trivial new sub-languages can be embedded into the host language. The enhanced-select does not pass this analysis, since it uses the same keyword at the beginning of the production as others in the host language. The other two do pass the analysis, however. Previous papers on context-aware scanning [16] and the modular determinism analysis [11] provide a more detailed description of context-aware scanning as used by COPPER.

3.2   Specification and Composition of Semantics

SILVER [14] is an extensible attribute grammar system with features that enable the composition of semantic analysis and translation specifications when they are specified as attribute grammars. It has many modern attribute grammar features (higher order, reference, and collection attributes, forwarding and aspect productions) borrowed from the attribute grammar literature, see [14] for details. It also has features from functional programming languages (parametric polymorphism and pattern matching).

In an attribute grammar (AG) a context-free grammar is used to define the abstract syntax. The nonterminals of the grammar are decorated with attributes (not unlike fields in records or objects) that are computed to store some semantic information for the AST. For example, a nonterminal may be decorated with an *errors* attribute, for example, that contains a list of semantic errors detected on a node (of that nonterminal type) or its descendants in the AST. Productions are seen as tree-constructing functions that specify equations for computing the values of the attributes defined on the constructed tree's root node and the nodes of its immediate children.

Consider the assignment production in the host language as shown below:

```
abstract production defaultAssign
s::Stmt ::= lhs::Expr rhs::Expr
{ s.pp = lhs.pp ++ " = " ++ rhs.pp ++ " ;\n" ;
  lhs.env = s.env;    rhs.env = s.env;      s.defs = emptyDefs();
  s.errors := lhs.errors ++ rhs.errors ;      }
```

The abstract production, named defaultAssign, has a statement nonterminal (Stmt) on the left and on the right has two expression nonterminals (Expr) for the left and right hand side of the assignment operator, which is abstracted away here. The pretty-print string attribute pp is defined on an assignment as the concatenation (++) of the pp attribute values on the children with the expected punctuation. This is a *synthesized* attribute as its value is synthesized from values on child nodes. The environment attribute env plays the role of a symbol table and passes bindings on names to their declarations down the tree; such attributes are called *inherited*. Since assignments do not alter the environment the value passed to the statement (s.env) is copied to its children. A corresponding synthesized attribute, defs, collects declarations to populate the env attribute, but since assignments do not declare names this attribute is the empty set of definitions. Any errors that occur on the children (such as an undeclared variable) are passed up the tree in the synthesized attribute `errors`. Recall the type checking is done in the `typeChecking` extension (described below) so no type errors are added here. The operator `:=` is used for collection attributes and is described below; for now it can be seen as the same as `=`. Attribute evaluation is the process of computing the values for attributes from these equations.

The abstract syntax for the host language in ABLEP is defined in SILVER using productions similar to the one shown above. It implements the scope rules as found in SPIN version 6 to bind variable uses to their declarations using reference attributes. These can be seen as pointers to remote nodes in the tree. The `env` attribute maps names to references to variable declarations; variable references look up their name in the `env` attribute to get the reference, if it exists, to their declaration. If it is not found an error is placed into the `errors` attribute and propagated up the tree to be reported by ABLEP.

The attribute grammar specifications of the extensions are easily composed with the host language specification since the specifications are seen as sets: sets of nonterminals, sets of terminals, sets of productions, sets of attribute equations on productions, etc. Thus, simple set union over these sets from the host and extension creates the composed language. In the case of the enhanced-select extension, it defines new productions for the concrete and abstract syntax of the new statements. These are then composed with those in the host language to create an extended grammar. These productions do basic type checking on the new constructs and thus extend both the host language and the type checking extension, which we thus discuss first.

Type Checking: The type checking extension performs basic type checking of Promela models and makes use of the variable-use-to-declaration binding that is done in the host language. It is certainly more natural, and common, to consider this as part of the host language. Here we have pulled it out as an extension to illustrate that tools such as ETCH can be implemented as extensions in ABLEP.

This extension adds no new concrete syntax. Instead it adds new attributes that decorate existing host language nonterminals and new attribute equations to provide values for these attributes. Specifically, a `typerep` attribute decorates expressions and declarations to represent the type of the expression and the type of the variable declared on the declaration. In Fig. 4 *aspect productions* are provided for the abstract productions `varRef` and `defaultAssign` that exist in the host language. These allow new attributes to be defined on existing productions. On the `varRef` production, the `typerep` of the variable is found by looking up its declaration in the environment and getting its type from it. This code is elided for space reasons, but is straightforward. On `defaultAssign`, the `typerep` attribute on the child expressions is used to determine if the types are compatible. If they are not, it adds a new error to the list of those in the `errors` attribute, defined in the host language. In the host language, `errors` is defined as follows:

```
synthesized attribute errors :: [ Error ] with ++ ;
```

```
grammar edu:umn:cs:melt:ableP:extensions:typeChecking ;
synthesized attribute typerep::TypeRep occurs on Expr, Decls ;
aspect production varRef
e::Expr ::= id::ID
{ e.typerep = ... retrieve from declaration found in e.env ... ;    }


aspect production defaultAssign
s::Stmt ::= lhs::Expr rhs::Expr
{ s.errors <- if isCompatible(lhs.typerep, rhs.typerep) then [ ]
              else [ mkError ("Incompatible types on assigment ...") ]; }
```

Fig. 4. Partial SILVER specification of simplified ETCH-like error checking

This attribute is a list of Error values that are constructed uses in mkError function, the details of which are not important here. What matters is that this is a *collection attribute* [2], as indicated by the with ++ clause. This specifies that when aspect productions contribute additional values, using the <- assignment operator, they are combined with the base value for errors, specified using the := operator that we saw above. These different values are then folded together using the ++ operator, which is both string and list concatenation. Any errors that this aspect production finds will be folded into the errors defined in the host language. Thus, it is important that the host language define errors as a collection attribute so that the extensions can "plug into it" to provide additional or improved semantic analysis on the model.

While this extension does not perform the same sophisticated analysis that is done by ETCH, it demonstrates how such analyses can be implemented as modular and composable language extensions. By doing so, such analyses do not need to be implemented as stand alone tools that require building their own scanner and parser, as ETCH has done.

Enhanced select and boolean tables: The enhanced-select extension provides two new versions of select, but we discuss just the select-from version that was used to assign to altQuality. Its concrete syntax specification was shown above; its abstract syntax production is given in Fig. 5. This (new) production defines its pretty print attribute pp as expected and computes type errors based on the typerep attributes introduced in the type-checking extension. This check is straightforward and more verbose than interesting, and thus elided here. Since this is a new production, not an aspect, we see that the definition of errors uses the := operator to assign the base value for errors, consisting of errors on the children v and es and errors detected on the select statement itself.

What is of specific interest here is the "forwards to" clause. This clause specifies a tree (of the same nonterminal type as on the left hand side of the production) that is defined as being *semantically equivalent* to the "forwarding" tree. When the forwarding tree (node s, here) is queried for an attribute for which the production does not have a defining equation, that query is passed to the forwards-to tree. In the case of the assignment to altQuality from above, the forwards-to tree is the if statement with three options, one for each possible

```
grammar edu:umn:cs:melt:ableP:extensions:enhancedSelect ;
abstract production selectFrom
s::Stmt ::= sl::'select' v::Expr es::Exprs
{ s.pp = "select ( " ++ v.pp ++ ":" ++ es.pp ++ " ); \n" ;
  s.errors := v.errors ++ es.errors ++
      if  ... check that all expressions in 'es' have same type as 'v' ...
      then [ mkError ("Error: select statement requires ... ") ]
      else [ ] ;
  forwards to ifStmt( mkOptions (v, es) ) ;              }
```

Fig. 5. SILVER specification of the semantics of the select-from extension

assignment, that was shown above in Section 2.1. The mkOptions function builds
the options for the if statement from the variable reference and expressions.

Consider removing the equation defining errors from the selectFrom production. If this were done, the query for the errors attribute would be forwarded
to the semantically equivalent if statement. This means that the user gets error
messages from code that he or she did not write, even though they would be
semantically correct. The boolean tables extension follows this same pattern.
Abstract productions for tables and the component rows perform type checking
and compute the less-readable semantically equivalent boolean expression of &&
and || operators that the table will forward to. In this case however, providing
a definition of the errors attribute is more critical since from the translation
down to the equivalent boolean expression it may not be able to detect when the
rows in the table are of different lengths. Forwarding provides a mechanism for
implicitly specifying the semantics (attributes) for a new construct when *explicit*
specifications for them are not provided by the production.

Discrete Time: Collection attributes and forwarding as described above play
important roles in defining the discrete-time language extensions and we need
not introduce any additional SILVER features. Because of this, and space limitations, we only describe the implementation of this extension. The new constructs
(set, expire, and delay) are defined as one would expect. The use of the existing assignment operator for assignments to timers, however, is more interesting.
Overloading on assignment is accomplished by defining an abstract assign production that is used by the concrete syntax in building the abstract syntax tree.
This production has an overloads collection attribute of type [Stmt] that is
initialized to the empty list and which extensions can write aspects for that add
new trees into this list. The discrete-time extension defines an aspect on assign
that checks if the expression on the right hand side of the assignment is of type
timer. If it is, it adds a Stmt tree to this overloads list that is built using a
new production for assignments to timers that is defined by the extension. The
"dispatching" assign production can then inspect this list in overloads and if
it contains a tree, it takes it from the list and forwards to it. If this list is empty,
the assign forwards to a tree constructed using the defaultAssign production
shown above. (If the list contains more than one tree, then two extensions are
trying to overload the same syntax and an internal error is raised.) This provides

a "hook" in the host language that extensions can exploit to overload existing syntax. Here the timer-specific assignment is used to allow assignment between integer and timer types, which would otherwise not be allowed since the timer type is specified as being incompatible with numeric types in the host language. A similar mechanism is used to generate the `Timers` process and `init` clause which will run it. The root-level production for Promela models has a collection attribute to which extensions can add new global declarations that they want inserted at the end of the Promela program.

3.3   Solutions to Some Challenges in Promela

An interesting feature of Promela is that it allows C code to be embedded inside Promela specifications, as in, for example, c_code { ... *C code* ... } phrases. In SPIN this is accomplished by recognizing the C code as a single token, not by parsing the embedded C code. SPIN reports syntax errors in the C code not when SPIN runs but when the generated verifier program, pan.c, is compiled. In ABLEP, however, we can parse the embedded C code directly and report a syntax error in the C code just as a syntax error in the Promela code is reported. Context-aware scanning makes this possible. We create a single grammar that includes the Promela concrete syntax and a separate specification of ANSI C concrete syntax. Even though many terminal symbols overlap in their regular expressions this does not cause a problem. For example, the composed grammar has two terminals for recognizing the keyword int. But because the parser is in a different LR-state when parsing the C code than it is in when parsing Promela, none of these overlapping terminal symbols occur in the same set of valid terminals that are passed to the scanner. Thus the scanner is never asked to return, for example, a Promela int keyword or a C int keyword - even though these two distinct terminals exist in the combined language specification. This fact is verified by COPPER when the scanner and parser are generated. Besides allowing syntax errors in the embedded C code to be detected and reported in a natural way, it also means that the language specification for Promela with embedded C code is declarative and easy to understand.

Forwarding is used to handle inlining as specified by the inline keyword in Promela. The declaration of an statement to be inlined is parsed and added to the environment env attribute. A inlining use then looks up this statement in the environment, instantiates the statement with the arguments provided at the call site and the forwards to this instantiated statement.

4   Related Work

The extensible language framework is based on the same principles that our colleagues and we have used to build ABLEJ, an extensible framework for Java 1.4 [15], a framework for a subset of Lustre [8] and a ongoing effort to do the same for C. There have been many investigations into the modular specification of languages in the attribute grammar community. Of particular interest is the JastAdd system [6] that adds a attribute grammar layer on top of Java. It has been used to build an extensible specification of Java 1.5 [5]. Other recent attribute grammar systems aimed at language extensibility have been specified as embedded DSLs: UUAG [13] in Haskell and Kiama [12] in Scala. MetaBorg [3], an language embedding framework based on term rewriting, has been used to develop JavaBorg - an extensible specification of Java.

There have been many efforts to extend Promela, with with new features or to provide tools that do additional analysis. In fact, the CPP macro processor is commonly used for these purposes. We discuss ETCH [4] and DTSPIN [1] as examples here because the cover much of the spectrum from light- to heavy-weight approaches and from ones that add new syntax to others that add only semantic analysis. Other examples can be found in the literature, primarily in past editions of the Spin Workshop, see [9].

5   Conclusion

One challenge with ABLEP is that SPIN, when simulating or verifying the ABLEP-generated Promela model, will report errors or issues on the pure Promela model written in the host language, not the extended language. We do not have a general solution for this problem, but SPIN itself suffers from this with its parser-based implementation of the for and select constructs. Still, sometimes a verbose but direct translation to SPIN works rather well, as is the case with the select statement that may generate many if options since, as described in Section 2, this may provide a more intuitive interaction with the user than the translation to a do loop. Our longer range goals are to investigate this problem in a general setting and we anticipate that ABLEP will be a good testbed for this effort. Another challenge arises if engineers introduce many different unfamiliar extensions as this may make it more difficult to read the specification. But the same thing happens if too many libraries are used in traditional programs. A bit of discretion on the engineer's part may be sufficient to address this concern.

Overall, we believe that extensible language frameworks such as ABLEP provide a good solution to the challenges of extending and evolving languages. ABLEP is middle-weight solution that enables more static analysis and syntactic expressiveness than is possible with simple macros, but at the cost of requiring an explicit pre-processing step to analyze the extended specification and generate the pure Promela version. It also does not provide the capabilities that one has in modifying the SPIN source code, but this is a significant effort that many will want avoid. An extensible framework such as ABLEPcan also take some of the pressure off of the host language developer. New language constructs and analyses can be tried out as language extensions, allowing for users to experiment with them and provide feedback based on their hands-on experiences. After this, some features may migrate into the host language if that is warranted. For discrete-time constructs found in DTSPIN, this may be appropriate. In other cases, such as with the ETCH-like type analysis, the feature may be sufficient when packaged as a language extension.

References

1. Bosnacki, D., Dams, D.: Integrating real time into Spin: A prototype implementation. In: Proceedings of the FORTE/PSTV XVIII Conference, pp. 423–439. Kluwer, Dordrecht (1998); Reproduced in Bosnacki's thesis, http://www.win.tue.nl/~dragan/Thesis/
2. Boyland, J.T.: Remote attribute grammars. J. ACM 52(4), 627–687 (2005)
3. Bravenboer, M., Visser, E.: Concrete syntax for objects: domain-specific language embedding and assimilation without restrictions. In: Proc. of OOPSLA 2004 Conf., pp. 365–383. ACM Press, New York (2004)
4. Donaldson, A.F., Gay, S.J.: Type inference and strong static type checking for Promela. Science of Computer Programming 75, 1165–1191 (2010)
5. Ekman, T., Hedin, G.: The JastAdd extensible Java compiler. In: Proc. Conf. on Object Oriented Prog. Sys. and Applications (OOPSLA), pp. 1–18. ACM Press, New York (2007)
6. Ekman, T., Hedin, G.: The JastAdd system - modular extensible compiler construction. Science of Computer Programming 69, 14–26 (2007)
7. Gagnon, E., Hendren, L.J.: SableCC, an object-oriented compiler framework. In: Proc. of 26th Technology of Object-Oriented Languages and Systems, pp. 140–154. IEEE Computer Society Press, Los Alamitos (1998)
8. Gao, J., Heimdahl, M., Van Wyk, E.: Flexible and extensible notations for modeling languages. In: Dwyer, M.B., Lopes, A. (eds.) FASE 2007. LNCS, vol. 4422, pp. 102–116. Springer, Heidelberg (2007)
9. Holzmanm, G.: Spin - formal verification, http://www.spinroot.com
10. Holzmann, G.J.: The SPIN Model Checker:Primer and Reference Manual. Addison-Wesley Professional, London (2003)
11. Schwerdfeger, A., Van Wyk, E.: Verifiable composition of deterministic grammars. In: Proc. of ACM SIGPLAN Conference on Programming Language Design and Implementation (PLDI). ACM Press, New York (2009)
12. Sloane, A.M.: Lightweight language processing in kiama. In: Fernandes, J.M., Lämmel, R., Visser, J., Saraiva, J. (eds.) GTTSE 2009. LNCS, vol. 6491, pp. 408–425. Springer, Heidelberg (2011)
13. Swierstra, S.D., Alcocer, P.R.A., Saraiva, J., Swierstra, D., Azero, P., Saraiva, J.: Designing and implementing combinator languages. In: Swierstra, S.D., Oliveira, J.N. (eds.) AFP 1998. LNCS, vol. 1608, pp. 150–206. Springer, Heidelberg (1999)
14. Van Wyk, E., Bodin, D., Gao, J., Krishnan, L.: Silver: an extensible attribute grammar system. Science of Computer Programming 75(1-2), 39–54 (2010)
15. Van Wyk, E., Krishnan, L., Bodin, D., Schwerdfeger, A.: Attribute grammar-based language extensions for java. In: Bateni, M. (ed.) ECOOP 2007. LNCS, vol. 4609, pp. 575–599. Springer, Heidelberg (2007)
16. Van Wyk, E., Schwerdfeger, A.: Context-aware scanning for parsing extensible languages. In: Intl. Conf. on Generative Programming and Component Engineering (GPCE). ACM Press, New York (2007)

Program Sketching via CTL* Model Checking

Andreas Morgenstern and Klaus Schneider

University of Kaiserslautern
P.O. Box 3049
67653 Kaiserslautern, Germany
{morgenstern,schneider}@cs.uni-kl.de

Abstract. Sketching is an approach to automated software synthesis where the programmer develops a partial implementation called a sketch and a separate specification of the desired functionality. A synthesizer tool then automatically completes the sketch to a complete program that satisfies the specification. Previously, sketching has been applied to finite programs with a desired functional input/output behavior and given invariants. In this paper, we consider (non-terminating) reactive programs and use the full branching time logic CTL* to formalize specifications. We show that the sketching problem can be reduced to a CTL* model checking problem provided there is a translation of the program to labeled transition systems.

1 Introduction

Formal verification is mandatory for software in safety critical applications. In particular, this is the case for embedded systems that implement difficult and concurrent control problems. These systems are often reactive real-time systems that must react sufficiently fast to the stimuli of their environment. For this reason, their temporal behavior is of essential importance for their correctness.

In the past two decades, many verification procedures based on model checking the temporal behavior of reactive systems have been developed [12], and this research already lead to tools that are now routinely used in industry. One of the most popular specification logics is CTL* [5,6] that subsumes the well-known temporal logics LTL and CTL and is strictly more expressive than both of them.

In this paper, we want to go one step beyond CTL* model checking. Instead of developing a full implementation and afterwards checking that the implementation satisfies a specification, a programmer may develop a partial implementation, which is called a program sketch. It is the aim of this paper to develop a procedure that completes this partial implementation such that a given CTL* specification is satisfied. The motivation behind the sketching approach is that in many cases, programmers have an idea of an algorithm, but often fail to determine the full details that are required to implement that algorithm without errors. For example, loop bounds are often missed by plus or minus one, so that one often speaks of plus/minus one bugs, or expressions are used that are 'almost' the correct ones, but fail for some corner cases. Typically, programmers feel whether an expression

A. Groce and M. Musuvathi (Eds.): SPIN 2011, LNCS 6823, pp. 126–143, 2011.

may not be correct, but they usually have no means in programming languages to express their doubts. Hence, instead of forcing a human programmer to determine the error-prone details, we employ computers to solve this difficult task in that we want to develop a synthesis procedure that selects among a set of given program expressions one that satisfies the specifications.

The term "sketching" has been coined by Solar-Lezama et. al [15,16,17]. The difference to our approach is that we consider reactive systems, i.e., systems with typically non-terminating behaviors that are specified by temporal logic specifications. In contrast to that, Solar-Lezama considers finite programs with a finite input-output behavior and only invariance properties.

Clearly, there is also a relationship to the synthesis problem of strategies in infinite games [2,7,10,11]. However, we want to emphasize that we solve a completely different problem: In infinite games, the players may select in each position of the game among a set of inputs and there is no restriction on this set of inputs with respect to the previously chosen inputs. Our problem is totally different: we are looking for *one* program expression that is used in the desired occurrences of the program and this program expression must not change whenever we reenter this program position[1].

There is also a relationship to programming with angelic nondeterminism: in [3] the authors propose to use Floyd's nondeterministic choose operator to allow the formulation of nondeterministic (finite) programs. The question they consider is whether this choose operator can be replaced by a deterministic program expression such that the specification is fulfilled. However, their procedure is more or less an example-generator: given a partial (nondeterministic) program with choose operator their procedure generates a finite execution trace such that the specification is satisfied and the programmer is still left with the problem of determining the correct program expressions based on this execution trace. In contrast, we use the ability of model checkers to generate counterexamples to actually generate correct program expressions (respectively to select one among a list of given proposals).

To be independent of the underlying programming language, we develop our theory purely on the basis of Kripke structures which are labeled transition systems. Hence, one is able to use our approach with any programming language provided there is a translation to a transition system. In order to leave the freedom to choose between different program expressions, we endow the Kripke structure with a set of oracles and the synthesizer has to choose among these

---

[1] Moreover, the known algorithms for the solution of infinite games solve the synthesis problem in an unsatisfactory way: as they construct a strategy that solves the synthesis problem, their result is a (nondeterministic) Moore (or a Mealy) automaton reading the uncontrollable inputs and generating the controllable inputs of the system as its outputs. Deriving a program expression from this automaton to replace the controllable inputs is a challenging task, in particular, if the resulting automaton is given symbolically, e.g., as a BDD. While a hardware circuit can be directly derived from this description, a program expression at the level of the source code, where more abstract data types than booleans should be used, cannot be directly obtained.

oracles to fulfill the specification. We have implemented our approach for the Quartz programming language that is a descendant of Esterel, which is a very good choice for implementing reactive systems. Examples given in the paper have been worked out with our Averest[2] system.

The outline of the paper is as follows: In the next section, we motivate the problem considered in this paper and indicate how we solve it. Section 3 recalls the formal definitions of the temporal logic CTL*. We also formally define Kripke structures with oracles in that section. Section 4 contains the core of the paper where we prove that our problem can be polynomially reduced to CTL* model checking, so that the PSPACE-completeness of CTL* defines also the complexity class of our problem. In Section 5, we then show how we implemented the approach on top of our Averest system. We finally briefly discuss related and future work in our conclusions.

2   Motivating Example

As already stated, we consider the situation where a programmer has an idea of how the algorithm should work, but fails to provide the full details in terms of correct program expressions. For an example, consider the faulty implementation of the well-known binary search algorithm. In Figure 1, we have chosen an implementation in the synchronous programming language Quartz [13], but the choice of the programming language is not relevant for the errors on the program. The algorithm searches a desired value v in a sorted array a and returns the index i of the array element a[i] if v is contained in a, and otherwise terminates with i==N which is no legal array index, since the array has elements a[0], ..., a[N-1].

The local variables left and right store the borders of the sub-array a that has to be searched through in future iterations. Hence, initially, we have left==0 and right==N-1 so that the entire array is searched through. Since a is sorted, the idea is to compare the middle element of the current sub-array with the desired value v. To this end, the index of the middle position mid is computed as mid = (left + right) / 2. If a[mid] is less than v, one assigns left=mid+1 and if a[mid] is greater than v , one assigns right=mid-1, and if a[mid] is equal to v, one assigns i = mid<N. These computations are iterated until left>=right or no longer i == N holds.

While this algorithm seems to be plausible, and while it is contained in many textbooks on algorithms, and is even taught (and verified!) each year in many courses in computer science, it is nevertheless wrong: For example, consider an array consisting of two elements 0 and 1 and the value searched for is v=1. The algorithm starts with left=0 and right=1 and computes then mid=0. We then have a[mid] == 0 < 1 == v, so that left is assigned the value mid+1, i.e., 1. Since we then have no longer left<right, the loop terminates,

---

[2] Available at http://www.averest.org.

```
macro M = 10;
macro N = 2;

module BinarySearch([N]int{M} ?a, int{M} ?v, nat{N+1} i) {
    nat{N} left,right ,mid;
    left  = 0;
    right = N − 1;
    i = N;
    while(left<right & i==N) {
        mid = (left + right) / 2;
        if (a[mid]<v)
            next(left)  = mid+1;
        else  if (a[mid]>v)
            next(right) = mid−1;
        else  // v has been found
            next(i) = mid;
        pause;
    }
}
```

Fig. 1. Faulty Implementation of Binary Search

but still i==N holds and thus, i points to the wrong index. The value is therefore not found even though it is contained in the array. This example suggests
that the loop condition should be rather left<=right & i==N instead of
left<right & i==N, so that another iteration is performed.

However, even with the modified loop condition left<=right & i==N, the
algorithm is still not correct: Assume a consists of the two values 2 and 3, and
we search for the value v=1 that is therefore not contained in the array. Again,
the algorithm starts with left=0 and right=1 and computes then mid=0. We
then have a[mid] == a[0] == 2 > 1 == v, so that right is assigned the
value mid−1, i.e., -1. This is very dangerous since this leads to an out-of-bound
error in the next iteration.

In a recent 'Google research blog', it has been reported [14] that almost all
binary search algorithms are broken. The problems are usually that arithmetic
over- and underflows may occur in the computation of the index of the middle
position. While it seems to be unavoidable at a first glance, [14] proves that
the expressions x+(y−x)/2 and (x+y)>>1 correctly implement that position
without overflows in case of signed integers, and the expression (x and y) +
(x xor y)/2 can be safely used in case of unsigned integers.

These problems with the binary search algorithm are well-known: In [9], it is
mentioned that the main idea of binary search has been published as early as
1946. However, the first correct implementation has been given probably in 1960
[9]. A similar problem with respect to integer arithmetic remained undiscovered
in the binary search implementation of the Java library for nearly 9 years. While
such problems are typically found by model checking, removing the errors is still
a hard and error-prone task.

Our approach to the problem is as follows: For example, it is pretty clear that the loop condition should contain either left<right or left<=right. Hence, the programmer might use (sel ? left<right : left<=right) by introducing a new boolean oracle variable sel. This condition equals to either left<right or left<=right depending on whether sel is true or false, respectively. In a similar manner, we might introduce new oracle variables add and sub that represent natural numbers (either 0 or 1) that are then used to increment or decrement the mid value.

The question we are going to solve in this paper is then to select constant values for the oracle variables sel, add, mul to replace the variables sel, add, mul.

3   Preliminaries

In this section, we recall the formal definitions required for the formulation of our problem. In particular, we start with the definition of the syntax and semantics of the temporal logic CTL* which we use for specifying the reactive programs that we want to develop. We will also consider a 'translation' from automata to Kripke structures (labeled transition systems). Finally, we provide a formal definition of Kripke structures with oracles which we use as a representative for incompletely specified programs.

3.1   Syntax and Semantics of CTL*

As already mentioned, we start the preliminaries with the definition of the syntax and semantics of the temporal logic CTL* [5]. The following mutually recursive definitions introduce the set of path formulas PF_Σ and the set of state formulas SF_Σ over a given finite set of variables V_Σ.

- The set of path formulas PF_Σ over the variables V_Σ is the least set which satisfies the following properties:
  - state formulas: each state formula is a path formula, i.e. $\mathrm{SF}_\Sigma \subseteq \mathrm{PF}_\Sigma$
  - boolean operators: $\neg\varphi$, $\varphi \wedge \psi$, $\varphi \vee \psi \in \mathrm{PF}_\Sigma$, if $\varphi, \psi \in \mathrm{PF}_\Sigma$
  - temporal operators: $\mathsf{X}\varphi$, $[\varphi \; \underline{\mathsf{U}} \; \psi]$, $[\varphi \; \mathsf{B} \; \psi] \in \mathrm{PF}_\Sigma$, if $\varphi, \psi \in \mathrm{PF}_\Sigma$
- The set of state formulas SF_Σ over the variables V_Σ is the least set which satisfies the following properties:
  - variables: each variable is a state formula, i.e. $V_\Sigma \subseteq \mathrm{SF}_\Sigma$
  - boolean operators: $\neg\varphi$, $\varphi \wedge \psi$, $\varphi \vee \psi \in \mathrm{SF}_\Sigma$, if $\varphi, \psi \in \mathrm{SF}_\Sigma$
  - path quantifiers: $\mathsf{E}\varphi, \mathsf{A}\varphi \subseteq \mathrm{SF}_\Sigma$ if $\varphi \in \mathrm{PF}_\Sigma$

The set of CTL* formulas over the set of variables V_Σ is the set of state formulas SF_Σ. CTL* formulas are interpreted over Kripke structures, which are labeled transition systems as defined below:

Definition 1 (Kripke Structures). *A Kripke structure $\mathcal{K} = (\mathcal{S}, \mathcal{I}, \mathcal{R}, \mathcal{L})$ for a finite set of variables $\mathcal{V}$ is given by a finite set of states $\mathcal{S}$, a set of initial states $\mathcal{I} \subseteq \mathcal{S}$, a transition relation $\mathcal{R} \subseteq \mathcal{S} \times \mathcal{S}$, and a label function $\mathcal{L} : \mathcal{S} \to 2^\mathcal{V}$ that maps each state to the set of variables that hold in this state.*

To define the semantics of CTL*, we have to define infinite paths through a Kripke structure:

Definition 2 (Paths). *Given a set of atomic propositions $\mathcal{V}$, an infinite path is a function $\pi : \mathbb{N} \to 2^{\mathcal{V}}$. We denote the i-th state of the path π as $\pi^{(i-1)}$ for $i \in \mathbb{N}$. Using this notation, paths are often given in the form $\pi^{(0)}\pi^{(1)} \ldots$. The path starting at t is moreover written as $(\pi, t) := \pi^{(t)}\pi^{(t+1)} \ldots$*

Note that a path as defined above is nothing but a sequence of assignments over the variables V_Σ. The semantics of path formulas is informally given as follows (see e.g. [12] for a full definition): $\mathsf{X}\varphi$ holds at a path π at position t_0 if φ holds at position $t_0 + 1$ on the path. $[\varphi\ \underline{\mathsf{U}}\ \psi]$ holds at t_0 iff ψ holds for some position $\delta \geq t_0$ and φ holds invariantly for every position t with $t_0 \leq t < \delta$ i.e. φ holds *until* ψ holds. The *weak before* operator $[\varphi\ \mathsf{B}\ \psi]$ holds at t_0 iff either φ holds before ψ becomes true for the first time after t_0 or ψ never holds after t_0. Finally, $\mathsf{E}\varphi$ holds in a state s of a Kripke structure if there is a path π starting in s such that φ holds on π, and analogously, $\mathsf{A}\varphi$ holds in a state s of a Kripke structure if all paths starting in s satisfy φ.

Finally, a Kripke structure satisfies a CTL* formula Φ if all initial states satisfy Φ [3].

3.2   Relating Automata to Kripke Structures

While Kripke structures are convenient for model checking, they are not useful in system design where state-based systems must still be executable for means of simulation and synthesis. To this end, we must distinguish between input and state variables, to keep track of the causality and the actors that determine the values of these variables. Thus, one typically prefers automata over Kripke structures, where in case of reactive systems, these automata read infinite words over letters chosen from an input alphabet:

Definition 3. *An automaton $\mathfrak{A} = (Q, \Sigma, Q_0, \Delta, \mathcal{L})$ over the alphabet Σ and a set of variables $\mathcal{V}$ is given by a finite set of states Q, a set Q_0 of initial states, a transition relation $\Delta \subseteq Q \times \Sigma \times Q$ and a labeling function $\mathcal{L} : Q \to 2^{\mathcal{V}}$.*

Obviously, there is a close relationship between automata and Kripke structures that is captured in the following definition [12]:

Definition 4 (Associated Kripke Structure of an Automaton). *Given an automaton $\mathfrak{A} = (Q, \Sigma, Q_0, \Delta, \mathcal{L})$ over the alphabet Σ, and a set of variables $\mathcal{V}$, we define the associated Kripke structure $\mathtt{Struc}(\mathfrak{A}) = (\mathcal{S}, \mathcal{I}, \mathcal{R}, \mathcal{L}')$ as follows*

---

[3] Other temporal operators can be defined as syntactic sugar in terms of the above ones: $\mathsf{G}\varphi := [0\ \mathsf{B}\ \neg\varphi]$, $\mathsf{F}\varphi := [1\ \underline{\mathsf{U}}\ \varphi]$, $[\varphi\ \mathsf{U}\ \psi] := [\psi\ \mathsf{B}\ (\neg\varphi \wedge \neg\psi)]$, $[\varphi\ \underline{\mathsf{B}}\ \psi] := [\neg\psi\ \underline{\mathsf{U}}\ (\varphi \wedge \neg\psi)]$, $[\varphi\ \mathsf{W}\ \psi] := [(\varphi \wedge \psi)\ \mathsf{B}\ (\neg\varphi \wedge \psi)]$, and $[\varphi\ \underline{\mathsf{W}}\ \psi] := [\neg\psi\ \underline{\mathsf{U}}\ (\varphi \wedge \psi)]$. For example, $[\varphi\ \mathsf{U}\ \psi]$ is the *weak until* operator that can be alternatively defined as $[\varphi\ \mathsf{U}\ \psi] := [\varphi\ \underline{\mathsf{U}}\ \psi] \vee \mathsf{G}\varphi$, i.e. the event ψ that is awaited for may not hold in the future. To distinguish weak and strong operators, the strong variants of a temporal operator are underlined in this paper (as done above).

- $\mathcal{S} = Q \times \Sigma$
- $\mathcal{I} = Q_0 \times \Sigma$
- $\mathcal{R}((q,\sigma),(q',\sigma')) \leftrightarrow \Delta(q,\sigma,q')$
- $\mathcal{L}'(q,\sigma) = q$.

Intuitively, the states of the associated Kripke structure consist of the configurations of an automaton, i.e., pairs (q,σ) consisting of a state q and an input letter σ that is read in that state. While automata are the natural result of translations of finite state programs, they are not well-suited for the definition of the semantics of temporal logics. For this reason, we make use of both automata and Kripke structures and use the above definition to relate both when necessary.

3.3   Kripke Structure with Oracles and Implementations

The previous subsection gives us a blueprint to define our problem: we assume that we are given an automaton where some of the inputs are oracle variables. Those oracle variables may represent "angelic" nondeterminism that may be resolved in favor to satisfy the specification. Hence we seek a deterministic implementation of those nondeterministic variables such that the specification is fulfilled. Translated to Kripke structures, we may assume that the state set of a Kripke structure $\mathfrak{A}$ is the product of a state set Q and a oracle set $\mathcal{O}$ and an implementation of $\mathfrak{A}$ is a Kripke structure that selects exactly one element of the oracle set and fixes this element throughout the execution.

Definition 5 (Kripke Structure with Oracles). *A Kripke structure with oracles is a Kripke structure $\mathcal{K} = (\mathcal{S}, \mathcal{I}, \mathcal{R}, \mathcal{L})$ as before where $\mathcal{S} = Q \times \mathcal{O}$ is the product of a state set Q with a oracle set $\mathcal{O}$.*
An implementation $\mathcal{K}_o = (\mathcal{S}_o, \mathcal{I}_o, \mathcal{R}_o, \mathcal{L})$ for some $o \in \mathcal{O}$ is a restriction of $\mathcal{K}$ given by

- $\mathcal{S}_o = \mathcal{S} \cap \{o\}$
- $\mathcal{I}_o = \mathcal{I} \cap \{o\}$
- $\mathcal{R}_o((q,\hat{o}),(q',\hat{o}')) \leftrightarrow \mathcal{R}((q,\hat{o}),(q',\hat{o}')) \wedge \hat{o} = \hat{o}' = o$

The question we are going to solve in this paper is to find an answer to the following question: Given a Kripke structure $\mathcal{K}$ with oracles and a CTL* formula Φ, is there an implementation $\mathcal{K}_o$ of $\mathcal{K}$ such that $\mathcal{K}_o \models \Phi$?

4   Implementations for Kripke Structures with Oracles

In this section, we show that the problem to determine whether a system has an implementation can be reduced to a CTL* model checking problem.

Theorem 1. *Let $\mathcal{K} = (Q \times \mathcal{O}, \mathcal{I}, \mathcal{R}, \mathcal{L})$ be a Kripke structure with oracle set $\mathcal{O}$ and a CTL* formula Φ. There exists a Kripke structure $\mathcal{K}' = (\mathcal{S}', \mathcal{I}', \mathcal{R}', \mathcal{L}')$ whose size is polynomial in the size of $\mathfrak{A}$ such that the following holds: there exists an implementation $\mathcal{K}_o$ of $\mathcal{K}$ satisfying Φ if and only if $\mathfrak{A}' \models \mathsf{EXAX}\Phi$.*

Proof. We define $\mathcal{K}' = (\mathcal{I}', \mathcal{S}', \mathcal{R}', \mathcal{L})$ by adding new states q_0 and q_{sel}^o for each value of the oracle set $o \in \mathcal{O}$ as follows:

- $\mathcal{S}' = \mathcal{Q} \times \mathcal{O} \cup \{q_0\} \cup \{q_{sel}^o \mid o \in \mathcal{O}\}$
- $\mathcal{I}' = \{q_0\}$
- $\mathcal{R}' = \begin{pmatrix} \{(q_0, q_{sel}^o) \mid o \in \mathcal{O}\} \cup \\ \{((q_{sel}^o, (q, o)) \mid q \in \mathcal{I} \wedge o \in \mathcal{O})\} \cup \\ \{((q, o), (q', o)) \mid ((q, o), (q', o)) \in \mathcal{R} \wedge o \in \mathcal{O}\} \end{pmatrix}$

The intuitive idea behind the construction of $\mathcal{K}'$ is as follows: The only initial state is q_0, and q_0 has transitions to every state q_{sel}^o for each value o of the oracle set $\mathcal{O}$. In each state q_{sel}^o, a choice is made for the oracle set that is kept invariant on all transitions of $\mathcal{K}'$: The transition relation $\mathcal{R}'$ of $\mathcal{K}'$ is defined such that from q_{sel}^o there are only transitions to states (q, o) where q is an initial state of $\mathfrak{A}$ and o is the value chosen by q_{sel}^o. Moreover, the transitions of $\mathcal{K}$ are pruned so that a transition leads from a state (q, o) to a state (q', o') only if $o = o'$ holds (and there was already this transition in $\mathcal{K}$). Hence the sub-structure starting at q_{sel}^o is bisimulation equivalent to the implementation $\mathcal{K}_o$.

Now remember that a Kripke structure $\mathcal{K}$ satisfies a CTL* specification Φ if and only if all initial states of $\mathcal{K}$ satisfy Φ. Hence there does exist a implementation $\mathcal{K}_o$ if and only if the sub-structure rooted at $q_{sel}^o \models \mathsf{AX}\Phi$ and accordingly if and only if $\mathcal{K}' \models \mathsf{EXAX}\Phi$.   □

The following corollary determines the complexity of the problem:

Corollary 1. *Deciding whether a Kripke structure with oracles has an implementation satisfying a CTL* property is PSPACE-complete.*

Proof. The problem of CTL* model checking (which is PSPACE-hard) can be reduced to the problem of deciding the existence of an implementation over a singleton Oracle set that has no effect. Hence PSPACE-hardness follows. The problem can be solved in polynomial space, since the constructed Kripke structure of the previous theorem is polynomial in the size of the original Kripke structure and CTL* model checking can be solved in polynomial time.   □

5   Sketching Programs in Practice

In this section, we show how a program in a synchronous reactive programming language has to be modified to obtain a Kripke structure with oracles. To this end, we make use of our synchronous language Quartz [13], a descendant of Esterel. As will be seen the changes are only needed in the program and can be moreover automatically done by a source code transformation. Moreover, note that the principle can be applied to any programming language, and it could also be performed on an automaton that has been obtained by translation of the program. We start with a short introduction to the synchronous language Quartz, and will then show how the construction given in Theorem 1 can be performed at the source code level of Quartz programs.

5.1 Essentials of the Synchronous Programming Language Quartz

Synchronous languages are becoming more and more attractive for the design and the verification of reactive real time systems. There are imperative languages like *Esterel*, data flow languages like *Lustre*, and graphical languages like certain Statechart variants like *SyncCharts*.

Synchronous languages are well-suited for the design of reactive systems since they provide language constructs for parallel execution of processes and a synchronous concurrency that matches with the product computation of automata and Kripke structures. Moreover, they have a formal semantics that allows one to translate synchronous programs to extended finite state machines, and if the program has only finite data types, then even to finite state automata. These translations allow one to directly apply model checking techniques to the automata obtained from synchronous programs or to generate hardware circuits that implement the desired automata.

The common paradigm of synchronous languages is the perfect synchrony [8,1] which means that the execution of programs is divided into macro steps that are usually interpreted as logical time. As this logical time is the same in all concurrent threads, the threads run in lockstep, which leads to a deterministic form of concurrency. Macro steps are divided into finitely many micro steps that are atomic actions of the programs. Moreover, variables change synchronously in macro steps, i.e., variables have unique values in each macro step.

In the following, we give a brief overview of the synchronous programming language Quartz. We do, however, not describe the entire language, and refer instead to [13]. Provided that S, S_1, and S_2 are statements, ℓ is a location variable, x is a variable, σ is a boolean expression, and α is a type, then the following are statements (keywords given in square brackets are optional):

- *nothing* (empty statement)
- $x = \tau$ and $next(x) = \tau$ (assignments)
- *assume*(φ) (assumptions)
- *assert*(φ) (assertions)
- [ℓ :]*pause* (start/end of macro step)
- *if* (σ) S_1 *else* S_2 (conditional)
- $S_1; S_2$ (sequential composition)
- *do* S *while*(σ) (iteration)
- $S_1 \parallel S_2$ (synchronous concurrency)
- *[weak] [immediate] abort* S *when* (σ) (abortion)
- *[weak] [immediate] suspend* S *when* (σ) (suspension)
- $\{\alpha\ x;\ S\}$ (local variable y with type α)

The ℓ : *pause* statement defines a control flow location ℓ which is a boolean variable that is true iff the control flow is currently at the statement ℓ : *pause*.

Since all other statements are executed in zero time, the control flow can only rest at these positions in the program, and therefore the possible control flow states are the subsets of the set of locations. Hence, the variables ℓ used to name these control flow locations are state variables that encode the control flow of the program.

There are two variants of assignments; and both evaluate the right-hand side τ in the current macro step. While immediate assignments $x = \tau$ immediately transfer the value of τ to the left-hand side x, delayed assignments $next(x) = \tau$ transfer this value in the following step.

In case the value of a variable is not determined by an assignment, a default value is determined by the declaration of the variable. To this end, declarations provide a storage class in addition to the type of a variable. There are two storage classes, namely *mem* and *event* that choose the previous value or a default value (determined by the type), respectively, in case no assignment determines the value of a variable. Available types are booleans, signed and unsigned integers (both with limited and unlimited bounds), bitvectors, as well as arrays and tuples of types.

In addition to the control flow constructs that are well-known from other imperative languages like conditionals, sequences and loops, Quartz offers synchronous concurrency $S_1 \parallel S_2$ and sophisticated preemption and suspension statements, as well as further statements to allow comfortable descriptions of reactive systems (see [13] for the complete syntax and semantics). In $S_1 \parallel S_2$, both statements S_1 and S_2 must run in lockstep as long as both are active, and the entire statement terminates when the last one of the contained statements terminates. Preemption statements attach a guard to a statement and either suspend or abort it if that guard is true. The immediate forms do already check for preemption at starting time, while the default is to check the preemption only after starting time. The weak variants allow all actions of the data flow to take place even at the time of preemption, while the strong variant forbids them at the time of preemption.

In Quartz programs, we may also add temporal logic specifications in section `satisfies` that follow a Quartz module (see examples below). The specifications listed in these sections can be endowed by an observer statement that makes it often easier to express properties that are otherwise hard to formulate in temporal logic alone. We consider however only specifications that stem from the temporal logic CTL* in this paper.

5.2   Examples

In Theorem 1, we have described a reduction of the oracle selection problem of CTL* properties to CTL* model checking. In this section, we show how that construction can be performed at the source code level of Quartz programs.

The Hello World Program of Sketching. To start with, consider the "Hello World" program of sketching that has been introduced in [15] which is reformulated in Quartz as follows:

```
macro N = 2;
module HelloWorld(nat{N} ?x, nat{N∗2} !y) {
    y = x ∗ ??;
}
satisfies {
    s1: assert (y == x+x);
}
```

We define an input x and an output y, both as natural numbers with a fixed range: x may take values $0, 1$, and y may take values $0, 1, \ldots 3$ [4]. The task of our synthesis procedure is to determine the value of the expression ?? such that the output y equals 2 times x in the initial step. To solve that problem, we divide our program into two modules. The first one is essentially the sketch given above where an additional input variable mul has been introduced to replace the ??. The second module implements the construction given in Theorem 1 and is responsible for choosing a proper value for mul:

```
macro N = 2;
module HelloWorldSketch(nat{N} ?x, nat{N∗2} !y,nat{3} ?mul,) {
    y = x ∗ mul;
}
```

```
module HelloWorldSelector(nat{N} ?x, nat{N∗2} !y,nat{3} ?mul,){
    nat{3} m;
    nothing; // here q_0 implicitly holds
    q_sel : pause;
    m = mul;
    q_1:pause;
    HelloWorldSketch(x,y,m);
}
satisfies {
    spec1: assert E X A X (y == x+x);
}
```

According to the construction described in the proof of Theorem 1, the state q_0 which does nothing starts in the first program line and terminates, leading to the next state(s) where q_sel holds. Note that in the above program, q_sel is a unique control flow state, that is however multiplied with the possible data values that can be stored in the new local variable m. Note further that we have added a new input variable mul. The idea is that the environment is able to determine the input mul in every possible way that is consistent with its type, i.e., mul may have any of the values 0,1,2. The program takes only care of this value when the control flow is at the pause statement q_sel, where the value of the input mul is stored in the local variable m. This local variable m is a memorized variable, and since there are no further assignments to m, this

---

[4] Clearly we could use arbitrary bounds but took N=2 to simplify figure 2.

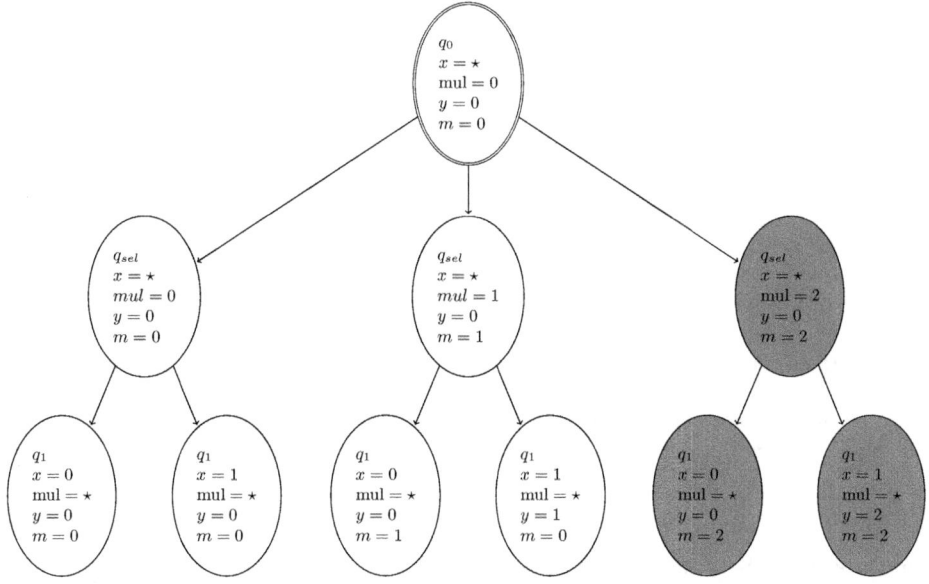

Fig. 2. Kripke structure for the Hello World Example

variable stores the value of the input variable mul at time t=1. Figure 2 shows the Kripke structure of the modified program.

In order to simplify the picture, we replaced each "don't care" variable with a $\star$. Hence, each state labeled with some $\star$ represents more than one state. For example, we have two initial states, one labeled with $x = 0$ and one with $x = 1$. As can be seen, this Kripke structure satisfies the modified specification: for all successor states of $q_{sel}, x = \star, mul = 2, y = 0, s = 2$, we have $y == x + x$. The idea behind this modified program is the same as in the previous section: In the selection state q_sel, the internal variable m stores the values of mul. Afterwards, m will never change and therefore stores the implementation if one exists (note that since mul is a input variable, every possibility is considered by the model checker). From each of those selection states, all initial states of the original program are reachable. Since we fixed the value of m, we try, in principle, each possible strategy in parallel.

It is not difficult to prove that the modifications we made lead to a program that is translated to an automaton whose corresponding Kripke structure is the result of the construction described in the proof of Theorem 1.[5] Thus, we can easily perform the construction as a source code transformation which is very convenient since the Quartz compiler performs the remaining translation, and thus, the essential construction of Theorem 1, implicitly for us.

---

[5] The only exception is that the initial state q_0 is multiplied with the input variables which however poses no problem.

```
macro M = 10;
macro N = 2;
module BinarySearchSketch([N]int{M} ?a, int{M} ?v, nat{N+1} i, ?sel, nat{1} →
    ? add,? sub) {
  nat{N} left,right,mid;
  left  = 0;
  right = N − 1;
  i = N;
  while((sel ?  left <right :  left <=right) & i==N) {
      mid = (left + right) / 2;
      if(a[mid]<v)
          next(left) = mid+add;
      else if(a[mid]>v)
          next(right) = mid−sub;
      else // v has been found
          next(i) = mid;
      w: pause;
  }
}
module BinarySearchSelector([N]int{M} ?a, int{M} ?v, nat{N+1} i, →
    ?sel,nat{1} ? add,? sub){
  bool s;
  nat{1} ad;
  nat{1} su;
  q_sel : pause;
  s  = sel;
  ad=add;
  su=sub;
  q_1:pause;
  BinarySearchSketch(a,v,i,s,ad,su);
}
```

Fig. 3. A Sketch for Binary Search

Checking this toy example with the model checker NuSMV is done in a couple of milliseconds and gives the correct result that the sketch can be completed to satisfy the specification. In order to actually synthesize a solution, all we have to do is to negate the specification. The values of each possible counterexample in the second state then determine a valid completion of the sketch.

A Sketch for Binary Search. In a same way, we obtain a sketch for the binary search algorithm we considered in Figure 1. The result is shown in Figure 3 where we replaced the problematic loop condition and the addition / subtraction of proper values by oracle variables. Again, those oracle variables are kept constant in a separate selector module so that we see how this principle "rewriting" on the source code level is performed. Solving the problem using NuSMV is done in under a minute and gives the correct values sel=false, add=1, sub=0.

```
macro N = 21;

module SingleRowNIMSketch(
    nat{N} numA, numB,
    nat{N+1} matches,
    nat{5} modulus,
    bool turnA
) {
    turnA = true;
    matches = N;
    while(matches>0) {
        if(turnA) {
            numA = (matches % modulus);
            next(matches) = matches−numA;
            next(turnA) = not turnA;
        } else {
            if(0<numB & numB<=matches) {
                next(matches) = matches−numB;
                next(turnA) = not turnA;
            }
        }
        pause;
    }
}

satisfies {
    A_always_wins: assert E X A X A G (modulus>0 & (matches==0 −> →
        !turnA));
}
```

Fig. 4. A Sketch for the Single Row NIM Game

Single Row NIM Game. In the single row NIM game, N matches are put on a desk. The game is played by two players A and B that take either 1,2, or 3 matches in alternating turns from this pile. The player who will take the last match has won. It is well-known that there is a optimal solution: the strategy is to choose a number of matches such that the remaining matches is a multiple of four. This is always possible for player A if initially the number of matches is not a multiple of four. Otherwise, player B will have the winning strategy.

Now suppose a programmer remembers that the solution has to do with some modulo operation. So, he might propose the sketch given in Figure 4 (where we omitted the selector module to safe space).

Notice that we have to additionally ensure that `modulus>0` to ensure that player A selects a value in the range 1,2,3. Again, checking that there does exist a implementation is done in a couple of seconds using NuSMV and generated a valid implementation with `modulus=4`. To see that this is the correct solution, remember from our hint that the number of remaining matches must be a multiple of four. Hence removing (matches mod 4) piles ensures this invariant.

```
macro red=0;
macro white=1;
macro blue=2;

macro N=10;

module DutchSketch ([N] nat{3} a,nat{3} op_loop,nat{7} op_inc){
    nat{N} i;
    nat{N} R;
    nat{N} B;
    i=0;
    R=0;
    B=N−1;
    while((op_loop==0) & (i<=(N−1)) |
          (op_loop==1) & (i<=R) |
          (op_loop==2) & (i<=B)){
        if (a[i]==red) {
            next(a[i])=a[R];
            next(a[R])=a[i];
            next(R)=R+1;
        }
        else if (a[i]==blue){
            next(a[i])=a[B];
            next(a[B])=a[i];
            next(B)=B−1;
        }
        if (
            (op_inc==0) |
            (op_inc==1) & (a[i]==red) |
            (op_inc==2) & (a[i]==white) |
            (op_inc==3) & (a[i]==blue) |
            (op_inc==4) & (a[i]!=red) |
            (op_inc==5) & (a[i]!=white) |
            (op_inc==6) & (a[i]!=blue)
            )
            next(i)=i+1;
        pause;
    }
}
satisfies {
    correct : assert E X A XA F ((forall (i=0 .. (N − 2)) (( (a[i]==white) −> →
        ( a[i+1] == white) | (a[i+1] == blue)) &
                            (a[i]==blue) −> a[i+1]==blue)));
}
```

Fig. 5. Dutch Flag Problem

The Dutch Flag Problem. Dijkstra presents the Dutch Flag Problem in [4], we follow here the description given in [3]): given an array of n pebbles, each of which is either red, white or blue, the algorithm must sort them in-place, in order of the colors in the Dutch flag: first red, then white, then blue. The algorithm may inspect at most one pebble at once and can only move the pebbles by swapping. A crucial constraint is that only a constant amount of storage can be used to remember the color of pebbles that have been examined.

We propose to use the sketch given in figure 5. The intended meaning of the variables is that i is the index-variable that is used to swap the array indices, all pebbles to the left of R are red and all pebbles to the right of B are blue.

There are two problematic program expressions: the first one is the loop condition while the second is when to increment i. We solve the problem using sketching by introducing two new oracle variables op_loop and op_inc that encode the right expression for the problematic cases. A natural guess would be that i should be incremented always. However, this is not true: whenever we found that position i contains a blue pebble, it is swapped with some other pebble from the right for which we have not yet determined the color. So it may be the case that we have to swap this pebble again. So can you imagine a right condition? With sketching, a programmer need not. He can simply let this hard work done by a computer as done in figure 5. The loop condition is not as problematic as the i increment condition, however looping until N-1 is not true: instead we have to loop until i>B, since otherwise we would overwrite the blue zone.

Solving this sketching problem is harder than the previously considered: it took approximately 12 minutes on a 3.0 GHz Quad Core Pentium Duo which is however still acceptable and indeed, NuSMV generated us the correct program expressions **while** (i<=B) {...} and **if** (a[i]!=blue) next(i)=i+1 .

6   Conclusions

We considered the problem how one can determine desired program expressions of a synchronous reactive program so that given temporal logic specifications in CTL* are satisfied. We proved that the problem can be reduced to CTL* model checking, so that we can employ model checkers for the solution of the obtained CTL* model checking problems. We then have shown how the reduction to CTL* model checking can be even performed at the source code level of programs so that existing compilers actually perform this construction for us. All that has to be done is to introduce a new control flow location q_sel at the point of time where the choices for the oracle variables are made and these choices are stored in local variables at that position. These local variables are kept invariant in the following so that the right solution is stored in those local variables. Using state-of-the-art model checkers, we are then able to check whether a suitable choice exists, and if so, we can determine one by means of counterexample generation offered by model checkers.

Our work has been inspired by the sketching approach to program synthesis [15,17,16] that describes how a partial finite program can be completed such that a specification is satisfied after termination of the program. However, in contrast to [15,17,16], we consider reactive programs that have non-terminating behavior specified by temporal logic formulas which makes our problem harder than the one imposed in [15,17,16].

We therefore proposed an efficient solution to the automatic synthesis of program expressions that can be used to significantly simplify programming of difficult concurrent reactive programs. We see future work in two directions: the first direction is to define new language constructs that allow to automatically derive sketches. So instead of manually adding a oracle variable to encode different program expressions, we want the compiler to construct the expressions with the oracle variables based on more convenient expressions that only list the potential choices. Those constructs should then be employed to develop new examples that cover the full power of our construction. The given examples have been chosen to be easily understandable and give an intuitive idea how sketching works. Therefore we restricted us to finite programs and invariance properties. However in future works we should come up with non-terminating programs involving more complex specification like e. g. fairness.

The more challenging future work is to develop new procedures so solve the sketching problem. It is well-known that SAT-based model checking procedures do often scale better in comparison to BDD-based model checking procedures. This is especially the case when there are many variables (which we introduce whenever many oracle variables are needed). A slightly modified bounded model checker may be a good starting point to simplify the problem so that on this simplified problem, BDD-based model checkers might succeed.

References

1. Benveniste, A., Caspi, P., Edwards, S., Halbwachs, N., Le Guernic, P., de Simone, R.: The synchronous languages twelve years later. Proceedings of the IEEE 91(1), 64–83 (2003)
2. Bloem, R., Galler, S., Jobstmann, B., Piterman, N., Pnueli, A., Weiglhofer, M.: Specify, compile, run: Hardware from PSL. Electronic Notes in Theoretical Computer Science (ENTCS) 190, 3–16 (2007)
3. Bodík, R., Chandra, S., Galenson, J., Kimelman, D., Tung, N., Barman, S., Rodarmor, C.: Programming with angelic nondeterminism. In: Hermenegildo, M., Palsberg, J. (eds.) Principles of Programming Languages (POPL), Madrid, Spain, pp. 339–352. ACM, New York (2010)
4. Dijkstra, E.: A Discipline of Programming. Prentice Hall, Englewood Cliffs (1976)
5. Emerson, E.A.: Temporal and modal logic. In: van Leeuwen, J. (ed.) Handbook of Theoretical Computer Science, volume B: Formal Models and Semantics, ch.16, pp. 995–1072. Elsevier, Amsterdam (1990)
6. Emerson, E.A., Lei, C.-L.: Modalities for model checking: Branching time strikes back. In: Principles of Programming Languages (POPL), pp. 84–96. ACM, USA (1985)
7. Filiot, E., Jin, N., Raskin, J.-F.: Compositional algorithms for LTL synthesis. In: Bouajjani, A., Chin, W.-N. (eds.) ATVA 2010. LNCS, vol. 6252, pp. 112–127. Springer, Heidelberg (2010)

8. Halbwachs, N.: Synchronous programming of reactive systems. Kluwer, Dordrecht (1993)
9. Knuth, D.: The Art of Computer Programming, vol. 2. Addison-Wesley, London (1998)
10. Morgenstern, A., Schneider, K.: A LTL fragment for GR(1)-synthesis. In: International Workshop on Interactions, Games and Protocols (IWIGP), Electronic Proceedings in Theoretical Computer Science (EPTCS), Saarbrücken, Germany (2011)
11. Schewe, S., Finkbeiner, B.: Bounded synthesis. In: Namjoshi, K.S., Yoneda, T., Higashino, T., Okamura, Y. (eds.) ATVA 2007. LNCS, vol. 4762, pp. 474–488. Springer, Heidelberg (2007)
12. Schneider, K.: Verification of Reactive Systems - Formal Methods and Algorithms. In: Texts in Theoretical Computer Science (EATCS Series). Springer, Heidelburg (2003)
13. Schneider, K.: The synchronous programming language Quartz. Internal Report 375, Department of Computer Science, University of Kaiserslautern, Kaiserslautern (2009)
14. Shade, E.: Size matters: lessons from a broken binary search. Journal of Computing Sciences in Colleges (JCSC) 24(5), 175–182 (2009)
15. Solar-Lezama, A.: Program Synthesis by Sketching. PhD thesis, University of California, Berkeley, California, USA (2008)
16. Solar-Lezama, A., Rabbah, R.,Bodík, R., Ebcioğlu, K.: Programming by sketching for bit streaming programs. In: Hall, M. (ed.) Programming Language Design and Implementation (PLDI), pp. 281–294. ACM, Chicago (2005)
17. Solar-Lezama, A., Tancau, L., Bodik, R., Saraswat, V., Seshia, S.: Combinatorial sketching for finite programs. In: Architectural Support for Programming Languages and Operating Systems (ASPLOS), pp. 404–415. ACM, USA (2006)

A Verification-Based Approach to Memory Fence Insertion in Relaxed Memory Systems*

Alexander Linden and Pierre Wolper

Institut Montefiore, B28
Université de Liège
B-4000 Liège, Belgium
{linden,pw}@montefiore.ulg.ac.be

Abstract. This paper addresses the problem of verifying and correcting programs when they are moved from a sequential consistency execution environment to a relaxed memory context. Specifically, it considers the TSO (Total Store Order) relaxation, which corresponds to the use of store buffers, and its extension x86-TSO, which in addition allows synchronization and lock operations.

The proposed approach uses a previously developed verification tool that uses finite automata to symbolically represent the possible contents of the store buffers. Its starting point is a program that is correct for the usual sequential consistency memory model, but that might be incorrect under x86-TSO. This program is then analyzed for this relaxed memory model and when errors are found (with respect to safety properties), memory fences are inserted in order to avoid these errors. The approach proceeds iteratively and heuristically, inserting memory fences until correctness is obtained, which is guaranteed to happen.

An advantage of our technique is that the underlying symbolic verification tool makes a full exploration possible even for cyclic programs, which makes our approach broadly applicable. The method has been tested with an experimental implementation and can effectively handle a series of classical examples.

1 Introduction

Model-checking tools such as SPIN [1] verify concurrent programs under the traditional *Sequential Consistency* (*SC*) memory model [2], in which all accesses to the shared memory are immediately visible globally. However, modern multiprocessor architectures implement relaxed memory models, such as *Total Store Order* (*TSO*) [3,4], which allow many more possible executions and thus can introduce errors that were not present in SC. Of course, one can force a program executed in the context of TSO to behave exactly as in SC by adding synchronization operations after every memory access. But this totally defeats

---

* This work is supported by the *Interuniversity Attraction Poles* program *MoVES* of the Belgian Federal Science Policy Office, and by the grant 2.4545.11 of the Belgian Fund for Scientific Research (F.R.S.-FNRS).

A. Groce and M. Musuvathi (Eds.): SPIN 2011, LNCS 6823, pp. 144–160, 2011.

the performance advantage that is precisely the motivation for implementing relaxed memory models, rather than SC. Thus, when moving a program to an architecture implementing a relaxed memory model (which includes most current multi-core processors), it is essential to have tools to help the programmer check if correctness is preserved and, if not, to minimally introduce the necessary synchronization operations.

Processor vendors do not publish formal definitions of the memory models their products implement, but rather document the memory model by describing sets of typical behaviors. This is not sufficient for building verification tools, but the problem has been well studied and quite simple models that cover the behaviors that can be seen in actual processors have been defined. These models can be axiomatic, giving constraints that characterize the possible behaviors, or operational, giving a program like description of the relaxed memory system. The model we will use is TSO [3,4], and its extension *x86-TSO* [5], which covers the possible behaviors of many current processors. In x86-TSO, just as in TSO, writes are buffered, and each processor can read its last buffered values before these become globally visible. In addition, x86-TSO includes a memory barrier instruction (*memory fence*) that can be used for synchronization, as well as a *global lock* allowing atomic operations on the shared memory. The operational model of x86-TSO is quite natural: each process writes to its own buffer from which it can also read, writes being nondeterministically committed to main memory.

Based on these models, several verification approaches and tools for concurrent programs executed under relaxed memory models have been developed. In [6], we proposed a technique that incorporates the TSO store buffers into the model and uses finite automata to represent the possibly infinite set of possible contents of these buffers. This representation coupled with acceleration techniques similar to those proposed in [7], as well as with the *sleep-sets* partial-order reduction techniques [8], allows a full exploration of the state space of programs, including cyclic programs. Other work on this topic includes [9], which proceeds by detecting behaviors that are not allowed by SC but might occur under TSO (or *PSO (Partial Store Order)* [4]). This is done by only exploring SC interleavings of the program, and by using explicit store buffers. The more theoretical work presented in [10] uses results about systems with lossy fifo channels to prove the decidability of reachability under TSO with respect to unbounded store buffers, but the undecidability of repeated reachability. Other approaches to verification, with respect to relaxed memory models, adopt the axiomatic definition of these models and exploit SAT-based bounded model checking [11,12], which of course pushes handling cyclic programs or unbounded buffers beyond their reach. Finally, [13] proposes an approach based on SPIN that uses a Promela model with (bounded) explicit queues and an explicit representation of the dependencies on memory accesses that are implied by the relaxed model *RMO (Relaxed Memory Order)* [4].

This paper focuses on porting a program, verified under SC to x86-TSO, while preserving its safety properties. The approach is based on the verification tool presented in [6], which makes it applicable to cyclic programs. A first contribution is to show that the performance of this tool can be improved by a more complete use of partial-order techniques. The improvement is such that the number of states explored while verifying under the relaxed memory model is often not significantly larger than the number of states explored in a verification under SC.

The second contribution of the paper is the method developed for safely porting programs from SC to x86-TSO. It starts by attempting to verify the program under x86-TSO and, if an undesirable state is found to be reachable, memory fences are inserted. The insertion policy is based on the observation that if no process can execute a *load* after a *store* without going through an *mfence* (memory fence), then every safety (unreachability of undesirable states) property satisfied under SC is also satisfied under x86-TSO. Exploiting this, we develop a heuristic iterative approach, which is guaranteed to converge.

2   Concurrent Programs and Memory Models

We consider a very simple model of concurrent programs in which a fixed set of finite-state processes are interacting through a shared memory. Such a concurrent system is thus defined by a finite set of processes $\mathcal{P} = \{p_1, \ldots, p_n\}$ and a finite set of memory locations $\mathcal{M} = \{m_1, \ldots, m_k\}$, the initial content of the shared memory being defined by a function $\mathcal{I} : \mathcal{M} \to \mathcal{D}$, $\mathcal{D}$ being the domain of memory values.

The definition of each process p_i includes a finite set of control locations $\mathcal{L}(p_i)$, an initial control location $\ell_0(p_i) \in \mathcal{L}(p_i)$ and a set of transitions labeled by operations taken from a set $\mathcal{O}$. The transitions of a process p_i are thus elements of $\mathcal{L}(p_i) \times \mathcal{O} \times \mathcal{L}(p_i)$, also written as $\ell \xrightarrow{op} \ell'$, where both $\ell, \ell' \in \mathcal{L}(p_i)$.

The set $\mathcal{O}$ of operations contains the two following memory operations:

- $store(p_i, m_j, v)$, the meaning of which is that process p_i stores the value $v \in \mathcal{D}$ to the memory location m_j,
- $load(p_i, m_j, v)$, the meaning of which is that process p_i loads the value stored in memory location m_j and checks if that value is equal to v. The operation is possible only if the values are equal, otherwise it does not go through and execution is blocked.

Under the SC memory model, the semantics of such a concurrent program is the one in which the possible behaviors are all the interleavings of the operations executed by the different processes, and in which the store operations become immediately visible to all processes.

In TSO, each process executing a store operation can directly load the value saved by this store operation, but other processes cannot always immediately see that value and might read an older value stored in shared memory. This can lead to executions that are not possible on a sequential consistency memory system. For example, in the program given in Table 1, both processes can run through and finish their execution if run on a TSO memory system, but this

Table 1. Intra-processor forwarding example from [14]

initially:	
x = y = 0;	
Process 1	Process 2
$store(p_1, \mathrm{x}, 1)$ (s_1)	$store(p_2, \mathrm{y}, 1)$ (s_2)
$load(p_1, \mathrm{x}, 1)$ (l_1)	$load(p_2, \mathrm{y}, 1)$ (l_3)
$load(p_1, \mathrm{y}, 0)$ (l_2)	$load(p_2, \mathrm{x}, 0)$ (l_4)

cannot happen on an SC memory system, where at least one process would find the value 1 in its last load operation, which would thus not go through.

The x86-TSO memory model [15,5] is an extension of TSO in which operations such as *atomic writes* and *flushing* (emptying) *the buffer content* to the shared memory, have been added. In spite of its name, x86-TSO is not an exact model of a given architecture, but is an abstract programmer's model that covers the documented behaviors of a wide range of processors. One can thus safely assume that a program verified under x86-TSO will run correctly on the corresponding processors.

The formal definitions of the memory models use the concepts of *program order* and *memory order* [3,16]. Program order ($<_p$) is a partial order in which the instructions of each process are ordered as executed, but instructions of different processes are not ordered with respect to each other. Memory order ($<_m$) is a total order on the memory operations, which is fictitious but characterizes what happens during relaxed executions.

Let *op* denote any load or store operation, l any load operation, s any store operation, l_a a load operation on location a, and s_a a store operation on location a. Furthermore, let $val(l)$ be the value returned by the load operation l and let $val(s)$ be the value stored by the store operation s.

An SC execution is one for which there exists a memory order satisfying the following constraint for each process p_i:

1. $\forall op_i, op_j : op_i <_p op_j \Rightarrow op_i <_m op_j$

This means that the memory order is an interleaving of the program orders. The result of a load operation is then simply the value of the most recent (in memory order) store to the same location.

On the other hand, a TSO execution is then one for which there exists a memory order satisfying the following constraints:

1. $\forall l_a, l_b : l_a <_p l_b \Rightarrow l_a <_m l_b$
2. $\forall l, s : l <_p s \Rightarrow l <_m s$
3. $\forall s_a, s_b : s_a <_p s_b \Rightarrow s_a <_m s_b$
4. $val(l_a) = val(\max_{<_m}\{s_a \mid s_a <_m l_a \vee s_a <_p l_a\})$. If there is no such a s_a, $val(l_a)$
   is the initial value of the corresponding memory location.

The first three rules specify that the memory order has to be compatible with the program order, except that a store can globally be postponed after a load

Table 2. Possible operation sequence and memory order

Operation sequence	Associated memory orderings
$store(p_1, x, 1)$ (s_1)	-
$load(p_1, x, 1)$ (l_1)	l_1
$load(p_1, y, 0)$ (l_2)	$l_1 <_m l_2$
$store(p_2, y, 1)$ (s_2)	$l_1 <_m l_2$
$load(p_2, y, 1)$ (l_3)	$l_1 <_m l_2 <_m l_3$
$load(p_2, x, 0)$ (l_4)	$l_1 <_m l_2 <_m l_3 <_m l_4$
-	$l_1 <_m l_2 <_m l_3 <_m l_4 <_m s_1$
-	$l_1 <_m l_2 <_m l_3 <_m l_4 <_m s_1 <_m s_2$

that is executed within the same process later than the store, this is known as the *store* $\rightarrow$ *load* order relaxation. The last rule specifies that the value retrieved by a load is the one of the most recent store in memory order that precedes the load in memory order or in program order, the latter ensuring that a process can see the last value it has stored. If there is no such store, the initial value of that memory location is loaded.

For the example of Table 1, a possible memory order is given in Table 2. The first process starts its execution by its store operation, which is not directly added to the memory order. The following load operations are directly added to the memory order, and the first process finishes its execution without being blocked. Then, the second process starts its execution with its store operation, which is not directly added to the memory order. The following load operations are then executed and added to the memory order. Finally, the stores of both processes are eventually transferred to main memory and introduced in the memory order.

The characterization of TSO we have just given is useful in dealing with TSO axiomatically, but not adapted for applying state-space exploration verification techniques. Fortunately, there exists a natural equivalent operational description of TSO, as well as of x86-TSO. In this description (see Fig. 1), stores from each process are buffered and eventually transferred to shared memory in an interleaved way. A store only takes effect globally when it is transferred (or committed) to shared memory, which is also when it is introduced into the memory order. Committing to shared memory is an internal operation, which is assumed to be executed nondeterministically. When a process executes a load, it will read the most recent value in its own store buffer or, if there is no such buffered store, the value found in shared memory.

In x86-TSO, a global lock is added to enable the processes to gain exclusive access to the shared memory. While this global lock is held by a given process, no other process can obtain the lock or execute a load operation, and the only commit operations that can be executed are those of the process holding the lock. An *unlock* operation is only possible if the process executing it holds the lock and if the store buffer of that process is empty. Additionally, a new operation called *mfence* is added to the set of operations. An mfence operation simply blocks the process executing it until its store buffer is empty.

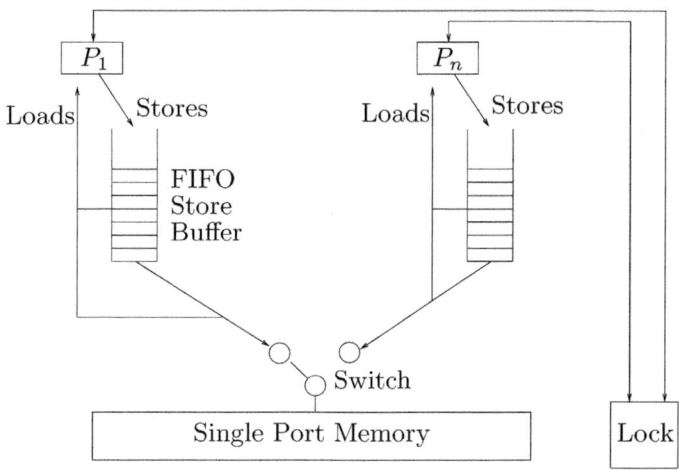

Fig. 1. Operational definition of x86-TSO of [5]

The formal operational model of x86-TSO is obtained by extending the program as follows. A set

$$\mathcal{B} = \{b_{p_1}, \ldots, b_{p_n}\}$$

of store buffers are introduced, one for each process[1]. One also adds a global lock L whose value can be a process p, or undefined ($\bot$). A global state is thus the composition of the content of the memory, the value of the global lock, and, for each process p, a control location and the content of its store buffer $[b_p]$, which is a word in $(\mathcal{M}, \mathcal{D})^*$.

The precise semantics of the operations can then be described as follows.

store operation : $store(p, m, v)$:

$$[b_p] \leftarrow [b_p](m, v).$$

load operation : $load(p, m, v)$:

If ($[L] \neq\bot$ and $[L] \neq p$), then $load(p, m, v)$ cannot be executed; otherwise, let $[b_p] = (m_1, v_1)(m_2, v_2)\ldots(m_f, v_f)$ and let $i = \max\{j \in \{1 \ldots f\} \mid m_j = m\}$. If i exists, then the result of the load is the test $d_i = d$. If not, it is the result of the test $[m] = v$, where $[m]$ denotes the content of the memory location m.

mfence operation : $mfence(p)$:

If ($[b_p] = \varepsilon$) then $mfence(p)$ is enabled;

---

[1] Note that we introduce a buffer per *process* rather than by *processor*. This approach is safe for verification since it allows more behaviors than a model in which some processes (could) share the same buffer. Furthermore, it is impossible to know which process will run on which processor when analyzing a program.

otherwise $mfence(p)$ cannot be executed.

lock operation : $lock(p)$:

If $([L] = \bot$ or $[L] = p)$ then $lock(p)$ is enabled;
otherwise, $lock(p)$ cannot be executed.

unlock operation : $unlock(p)$:

If $([L] = p \wedge [b_p] = \varepsilon)$ then $[L] \leftarrow \bot$ (the lock is released);
otherwise $unlock(p)$ cannot be executed.

commit operation : $commit(p)$:

If $([L] \neq \bot$ and $[L] \neq p)$, then $commit(p)$ cannot be executed;
otherwise, let $[b_p] = (m_1, v_1)(m_2, v_2) \ldots (m_f, v_f)$. Then, if $[b_p] \neq \varepsilon$, the result
of the commit operation is

$$[b_p] \leftarrow (m_2, v_2) \ldots (m_f, v_f)$$

and

$$[m_1] \leftarrow v_1, \text{ or}$$

if $[b_p] = \varepsilon$, the commit operation has no effect.

Note that $commit(p)$ is not an operation that can appear in a program, but
is assumed to be always enabled and nondeterministically interleaved with the
actual program operations. Thus, when an $mfence(p)$ or $unlock(p)$ operation
is blocked because the process buffer is nonempty, the implicit execution of
$commit(p)$ operations makes it possible to empty the buffer and enable this
operation.

3   Representing Sets of Buffer Contents and State Space Exploration

Verifying a program under the x86-TSO memory model can be done with a tool
such as SPIN. However, this leads to two problems. First, one must bound the
size of the buffers in order to keep the model finite-state. Second, the size of the
state space quickly explodes as the size of the buffers grows.

These problems were addressed in [6] as follows. To start with, rather than
limiting buffers to a fixed size, finite automata are used to represent possibly
infinite sets of buffer contents. This allows unbounded buffer contents to be
taken into account and, with the help of acceleration techniques similar to those
of [17] and [7], to explore the full state space of programs, even if they include
memory accesses (especially memory writes) in cycles that can be indefinitely
repeated.

This approach, with the help of *partial-order* techniques, was also quite helpful
in coping with the problem of the size of the state space. Indeed, the automata

representing buffer contents stay reasonably small, since their size is only of the order of the one of the program for the process writing to the buffer. Furthermore, buffering memory write operations introduces a lot of independence between the actions of the various processes, which makes the use of partial-order reduction techniques especially effective. This was exploited in [6] by using *sleep-sets*, as well as other optimization such as only executing commit operations just before operations with which they are dependent, namely load, mfence and unlock operations.

The version of the tool used for this paper goes further and fully implements the *persistent-sets* reduction of [8,18]. Persistent sets are formally defined as follows.

Definition 1. *A set* T *of transitions enabled in a state* s *is persistent in* s *iff, for all nonempty sequences of transitions*

$$s = s_1 \xrightarrow{t_1} s_2 \xrightarrow{t_2} \dots \xrightarrow{t_{n-1}} s_n \xrightarrow{t_n} s_{n+1}$$

from s *in the transition system and including only transitions* $t_i \notin T, 1 \leq i \leq n, t_n$ *is independent in* s_n *with all transitions in* T.

Our implementation uses a simple greedy algorithm for computing persistent sets and handles the *ignoring problem*[2] described in [19,8], by using a *proviso condition* as suggested in these references. The proviso condition we use imposes that, if none of the transitions to be explored from a state leads to a state that is not on the current search stack, then all transitions from that state must be explored. However, this only guarantees the reachability of local states, some global states potentially being left unexplored. Thus, to force the detection of global error states, we consider as dependent with transitions of other processes all transitions leaving a local state that is part of an error state.

The procedure to compute a persistent set satisfying the proviso condition is the following. One searches for a process whose enabled operations are only store or local operations and satisfy the proviso condition, i.e. contain at least one operation leading to a state that is not on the search stack. If furthermore the local state of this process is not part of a global error state, the persistent set is taken to be the set of enabled transitions of this process. Indeed, this set will be independent with all operations of the other processes, as well as with respect to all possible commit operations. If such a process cannot be found, the persistent set is taken to be the whole set of enabled transitions (including commits).

4   From SC to TSO

We turn to the problem of preserving the correctness of a program when it is moved from an SC to an x86-TSO memory environment. By correctness,

---

[2] A partial-order search might "ignore" a process and thus leave it totally inactive at some point.

we mean preserving state (un)reachability properties. Note that this captures safety properties, since safety can always be reduced to state (un)reachability in an extended model.

An obvious way to make sure a program can safely be moved from SC to x86-TS0 is to force writes to be immediately committed to main memory by inserting an mfence after each store, thus precluding any process from moving with a nonempty store buffer. The obvious drawback of doing so is that any performance advantage linked to the use of store buffers in the implementation is lost.

However, this is more than is necessary to guarantee that the executions that can be seen under x86-TSO are also possible under SC. Recall that the difference between the axiomatic definition of SC and of TSO is the absence of the following store-load constraint in TSO:

$$\forall l, s : s <_p l \Rightarrow s <_m l \qquad (1)$$

Thus stores can be postponed in memory order, which leads to executions that are not possible in SC. To avoid this it is sufficient to make sure that no process can execute a load after a store without going through an mfence. Indeed, even though successive stores might be buffered, they will be committed to main memory before any later load and hence the constraint (1) will be satisfied by the memory order, just as in SC. The memory order then becomes an interleaving of the program orders and the execution semantics thus match SC. We formalize this in the following lemma.

Lemma 1. *Given an x86-TSO execution, if in the program order of each process, an* mfence *is executed between each* load *and any preceding* store, *the memory order satisfies all the SC constraints.*

Proof. The semantics of mfence operations can be formalized by introducing these operations in the memory order with the following constraints, s, l and m representing store, load, and mfence operations respectively:

1. $\forall s, m : s <_p m \Rightarrow s <_m m$
2. $\forall s, m : m <_p s \Rightarrow m <_m s$
3. $\forall l, m : l <_p m \Rightarrow l <_m m$
4. $\forall l, m : m <_p l \Rightarrow m <_m l$

In the conditions of the lemma, we have that if $s <_p l$, there is an mfence m such that $s <_p m$ and $m <_p l$. And thus we have that $s <_m l$, using the semantics of memory fences.

The memory order thus satisfied all constraints of an SC order.

Remark 1. Using Lemma 1, one can deduce that for any algorithm that writes to memory exclusively with processor instructions that include an implicit memory barrier (such as *CAS* (compare-and-swap) or *TAS* (test-and-set)), moving this algorithm from an SC to a TSO architecture will preserve its correctness.

The Michael-Scott non-blocking queue [20] is such an algorithm, in which all store operation to shared memory are implemented by CAS operations, and thus will run correctly under x86-TSO. This is consistent with the results in [21].

We now have a sufficient condition for guaranteeing correctness while moving from SC to x86-TSO. The condition is expressed on executions, but can easily be mapped to a condition on programs: in the control graph of the program, an mfence must be inserted on all paths leading from a store to a load. This is sufficient, but can insert many unnecessary mfence instructions. We now turn to an approach that aims at only inserting the mfence instructions that are needed to correct errors that have actually appeared when moving the program to x86-TSO.

5   An Iterative mfence Insertion Algorithm

Our method is quite simple:

- The explicit state verification algorithm, presented in [6] and extended with the *persistent-set* partial-order reduction, is run until a state violating a correctness criterion is found;
- A search for a place in which to insert an mfence in order to make the undesirable state unreachable is performed and the mfence instruction is added to the program;
- The procedure is repeated until no further undesirable state can be reached.

The central algorithm is Algorithm 2. It is the algorithm used in [6] with a call to the function *insertMfence()* being executed when an incorrect state is reached. When this happens the function *DFS()* returns *false*, which is passed back up the recursive call chain. Otherwise, *DFS()* returns *true*.

The main program is presented in Algorithm 1. It simply initializes the search and repeats it until *DFS()* returns *true*.

Algorithm 1. Iterative initialization and call of depth-first search with error handling

---

1: **repeat**
2:    init(Stack)
3:    init(H) /* Table of visited states */
4:    s_0 = initial state
5:    $s_0.Sleep = \emptyset$
6:    $delay(s_0) = \emptyset$
7:    push s_0 onto Stack
8: **until** (DFS())

We now describe the method used in the *insertMfence()* procedure. Since we started with an algorithm that is correct under SC, an undesirable state can only be reached because of the relaxed memory model. Comparing x86-TSO and SC, and using the same line of reasoning as that leading to Lemma 1, this can only happen if a load is performed when the corresponding buffer is nonempty.

Thus, the procedure *insertMfence()* starts from the detected error state and searches backwards through the current search path for such a situation. We

Algorithm 2. Recursive DFS() procedure with error detection and mfence insertion

```
 1: s = top(Stack)
 2:
 3: /* if s is an error state: */
 4: /*    search for the last relaxation in the current search path */
 5: /*    and insert a mfence to avoid this relaxation, and return false */
 6: if (s is an error state) then
 7:     insertMfence()
 8:     return  false
 9: end if
10:
11: /* Go through stack from top to bottom, looking for cycles */
12: for all ss in (Stack \ top(Stack)) do
13:     if (cycleCondition(ss,s)) then
14:         s = cycle(ss,s)
15:         break
16:     end if
17: end for
18:
19: if (∃sI ∈ H | s ⊆ sI) then
20:     iSleep = ⋂∀sI∈H|s⊆sI H(sI).Sleep
21:     T = {t | t ∈ iSleep ∩ t ∉ s.Sleep}
22:     s.Sleep = s.Sleep ∩ iSleep
23:     if (s ∈ H) then
24:         H(s).Sleep = s.Sleep
25:     else
26:         enter s in H
27:     end if
28: else
29:     enter s in H
30:     T = Persistent_Set_satisfying_Proviso(s)\s.Sleep
31: end if
32:
33: for all t ∈ T do
34:     ssucc = succ(s,t)
35:     ssucc.Sleep = {tt | tt ∈ s.Sleep ∧ (t, tt) independant in s}
36:     push ssucc onto Stack
37:
38:     /* if an error is encountered, return false */
39:     if (!DFS()) then
40:         return  false
41:     end if
42:
43:     s.Sleep = s.Sleep ∪ {t}
44: end for
45: pop(Stack)
46: return  true
```

could directly insert an mfence just before the offending load in the code of the process executing it, but this would be suboptimal if the previous instruction was a load and not a store given that only store to load transitions are problematic. The backwards search is thus continued until a store executed by the same process as the offending load is found. When this operation is detected, we insert an mfence operation right after it in the control graph of the process.

Note that we just insert one mfence at each run of the verification procedure. This means that the procedure will usually be run repeatedly, but since the number of possible mfence insertions is bounded by the program size, the iterative process will always terminate. Moreover, as we only insert necessary mfence operations, the number of fence instructions inserted is in this sense optimal, but the optimal is local: there is no proof that we always reach a globally minimal number of mfence insertions.

6   Experimental Results

The memory fence insertion technique presented in this paper has been implemented within the prototype tool described in [6]. The input language for this tool is a simplified version of Promela. It is implemented in Java and uses the BRICS automata-package [22] for handling the automata representing buffer contents.

This prototype has been tested on examples, most of which are mutual exclusion algorithms: Dekker's and Peterson's algorithm for mutual exclusion, and Lamport's Bakery algorithm. We also considered all the litmus tests proposed in [5] together with the definition of x86-TSO. These litmus tests are sample programs provided by processor vendors for illustrating possible behaviors of the memory system. Our tool was used in several ways on these litmus tests. First, it was checked that the possibility/impossibility scenarios given for the litmus tests fell respectively within/outside the behaviors considered possible by our tool. The second was to consider non SC behaviors allowed by the litmus tests to be errors and to use the approach of this paper to insert memory fences in order to eliminate these behaviors. All this was performed successfully.

For mutual exclusion, both a single entry version and a repeated entry version were considered for Dekker's and Peterson's algorithms. In the single entry version, each process only attempts to enter the critical section once, whereas in the repeated entry version, each process repeatedly attempts to enter the critical section. A single entry version of the generalized Peterson's algorithm with 3 processes was also analyzed, as well as Lamport's Bakery with 2 processes. Also notice that the loop executed in that protocol was unrolled, which explains why 6 locations for memory fence insertion are found, rather than the 3 required. Given this, the number of mfence operations operations inserted by our algorithm is, for all the examples we have handled, optimal.

For Lamport's Bakery algorithm, the counter used pushes the repeated entry version beyond the scope of our tool.

The results with and without error correction are given in Table 3. Column 2 defines the entry version (single or repeated), Column 3 gives the number of

Table 3. Experimental results for Dekker's and Peterson's Algorithm for mutual exclusion and for Lamport's Bakery with and without memory fence insertion

Program	entry-vers	#Proc	without err. corr.		with err. corr.			
			#St	t	#St	#it	#f	t
Dekker	single	2	118	0.84s	92	3	2	0.80s
Dekker	repeated	2	5468	12.70s	213	5	4	0.41s
Peterson	single	2	108	0.09s	52	3	2	0.03s
Peterson	repeated	2	400	0.58s	54	3	2	0.05s
Gen. Peterson	single	3	15476	44.42s	1164	7	6	1.55s
Lamport's Bakery	single	2	775	0.58s	340	5	4	0.15s

processes. Columns 4 and 5 give information (number of states and time respectively) about the state-space exploration when no fences are inserted. Columns 6 to 9 give information about the exploration with error correction. Column 7 gives the number of iterations needed to insert enough memory fences to correct the program (and do a last check of its correctness) and Column 6 gives the number of states in the final program. The 8th Column gives the number of memory fences inserted, and the last Column gives the total amount of time needed to insert iteratively the fences and to finally verify that the safety property holds again. Very interestingly, even though it involves several iterations, this time is, in almost every case, lower than the time needed to explore the full state space of the uncorrected version.

For Dekker's algorithm, it is important to work with the repeated entry version, since with the single entry version, only 2 memory fences need to be inserted, whereas 4 are essential for the repeated entry version. Note that in [21], only 2 memory fences for Dekker under TSO are detected. This appears to be the linked to the fact that they are using the version of Dekker's algorithm given in appendix J of [4], where it is classified as not deadlock-free. The version we consider is deadlock-free and guarantees freedom of non-progress cycles.

All experimental results were obtained by running our Java-program on a 2.0GHz Intel Core Duo laptop running Ubuntu Linux.

Interestingly, compared to results that can be obtained for the SC memory model, our results show that the exploration of a state space considering the TSO memory model can be performed with a limited increase in the number of states to be explored. Table 4 compares the size of the state-space computed by SPIN (with partial-order reduction) for the SC memory model to the size of the state space computed by our prototype for the x86-TSO memory model, both when the full state-space is explored and when error correction is applied. It might seem surprising that in the latter case, the number of stored states is sometimes smaller than when doing verification under SC. However, this is due to the combination of the partial-order techniques and of the additional independence between the actions of the various processes that comes from delaying stores until they are needed for a load, an mfence or an unlock operation.

Table 4. Comparison of state spaces computed by SPIN for SC and by our implementation for TSO

			SPIN-SC		Our Prototype-TSO without err. corr.	
Program	entry-vers	#Proc	#St stored	#St visited	#St stored	#St visited
Dekker	single	2	105	165	118	160
Dekker	repeated	2	179	214	5468	11322
Peterson	single	2	22	47	108	134
Peterson	repeated	2	24	49	400	640
Gen. Peterson	single	3	1901	4315	15476	46302
Lamport's Bakery	single	2	238	414	775	1186

			SPIN-SC		Our Prototype-TSO with err. corrected	
Program	entry-vers	#Proc	#St stored	#St visited	#St stored	#St visited
Dekker	single	2	105	165	92	117
Dekker	repeated	2	179	214	213	365
Peterson	single	2	22	47	52	68
Peterson	repeated	2	24	49	54	89
Gen. Peterson	single	3	1901	4315	1164	2697
Lamport's Bakery	single	2	238	414	340	407

Finally, it is worth noting that only one mfence is inserted at each iteration, whereas more could be inserted by matching similar code in the various processes. This could lead to a further reduction of the number of required iterations.

7   Conclusions and Comparison with Other Work

Besides our work, several fence insertion algorithms have been proposed. The main originality of our approach is that it is based on a tool that can analyze cyclic programs under x86-TSO and thus that it can infer fence insertion in this context.

In [21] a fence insertion algorithm described as "maximal permissive", i.e. producing an algorithm with the least possible set of restrictions on its behaviors, is proposed. The approach is based on bounded model-checking. It works by propagating through the state graph constraints that represent relaxations that could be removed by an mfence. Once an undesirable state is reached, one can use the associated constraints in order to determine how to make that state unreachable. This approach cannot be applied to cyclic programs and it is not compatible with partial-order reductions, which does not make it possible to transfer it to our context.

Another automatic fence insertion algorithm, using bounded model-checking is given in [23]. This approach is targeted to programs written in *C#*, whose memory model is more relaxed than SC, and hence can lead to surprises when programs are ported to a non SC environment. They use the *maxflow-mincut*

algorithm [24] to decide where to insert memory fences in oder to ensure that
error states are not reached. No claim is made about the minimality of the set
of inserted fences. Along related lines, [25,26] considers the *Java* language and
aims at preserving its semantics when the program is run under a memory model
that is more relaxed then the one specified in the *Java* model.

A less automatic approach was presented in [11], in which the tool could find
errors, print the corresponding traces, but leave it to the programmer to decide
where to insert memory fences. This approach can only handle finite exploration
graphs.

Less directly related work on guaranteeing correct execution under TSO includes [27], which shows that under special conditions, such as the *triangular
race freedom* introduced in [28], all behaviors possible in TSO are also possible
in SC. However, we are not aware of any automated tool to detect triangular
races and achieve freedom of these races. Furthermore, even if a program includes a triangular race this does not imply that it will have incorrect behaviors,
with respect to a safety property, under a relaxed memory model.

As conclusions, we first claim that we have shown that with the right combination of techniques (automata for representing buffer contents and partial-order
reductions), using explicit state enumeration to verify programs under relaxed
memory models can be done with limited penalty compared to verification under SC. Retrospectively, this is not really surprising since using store buffers
introduces a lot of independence, which is tamed by the partial-order methods.
Our second claim is that we have shown that this can be effectively exploited in
order to find which memory synchronization operations need to be introduced
to guarantee that correctness is preserved when moving a program from SC to
x86-TSO.

References

1. Holzmann, G.J.: The SPIN Model Checker: Primer and Reference Manual.
   Addison-Wesley Professional, London (2003)
2. Lamport, L.: How to Make a Multiprocessor Computer That Correctly Executes
   Multiprocess Programs. IEEE Trans. Computers 28(9), 690–691 (1979)
3. SPARC International Inc., C.: The SPARC architecture manual: version 8.
   Prentice-Hall Inc., Upper Saddle River (1992)
4. SPARC International, Inc., C.: The SPARC architecture manual (version 9).
   Prentice-Hall, Inc., Upper Saddle River (1994)
5. Sewell, P., Sarkar, S., Owens, S., Nardelli, F.Z., Myreen, M.O.: x86-TSO: a rigorous
   and usable programmer's model for x86 multiprocessors. Commun. ACM 53, 89–97
   (2010)
6. Linden, A., Wolper, P.: An automata-based symbolic approach for verifying programs on relaxed memory models. In: van de Pol, J., Weber, M. (eds.) Model
   Checking Software. LNCS, vol. 6349, pp. 212–226. Springer, Heidelberg (2010)
7. Boigelot, B., Godefroid, P., Willems, B., Wolper, P.: The Power of QDDs (Extended
   Abstract). In: Hentenryck, P.V. (ed.) SAS 1999. LNCS, vol. 1302, pp. 172–186.
   Springer, Heidelberg (1997)

8. Godefroid, P.: Partial-Order Methods for the Verification of Concurrent Systems. LNCS, vol. 1032. Springer, Heidelberg (1996)
9. Burnim, J., Sen, K., Stergiou, C.: Sound and complete monitoring of sequential consistency in relaxed memory models. Technical Report UCB/EECS-2010-31, EECS Department, University of California, Berkeley (March 2010)
10. Atig, M.F., Bouajjani, A., Burckhardt, S., Musuvathi, M.: On the verification problem for weak memory models. In: Hermenegildo, M.V., Palsberg, J. (eds.) Proceedings of the 37th ACM SIGPLAN-SIGACT Symposium on Principles of Programming Languages, POPL 2010, Madrid, Spain, January 17-23, pp. 7–18. ACM, New York (2010)
11. Burckhardt, S., Alur, R., Martin, M.M.K.: Checkfence: checking consistency of concurrent data types on relaxed memory models. In: Ferrante, J., McKinley, K.S. (eds.) Proceedings of the ACM SIGPLAN 2007 Conference on Programming Language Design and Implementation, San Diego, California, USA, June 10-13, pp. 12–21. ACM, New York (2007)
12. Burckhardt, S., Musuvathi, M.: Effective program verification for relaxed memory models. In: Gupta, A., Malik, S. (eds.) CAV 2008. LNCS, vol. 5123, pp. 107–120. Springer, Heidelberg (2008)
13. Jonsson, B.: State-space exploration for concurrent algorithms under weak memory orderings (preliminary version). SIGARCH Comput. Archit. News, 65–71 (June 2009)
14. Intel Corporation: Intel®64 and IA-32 Architectures Software Developer's Manual. Specification (2007)
15. Owens, S., Sarkar, S., Sewell, P.: A better x86 memory model: x86-TSO. In: Berghofer, S., Nipkow, T., Urban, C., Wenzel, M. (eds.) TPHOLs 2009. LNCS, vol. 5674, pp. 391–407. Springer, Heidelberg (2009)
16. Loewenstein, P., Chaudhry, S., Cypher, R., Manovit, C.: Multiprocessor memory model verification (2008)
17. Boigelot, B., Wolper, P.: Symbolic Verification with Periodic Sets. In: Dill, D.L. (ed.) CAV 1994. LNCS, vol. 818, pp. 55–67. Springer, Heidelberg (1994)
18. Godefroid, P., Pirottin, D.: Refining dependencies improves partial-order verification methods (extended abstract). In: Courcoubetis, C. (ed.) CAV 1993. LNCS, vol. 697, pp. 438–449. Springer, Heidelberg (1993)
19. Valmari, A.: Stubborn sets for reduced state space generation. In: Rozenberg, G. (ed.) APN 1990. LNCS, vol. 483, pp. 491–515. Springer, Heidelberg (1991)
20. Michael, M.M., Scott, M.L.: Simple, fast, and practical non-blocking and blocking concurrent queue algorithms. In: Proceedings of the Fifteenth Annual ACM Symposium on Principles of Distributed Computing, pp. 267–275. ACM, New York (1996)
21. Kuperstein, M., Vechev, M., Yahav, E.: Automatic inference of memory fences. In: Formal Methods in Computer Aided Design (2010)
22. Møller, A.: brics/automaton DFA/NFA Java implementation.
23. Huynh, T.Q., Roychoudhury, A.: A memory model sensitive checker for C#. In: Misra, J., Nipkow, T., Karakostas, G. (eds.) FM 2006. LNCS, vol. 4085, pp. 476–491. Springer, Heidelberg (2006)
24. Ford, L.R., Fulkerson, D.R.: Maxumum flow through a nework. Canad. J. Math. 8, 399–404 (1956)
25. Sura, Z., Wong, C.L., Fang, X., Lee, J., Midkiff, S.P., Padua, D.A.: Automatic implementation of programming language consistency models. In: Pugh, B., Tseng, C.-W. (eds.) LCPC 2002. LNCS, vol. 2481, pp. 172–187. Springer, Heidelberg (2005)

26. Fang, X., Lee, J., Midkiff, S.P.: Automatic fence insertion for shared memory multiprocessing. In: Proceedings of the 17th Annual International Conference on Supercomputing (ICS 2003), pp. 285–294. ACM, New York (2003)
27. Attiya, H., Guerraoui, R., Hendler, D., Kuznetsov, P., Michael, M.M., Vechev, M.: Laws of order: expensive synchronization in concurrent algorithms cannot be eliminated. In: Proceedings of the 38th annual ACM SIGPLAN-SIGACT Symposium on Principles of Programming Languages (POPL 2011), pp. 487–498. ACM, New York (2011)
28. Owens, S.: Reasoning about the implementation of concurrency abstractions on x86-TSO. In: D'Hondt, T. (ed.) ECOOP 2010. LNCS, vol. 6183, pp. 478–503. Springer, Heidelberg (2010)

Model Checking Industrial Robot Systems

Markus Weißmann[1], Stefan Bedenk[2], Christian Buckl[3], and Alois Knoll[1]

[1] Technische Universität München, Fakultät für Informatik
Boltzmannstrasse 3, 85748 Garching, Germany
weissmann@ini.tum.de, knoll@in.tum.de
[2] AUDI AG
85057 Ingolstadt, Germany
stefan.bedenk@audi.de
[3] fortiss GmbH
Guerickestr. 25, 80805 München, Germany
buckl@fortiss.org

Abstract. Modern production plants are highly automated complex systems consisting of several robots and other working machines. Errors leading to damage and stop of production are extremely expensive and must be avoided by all means. Hence, the state of practice is to test control programs in advance which implies high effort and comes with high costs. To increase the confidence into the control systems and to reduce the necessary effort, this paper proposes to use model checking to verify certain properties. It presents a compiler that can transform industrial robot programs into PROMELA models. Since the statements of the robot programming language can not be mapped directly into PROMELA statements, we apply compiler optimization techniques to close the semantic gap. In case of a specification violation the trace is mapped to the original context so that the robot programmer can reconstruct the problem. As a case study we applied the tool to verify the absence of collisions and deadlocks. We were able to detect one deadlock in a car-body welding station with 9 robots, correct the program and verify the correctness of the resulting system.

Keywords: model checking, abstract interpretation, industrial robots, distributed systems.

1 Introduction

Modern production plants are highly automated, complex systems. They use industrial robots for lifting, welding, bonding and other tasks for which the robots may have to work in the same area. Design errors resulting e. g. in collisions or deadlocks can lead to downtime of the plant which are extremely expensive. This is especially true for modern production plants that use just in time production; in these systems each industrial robot system easily becomes a single point of failure the outage of which can quickly result in an outage of the whole production line.

A. Groce and M. Musuvathi (Eds.): SPIN 2011, LNCS 6823, pp. 161–176, 2011.

To address this problem upfront, the control programs are tried to be kept as simple as possible. This approach is counteracted upon by the necessity for more and more dynamic production processes. For example car body production plants are used to produce different variants of cars, e. g. a fastback and station wagon, different numbers of doors, etc. This flexibility has to be provided by the control programs.

Virtual commissioning is an approach to find problems in the programming upfront, before the plant is built. Most commonly it is carried out as a computer simulation of the industrial robot system. Different levels of detail on the physical part of the plant are used, reaching from a plain emulation of the programs to 3D simulations with a hardware-in-the-loop setup of the controllers. Using this simulation the programs can be tested. However this approach implies great testing effort and does not guarantee the correctness of the system.

To target this issue, this paper proposes the use of model checking techniques to verify the correctness of the system with respect to certain properties. This approach has the advantage that it can prove the absence of errors – in contrast to tests. To apply model checking on the control programs, they must first be transformed into a formal model. Since engineers without a background in formal verification should be able to apply this method, too, a manual creation of this formal model is not feasible. An automated translation solves this problem and also the need to keep the formal model and the original robot programs synchronized.

This paper presents a compiler that can transform industrial robot programs into PROMELA models as input for the SPIN model checker [12]. Since the statements of the robot programming language can not be mapped directly into PROMELA statements, we apply compiler optimization techniques to close the semantic gap. To verify certain properties our tool extends the PROMELA code with assertions. The engineer can add further properties in form of linear temporal logic (LTL) formulas. To simplify the formulation of these LTL formulas, LTL patterns for each property to verify are provided.

If SPIN detects a violation of one property, it generates an error trace leading to the violation in the PROMELA model. To help a robot programmer understand the result of the analysis, the presented tool-chain provides a projection of the error-trace in the model back to the original robot programs.

As a case study we applied the tool to verify the absence of collisions and deadlocks. We were able to detect one deadlock in a car-body welding station with 9 robots, correct the robot control programs and verify the correctness of the resulting system.

The structure of the paper is as follows: Section 2 contains preliminaries on the problem and gives an overview of previous work; Section 3 discusses the problem details; our solution is presented in section 4. The results of our analysis of two industrial robot systems can be found in section 5. We conclude in section 6.

2   Background

An industrial robot system typically consists of a programmable logic controller (PLC) and several robots. The PLC and the robots are running the control programs. They control further devices like welding guns and riveting systems, which are not programmable devices; they are either controlled by the PLC or a robot. The PLC controls the system as a whole; it tells the robots which control program to use for the current process. The PLC is also the master hub of the industrial robot system: All up-stream communication from the system devices is routed through the PLC; hence the network topology of the system is a tree.

To reduce costs, increase reliability and to shorten product cycles, manufacturers want to have a high quality control software before starting the commissioning process. The current approach is to model the industrial robot system in a hardware-in-the-loop (HIL) simulation, the so-called virtual commissioning. This method allows testing up-front, but finding bugs is still a tedious task and the absence of bugs can not be shown. To address this problem, we want to introduce formal verification to analyze the control software.

Several approaches to formal verification for embedded systems [7] and more specifically industrial control systems using PLCs [19] are available. A common solution is to use model checking, e.g. with the SPIN model checker; other approaches include abstract interpretation [17] or manually created, computer based proofs [18].

A basic solution for making use of a model checker is to manually create a model of the PLC program, then use a model checker to verify it [14]. As our goal includes providing a system for non-experts in verification, manually created proofs are not a suitable option. More advanced approaches use automatic translation from PLC programs in Instruction List (IL) [4,15] or in Sequential Function Charts (SFC) [1]. This method is suitable not only for PLC programming languages: The Java PathFinder can be used to verify Java programs [11] by compiling them to PROMELA, the modeling language of SPIN. Bandera follows a similar approach and can analyze Java programs; it uses an optimizing compiler to translate them to either a Spin or NuSMV model [5]. This has also been done with programs written in C with a mixed-mode translation; the programs are compiled and combined with manually written system calls [8]. Care has to be taken that the extraction provides a faithful model of the system [10].

A remaining problem of the automatic model extraction [13] is that there is still the need for an expert to interpret the resulting trace in case of an error. This problem can be solved by creating highly specialized model checkers that can use the original program as model, e.g. in C [2] and in PLC/IL language [16].

Abstract interpretation has been used on modeling languages [9] and also on PLC/IL programs to perform range analysis [3].

Our approach uses model extraction on the robot programs, while the PLC task is generated. The resulting model consisting of multiple processes can then be verified. In case an error is found in the model, the resulting error-trace is projected back to the original context. Example properties that can be checked are deadlocks, collisions and kill-switch violations.

3 Problem Statement

In this section we provide an overview of the system we want to verify. We will discuss the robot programming language and the interlock algorithm provided by the PLC.

An industrial robot system typically consists of up to 10 robots and a PLC which communicate over field bus. This distributed system shares common resources in the form of physical space that can be occupied by a single robot only. If more than one robot tries to use the same area at the same time, this behavior leads to a collision of the robots. To avoid this behavior the robots use a software locking mechanism with the PLC as central arbiter.

Before an industrial robot system's start of production (SOP) its behavior is tested to assure it is working correctly, e. g. it is free of collisions. This testing is tedious, expensive and can not guarantee the absence of errors.

Our goal is to provide a system that:

- does not require much effort to set up for a concrete industrial robot system
- can quickly verify the absence of certain programming errors
- is easy to use for a robot programmer, i. e. does not require expertise in formal verification

3.1 Robot Programming Language

The robot control language (VKRC) is an imperative, sequential language. Our compiler handles the core language, which is sufficient to detect the faults we want to find. This core language includes assignments, control flow commands and movement commands for the robotic arm. For simplicity we will refer to this subset as VKRC.

Variables. The language only has boolean expressions. Depending on their type, variables can either store a boolean value or a boolean expression. Variables need not be declared, the set of variables is fixed. There are local variables, outgoing, incoming and symbolic variables; variables have a one-character prefix that determines their type followed by a natural number (see table 1). The outgoing and incoming variables are for communication with the PLC: Their contents are sent to the PLC by the robots runtime system, received from it respectively. This communication is completely transparent to the robot programmer. The symbolic variables can store an expression which gets evaluated when the symbolic variable is read. The kill-switch condition variable is a special purpose symbolic variable: When moving, the robot continuously checks this variable and triggers an emergency stop if the stored expression evaluates to false.

Statements. The assignment statement is the predominant command of VKRC programs. If the variable on the left-hand side is of type local or outgoing, the expression on the right-hand side gets evaluated and the result is stored in the target variable. If the target variable is a symbolic variable, the expression itself is stored without binding any values of the variables used in the expression.

Table 1. Types of variables in VKRC ($n \in \mathbb{N}^+$)

Variable	Semantics
Fn	Local variable
An	Outgoing variable
En	Incoming variable (read-only)
Mn	Symbolic variable (local)
FB SPS	Kill-switch condition (only on left-hand side)

Table 2. Statements of the VKRC language

Command	Semantics
variable = *expression*	Assignment of expression to variable
GOTO LABEL *id* = *expression*	Conditional jump to label *id*
LABEL *id*	Target of a jump
subroutine = *expression*	Conditional subroutine call of *subroutine*
REPEAT *subroutine* = n STOP = *expression*	Call subroutine n-times or unless condition is met
WARTE BIS *expression*	Wait until *expression* is met
n PTP	Move the robot arm to position n (point-to-point)
n LIN	Move the robot arm to position n (linear)
n, m CIRC	Move the robot arm to position m via n (circular)

For moving the robotic arm, VKRC has several movement commands that will make the runtime system move the arm to the designated target coordinate. The different commands are used for specifying the movement trajectory with which the robotic arm is moved. The movement commands feature a plethora of arguments with which the movement can be further specified. As we do not take into account all available options that fine-tune the movement, the movement commands presented here are simplified.

The VKRC language has subroutine calls. VKRC subroutines do not take parameters nor do they return a value. The subroutine call is only available as a conditional call for which the programmer must provide a condition expression. Subroutines must not be called recursively.

Control flow statements provide a conditional jump similar to a C goto/label. Furthermore the repeat statement lets the programmer call a subroutine several times or unless a given condition is met. At last there is a blocking wait statement that will block until the given expression evaluates to true.

Communication. The robot uses the input and output variables to communicate with the PLC; this communication is handled by a field bus. This communication is completely transparent to the robot programmer; to him the robot appears to have a shared memory with the PLC.

The PLC can either handle the incoming and outgoing variables of the robot with a PLC program, or just map the outgoing variables to incoming ones of another robot.

Table 3. Boolean functions in VKRC

Boolean Expression	Semantics
expression & *expression*	Logical and of two expressions
expression + *expression*	Logical or of two expressions
! *expression*	Logical inversion of expression
(*expression*)	Brackets for changing order of precedence
variable	See table 1
AUS	false (literally *off*)
EIN	true (literally *on*)

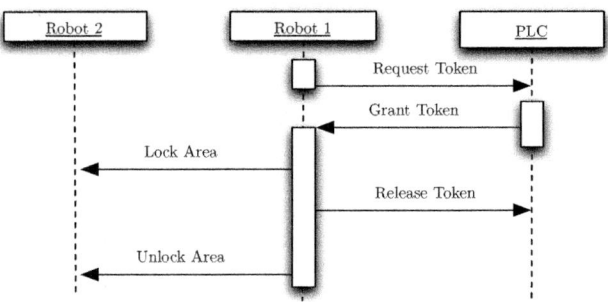

Fig. 1. Robot 1 successfully locks a shared working area

```
--- request token from the PLC
A81 = EIN
--- block until area is free and token is granted
WARTE BIS E41 & E81
--- lock area
A41 = AUS
--- return token
A81 = AUS

--- may now operate in shared working area
...

--- unlock area
A41 = EIN
```

Fig. 2. Robot program code to lock area 41/81

3.2   Interlock Algorithm

The robot programming language does not have lock/unlock primitives. The robot programs rely on the PLC as an arbiter to guarantee that a lock can only be taken by a single robot. The actual lock is between two robots only; the PLC only manages the token which allows a robot to acquire a lock.

If a robot wants to lock a certain area, it first requests the corresponding token from the PLC. The PLC will hand out this token only to one robot at a time and will withdraw it only if the robot gives it back. A robot that has a token is allowed to take the actual lock – if it is not already taken. After obtaining the actual lock, the robot will give back the token. When it has left the corresponding area, the robot must unlock the area (see figure 1). The corresponding program code of the robot can be seen in figure 2.

4   Solution

Our tool chain (see Figure 3) allows a robot programmer to verify programs without requiring any knowledge in model checking. The VKRC compiler translates the robot programs into PROMELA code. Together with the PLC logic and the error description, this forms our model. This model is then verified with SPIN. If an error is found, we transform the trace back into a VKRC trace.

4.1   VKRC to PROMELA Compiler

The VKRC compiler translates one robot program into a PROMELA process and a corresponding variable declaration list. The compiler is written in OCaml. It uses a classic lexer/parser front-end that first generates an abstract syntax tree (AST) from which a control flow graph (CFG) is built. The statements in the CFG are then translated from VKRC to PROMELA. Eventually the PROMELA CFG is used to generate PROMELA code.

The compiler is used to translate each robot program into a PROMELA process. The generated processes and variable declaration lists can then be combined with the process of the PLC to form a model of the industrial robot system.

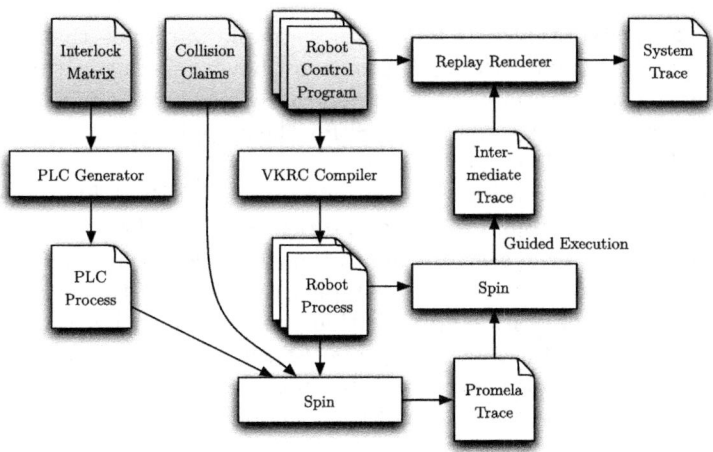

Fig. 3. Architectural Overview

Locations. The lexer passes the location information about the origin of lexer tokens to the parser. The parser embeds this information into each statement of the AST, so that we know the corresponding file and line of each statement. This information is kept for each statement during all compiler phases. When the compiler backend generates PROMELA code, it not only creates PROMELA statements for the corresponding logic, but also print-statements. They print a line containing the location information and additional information about the values of the variables used in the statement (see table 4).

This allows the transformation of the SPIN trace into a VKRC trace by using the guided execution capability of SPIN with the error trace. During guided execution, SPIN executes the program in such a way that the fault is reached in the formal model. The execution of the print statements along this path generates a trace that can be directly mapped to the VKRC programs.

Loop unrolling, function inlining. The VKRC language features a repeat-statement that calls a subroutine a fixed number of times – or until an additional condition is not met. To avoid introducing an additional integer for the loop counter and to keep the control flow graph as simple as possible, these loops are always unrolled. As the number of times the subroutine is called is a fixed integer value, the loop unrolling always succeeds in completely removing the loop. The unrolling is performed during the translation from the AST to the CFG.

PROMELA does not have functions or subroutines whereas VKRC has subroutines. To solve this mapping problem, the compiler inlines all subroutine calls. This approach is feasible as recursion is not allowed in VKRC. The VKRC subroutines do not take parameters which makes this inlining process straight forward: The compiler replaces the calls to subroutines by their body until the program is free of subroutine calls.

With all subroutine calls removed, the compiler also does not need to perform inter-function analysis during the next step. Inlining is performed with all subroutines being available in the VKRC CFG form.

Abstract Interpretation. VKRC has symbolic variables that can store a boolean expression while PROMELA does not have a similar feature. The compiler uses abstract interpretation [6] to remove the need of the symbolic variables from the source language. If this is successful, the mapping of the resulting VKRC program to PROMELA is easy.

The abstract interpretation is performed on the VKRC CFG; The compiler can perform *constant evaluation, copy propagation* and *dead code elimination*: The goal is to remove the assignments to the symbolic variables. First the compiler performs constant evaluation to simplify the CFG. With this simplification in place, the copy propagation optimization can determine the value of the symbolic variables in the statements they are used in. After the copy propagation, the symbolic variables occuring in right-hand side values are replaced by their value. This step removes the usage of the symbolic variables in right-hand side values.

This in turn makes the assignments to the symbolic variables unnecessary. The dead code analysis can now determine which assignments are unnecessary and

Table 4. Translation of VKRC statements, examples

VKRC	PROMELA
A23 = F17 + E12	atomic{ A23=F17||E12; printf("UP1.vkrc::24") }
GOTO LABEL 4 = EIN	*via control flow graph*
LABEL 4	*via control flow graph*
MAKRO20 = EIN	*inline contents of subroutine*
REPEAT MAKRO20 = 5 STOP = E9	*unroll loop (5x), then inline contents*
WARTE BIS E78	atomic{ (E78); printf("MAKRO20.vkrc::25") }
7 PTP	atomic{ location=7; printf("UP1.vkrc::23") }
19 LIN	atomic{ location=19; printf("UP1.vkrc::34") }
20, 21 CIRC	atomic{ location=21; printf("UP2.vkrc::72") }

remove them. After this step, no symbolic variables should appear on left-hand side values anymore either.

The abstract interpretation allows us to get rid of the symbolic variables, so that no PROMELA code needs to get generated for them. Unfortunately, this method might not work for all VKRC programs. Examples are goto loops including symbolic variables. However, the method worked for all robot control programs we analyzed as such a construction contradicts typical programming standards. If this method does not succeed, this could well be a programming error.

The compiler can be told to only perform the optimizations on the symbolic variables instead of all variables. This can lead to minor differences in the time required to verify the model as can be seen in section 5.

Movement commands. The robot control programs have movement commands. These commands will make the robotic arm move to the given position. The positions are given as integer numbers in the robot control program; a lookup-table exists where the actual movement coordinates are stored. We know from the CAD program the industrial robot system is planned in, which combinations of robots in which positions can lead to collisions.

The VKRC compiler translates the movement commands to assignments to a global position variable. The target points of the movements are enumerated already, so we use these numbers as right-hand side value of the assignment.

During movement, the robot continuously checks the kill-switch variable. This symbolic variable is evaluated and if returns false, will make the robot perform an emergency stop. To map this behavior, the compiler inserts an assert statement on the value of the kill-switch variable at the position of the movement command. This way the model checker will find a violation of this property.

4.2   PLC Generator

To verify the locking mechanism, a model of the PLC is required. We have written a code generator that creates this model based on the interlock configuration.

The PLC is modeled as a process that grants and removes locking-tokens based on the truth table in table 5. For every available lock between two robots, the

Table 5. Truth table of how the PLC grants and removes tokens T based on requests R

R_n	R_m	T_n	T_m	T'_n	T'_m	
0	0	0	0	-	-	
0	0	0	1	-	0	remove token from m
0	0	1	0	0	-	remove token from n
0	0	1	1	error		the token was granted to both robots
0	1	0	0	0	1	grant token to m
0	1	0	1	-	-	
0	1	1	0	0	1	
0	1	1	1	error		the token was granted to both robots
1	0	0	0	1	-	grant token to n
1	0	0	1	1	0	grant token to n, remove from m
1	0	1	0	-	-	
1	0	1	1	error		the token was granted to both robots
1	1	0	0	1	-	grant token to n
1	1	0	0	-	1	grant token to m
1	1	0	1	-	-	
1	1	1	0	-	-	
1	1	1	1	error		the token was granted to both robots

PLC process features one set of entries. One lock is always exclusively between two robots. The PLC therefore has to take into account all possible states of token-requested and token-granted for exactly two robots. We generate a PLC process for the final model in PROMELA from this table.

The PLC process consists of an event loop and decides non-deterministically which token to grant or withdraw; the two robots n and m can request their tokens T_n and T_m by sending requests R_n and R_m. For every lock in the system, we generate 8 lines for the PLC process: The truth table 5 has 17 rows; the row with both robots requesting the locking token has a non-deterministic result and for this reason appears twice. For the error-lines, where both robots have been granted the locking token, no code needs to be generated as they are unreachable. The lines for which the PLC process does not need to take any action, can also be omitted.

The actual locking bits are exchanged directly between the robots. A robot is only allowed to claim an area if it owns the locking token and the area is not already locked. The locking token is not required to release an area.

The robots can not directly communicate with each other, but all communication is handled via the PLC. In the original system, the PLC performs a mapping from the corresponding output variables of one robot to the input variables of the partner robot. We model this mapping by renaming the input variables to the output variables they are connected to.

4.3   Fault Description

We are searching for three classes of faults:

- Deadlocks
- Collisions
- Kill-switch violations

Deadlocks are searched for by SPIN automatically. We only need to specify that the PLC process does not have to terminate.

Collisions are found via the movement commands. We translate a movement command to an assignment of the unique movement point number to the `position` variable of the corresponding robot. The content of this variable specifies the coordinate, where the robot arm is heading. From the 3D model of the industrial robot system, we know which movement combinations of which robots can cause collisions. We use this information to formulate a never claim: Combinations of locations of two robots that would lead to a potential collision must not occur

The user has to supply a matrix of possible collisions based on the movement points of the robot programs. From this matrix we generate claims in LTL; for every possible collision between two robots – robot n at position i and robot m at position k – we add the claim:

$$\Box \neg ((\text{position}_n = i) \wedge (\text{position}_m = k))$$

Kill-switch violations are directly generated by the compiler as assertions in the PROMELA process. While in movement the robot continuously checks the `FB SPS` variable for its contents. If this is false, the robot will trigger an emergency stop. This kind of emergency situation must not occur during normal operation; hence, it is considered as an error in the model.

During translation the compiler determines the value of the `FB SPS` variable at each movement command. A movement command is then translated to the assignment to the position and a preceding PROMELA-assert statement. This assertion guarantees the expression in the kill-switch variable to be true during movement.

4.4 Putting the Model Together

To create a model for the entire industrial robot system, we combine the generated files: We create a main PROMELA file that first includes the variable declaration files of all robots. It then includes the files of the robot processes and of the PLC process. The verification engineer then has to add a never claim for the potential collision combinations. Finally we write a main process that initializes certain variables and then starts all robot processes and the PLC process.

As of now, we have several devices that are missing from our model, e. g. welding devices. To allow the robot program to work as intended, we manually set the variables that represent the feedback from those devices to their desired value. This means these events always succeed and the behavior of the system with these events failing is not taken into account.

4.5   Replay Trace

If the model checker finds a counter-example, it generates a trace leading to this error. This trace can be replayed in *guided execution*, executing the PROMELA program in such a way, that it leads to the found violation.

When executed in this way, the model checker will also execute the `printf` statements that were inserted by the compiler. The back-end of the compiler generates an accompanying `printf` statement for every statement generated. For a VKRC assignment, a PROMELA assignment is generated which is placed together with a `printf` statement inside an atomic block. This block then outputs the original location of the VKRC statement and the values of the variables used in the original statement.

This output is now a trace we can directly relate to the original robot control programs. The replay renderer takes this VKRC trace and generates a replay based on the robot programs. This replay shows the execution of the robot programs according to our trace; it displays the programs in the same way as in a teach panel, in a way the robot programmers are accustomed to. Variables in the VKRC program get colored depending on their current value.

The current replay can display two robot programs side by side, the current statement and the value of the variables. It consists of several HTML files so that a robot programmer does not need to install additional software to view the replay.

This replay allows a robot programmer to understand the way an error can occur in the system and help him find and remove the source of the problem. A screenshot of the current prototype can be seen in figure 4.

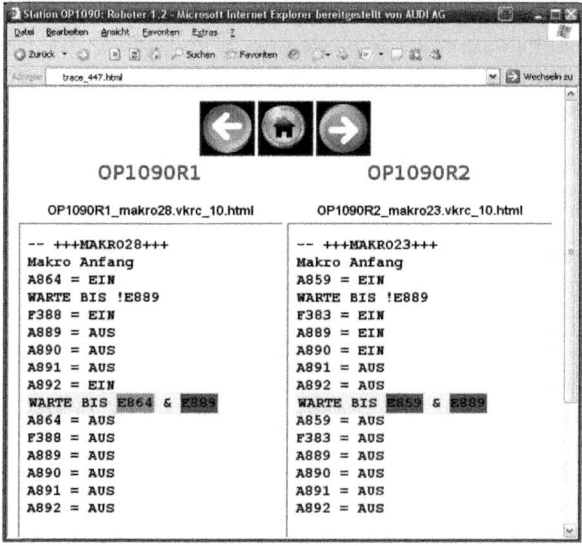

Fig. 4. Trace replay at the final deadlock situation between two robots

Table 6. Benchmarks of analyzed industrial robot systems

# of robots	2				9			
# of processes (robot/PLC)	3 (2/1)				10 (9/1)			
# of Variables (bit/byte)	214 (210/4)				936 (918/18)			
Contains deadlock	yes		no		yes		no	
Compiler optimizations	off	on	off	on	off	on	off	on
Number of transitions	179	179	45083	42742	2677	2677	24891214	30837984
CPU-time [sec]	0.030	0.061	0.077	0.140	0.061	0.108	119.640	132.718
Memory footprint [MByte]	2.501	2.501	3.184	2.989	4.161	3.868	909.786	909.883

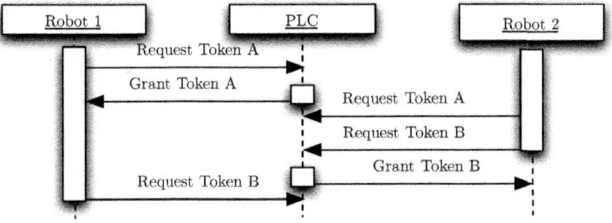

Fig. 5. Robot 1 and 2 deadlock each other trying to obtain two tokens concurrently

5   Evaluation

We conducted verification runs on a training station and on several recent car-body stations. The training station has 2 robots, while the car-body stations have 9.

We found a deadlock in the robot control programs of the training station. A robot programmer was able to quickly track the error with our replay tool and to remove the source of the error: A missing variable initialization. The results of the benchmarks on the training station (see table 6) were as expected: With the deadlock in place, the error was found with minimal amount of CPU-time. Without the deadlock, the verification run still finished in under 1 second. The activation of the optional compiler optimizations reduced the CPU-time required by 5%.

After the training station, we tried to verify several recent car-body stations with 9 robots each. We were able to find a deadlock in one of the welding stations. The preparation time to set up the model of the system was about 3 man-hours. With the deadlock in place, the verification run took well under one second. After removing the source of the deadlock, the verification itself took about 2 minutes. For this setup the optional compiler optimizations made the verification 11% more expensive in terms of CPU-time.

The deadlock of the welding station was due to a protocol error in the request of the locking tokens. The robot control programs requested two tokens before waiting for the arrival of the first one. As can be seen in figure 5, this can lead to a rare deadlock. The request for token *A* from robot *1* arrives first, which the PLC grants. Then the requests for token *A* and *B* from robot *2* arrive. The PLC has already handed out token *A* but token *B* is given to robot *2*. As both robots will block waiting for the arrival of both tokens, a classic deadlock situation occurs (see figure 5). To resolve this problem, both robots need to first wait for the arrival of token *A* before requesting token *B*.

6   Conclusion and Future Work

This paper proposed the use of model checking techniques to verify the correctness of industrial robot system with respect to certain properties. We presented a compiler to transform robot programs into extended PROMELA models. Furthermore the tool allows to map an error-trace created by SPIN back into the original context.

Using the suggested approach we could validate original robot control programs from Audi car body welding stations. In this process we found a protocol error in the robot programs that could eventually lead to a deadlock. Based on the generated error-trace it was possible to find and remove the error. We could show that model checking is a viable option for analyzing the control programs of large industrial robot system even with 9 robots.

In contrast to the simulation-based approach which is currently state-of-the-art in industry, the approach can guarantee the correctness with respect to certain properties, such as freedom of deadlocks and absence of collisions. The required effort to set up the modeling tool chain is also considerably smaller than the effort currently spent in testing these properties.

We are planning several improvements for the current tools to increase their applicability:

- Multi-language support; we want to analyze industrial robot system using robots from other manufacturers that use different programming languages.
- Higher degree of automation in setup process; if the barrier to use model checking can be lowered even further, the applicability will be higher.
- Replay-renderer for an arbitrary number of robots/processes
- Include support for more devices; we want to analyze if the robot programs handle external errors correctly, e. g. a welding problem

The case study presented in this paper showed that for current industrial robot system the performance scales well. However if further details are added to the formal model state space explosion can get a problem. Hence future work must also take into account techniques to limit the state space.

References

1. Bauer, N., Engell, S., Huuck, R., Lukoschus, B., Stursberg, O.: Stursberg: Verification of PLC Programs given as Sequential Function Charts. In: CICLing 2001. LNCS, pp. 517–540. Springer, Heidelberg (2004)

2. Beyer, D., Henzinger, T., Jhala, R., Majumdar, R.: The software model checker BLAST. International Journal on Software Tools for Technology Transfer (STTT) 9, 505–525 (2007); 10.1007/s10009-007-0044-z
3. Bornot, S., Huuck, R., Lakhnech, Y., Lukoschus, B.: Utilizing static analysis for programmable logic controllers. In: ADPM 2000: The 4th International Conference on Automation of Mixed Processes: Hybrid Dynamic Systems, pp. 183–187 (2000)
4. Canet, G., Couffin, S., Lesage, J.J., Petit, A., Schnoebelen, P.: Towards the automatic verification of PLC programs written in Instruction List. In: IEEE International Conference on Systems, Man and Cybernetics, pp. 2449–2454 (2000)
5. Corbett, J.C., Dwyer, M.B., Hatcliff, J., Laubach, S., Pasareanu, C.S., Zheng, H.: Bandera: Extracting Finite-state Models from Java Source Code. In: Proceedings of the 22nd International Conference on Software Engineering, pp. 439–448. ACM Press, New York (2000)
6. Cousot, P., Cousot, R.: Abstract interpretation: a unified lattice model for static analysis of programs by construction or approximation of fixpoints. In: Proceedings of the 4th ACM SIGACT-SIGPLAN Symposium on Principles of Programming Languages (POPL 1977), pp. 238–252. ACM, New York (1977)
7. Cousot, P., Cousot, R.: Verification of embedded software: Problems and perspectives. In: Henzinger, T.A., Kirsch, C.M. (eds.) EMSOFT 2001. LNCS, vol. 2211, pp. 97–113. Springer, Heidelberg (2001)
8. de la Cámara, P., del Mar Gallardo, M., Merino, P.: Model extraction for ARINC 653 based avionics software. In: Bošnački, D., Edelkamp, S. (eds.) SPIN 2007. LNCS, vol. 4595, pp. 243–262. Springer, Heidelberg (2007)
9. Dong, Y., Ramakrishnan, C.R.: An optimizing compiler for efficient model checking. In: Proceedings of the IFIP TC6 WG6.1 Joint International Conference on Formal Description Techniques for Distributed Systems and Communication Protocols (FORTE XII) and Protocol Specification, Testing and Verification (PSTV XIX), FORTE XII / PSTV XIX 1999, Deventer, The Netherlands, pp. 241–256. Kluwer Academic Publishers, Dordrecht (1999)
10. Duarte, L.M., Kramer, J., Uchitel, S.: Towards faithful model extraction based on contexts. In: Fiadeiro, J.L., Inverardi, P. (eds.) FASE 2008. LNCS, vol. 4961, pp. 101–115. Springer, Heidelberg (2008)
11. Havelund, K.: Java PathFinder, A Translator from Java to Promela. In: Dams, D.R., Gerth, R., Leue, S., Massink, M. (eds.) SPIN 1999. LNCS, vol. 1680, p. 152. Springer, Heidelberg (1999)
12. Holzmann, G.J.: The Model Checker SPIN. IEEE Transactions on Software Engineering 23, 279–295 (1997)
13. Holzmann, G.J., Smith, M.H.: An automated verification method for distributed systems software based on model extraction. IEEE Transactions on Software Engineering 28, 364–377 (2002)
14. Mazzolini, M., Brusaferri, A., Carpanzano, E.: Model-checking based verification approach for advanced industrial automation solutions. Emerging Technologies and Factory Automation (ETFA), 1–8 (2010)
15. Pavlovic, O., Pinger, R., Kollmann, M.: Automated formal verification of PLC programs written in IL. In: Conference on Automated Deduction (CADE), pp. 152–163 (2007)
16. Schlich, B., Brauer, J., Wernerus, J., Kowalewski, S.: Direct model checking of PLC programs in IL. In: 2nd IFAC Workshop on Dependable Control of Discrete Systems (DCDS), Bari, Italy (2009)
17. Seidl, H., Vojdani, V.: Region analysis for race detection. In: Palsberg, J., Su, Z. (eds.) SAS 2009. LNCS, vol. 5673, pp. 171–187. Springer, Heidelberg (2009)

18. Wan, H., Chen, G., Song, X., Gu, M.: Formalization and Verification of PLC Timers in Coq. In: Proceedings of the 2009 33rd Annual IEEE International Computer Software and Applications Conference, vol. 01, pp. 315–323. IEEE Computer Society, Los Alamitos (2009)
19. Younis, M.B., Frey, G.: Formalization of existing PLC programs: A survey. In: Proceedings of Computing Engineering in Systems Applications (CESA), Lille, France (July 2003)

EpiSpin: An Eclipse Plug-In for Promela/Spin Using Spoofax

Bob de Vos, Lennart C.L. Kats, and Cornelis Pronk

Delft University of Technology, The Netherlands
b.devos-1@student.tudelft.nl, {l.c.l.kats,c.pronk}@tudelft.nl

Abstract. This paper presents EpiSpin: an Eclipse plug-in for editing Promela models. It provides error markers as you type, various editor services and an interface to perform verification and simulation runs using Spin. An additional tool shows the static relations between channels, processes and global variables. These tools have been built using the Spoofax language workbench.

1 Introduction

Model Checking [6] is a technique used for state space exploration of a model of a system to determine whether it meets a given specification. In the past, model checking was performed on relatively small models. Currently, increasingly large models are routinely being constructed. Examples of such large models are given in [8,11,12]. In the latter paper a model consisting of more than 7000 lines of Promela code was developed and model checked. Current work on model checking FreeRTOS [3,14] will also lead to large programs. With these developments, it becomes increasingly important to provide state-of-the-art IDE support for efficient development and maintenance of Promela models.

In this paper, we introduce EpiSpin[1], an Eclipse plug-in for editing Promela programs and starting Spin verification and simulation runs. It includes several editor services like syntax highlighting, content completion, code folding and instant feedback on syntactic and semantic errors. Additionally, a tool is integrated which shows the static relations between processes, channels and variables.

Implementing state-of-the-art IDE support for a new language can be a challenge, requiring not only the implementation of a parser and semantic analysis, but also extensive knowledge of the sometimes complicated and highly interdependent APIs and extension mechanisms of an IDE framework. For EpiSpin, we use the locally developed Spoofax language workbench [7] for the development of an Eclipse plugin. As a language workbench, Spoofax abstracts over these implementation artifacts and provides a comprehensive environment that integrates syntax definition, program transformation, code generation, and declarative specification of IDE components.

We continue this paper with a brief introduction and background on Promela, the Spin Model Checker, the Spoofax language workbench and related work

---

[1] EpiSpin: Eclipse plug-in for Spin.

A. Groce and M. Musuvathi (Eds.): SPIN 2011, LNCS 6823, pp. 177–182, 2011.

inspiring this paper. The main development work on the Eclipse plug-in will be described in Section 3. Section 4 will describe the Static Communication Analyzer derived from the same Spoofax set-up. Testing the plug-in is covered in Section 5. The conclusions and some future work can be found in Section 6.

2 Background

Spin and Promela. Promela is a state of the art modeling language to describe verification models. These models can be analyzed by the iSpin model checker. A grammar definition of the complete Promela language (including version 6 constructs) and a more complete description of Promela and the Spin tool for which Promela has been developed can be found in [5].

Spoofax. Spoofax is a platform for the development of textual domain-specific languages with state-of-the-art IDE support. It combines the SDF syntax definition formalism [13] for the declarative specification of syntax with the Stratego [2] program transformation language for the specification of semantics.

Spoofax supports agile development of languages by allowing incremental, iterative construction of language and editor components. It shows editors for the language under development alongside its definition. As soon as a syntax definition has been written, an editor with default syntax highlighting and other syntactic editor services can be used, and customized. Stratego can be used to specify more sophisticated editor services as transformations on abstract syntax trees, to support e.g. semantic error markers or content completion.

Related Work. Our project is not the first endeavor to create an Eclipse plugin for Spin and Promela. Two other editors were created before by Rothmaier et al. [11] and Kovše et al. [8]. Those works used the standard, Java-based Eclipse API and follow a traditional architecture for editors, using regular expressions for editor services such as syntax highlighting and code folding. In the case of Kovše, the editor could also process the output of the Spin syntax checker to provide in-editor error markers. Our approach is fundamentally different: we emphasize rich, as-you-type editor feedback to aid developers of Promela models. We use a language workbench for our approach instead of the standard, rather low-level Eclipse API and regular expressions. Using Spoofax, new languages can be developed using a set of grammar production and transformation rules. From this, the workbench generates an editor with a parser that executes (in a background thread) with every change in a Promela model. Based on the parser our editor provides more accurate syntax highlighting and as-you-type syntactic error markers. Internally, it also creates abstract syntax trees used for analyses of the model. With these analyses we provide editor services such as inline error markers without requiring the user to manually invoke the Spin syntax checker. We also provide more editor sophisticated services such as reference resolving and content completion.

3   EpiSpin

EpiSpin includes the following features:

- Promela editor with full syntax support according to Promela language version 6 including the new `for` and `select` keywords, and support for inline specification of LTL properties,
- Instantaneous feedback on syntactic and semantic errors,
- Syntax highlighting, outline view, code folding, code completion and reference resolving,
- Interface to start the Spin verifier and simulator,
- Static Communication Analyzer (see Section 4).

The Spin simulator and verifier can be called from within EpiSpin directly. A Spin command is executed according to the options specified and the resulting textual output is shown in the Eclipse console. The Promela grammar from [4] has been used as a basis to form the SDF rules. Since only context-free grammars can be specified in SDF, EpiSpin currently does not provide full support for macros. As a work-around it is possible to call the Spin syntax checker or to open the model in iSpin.

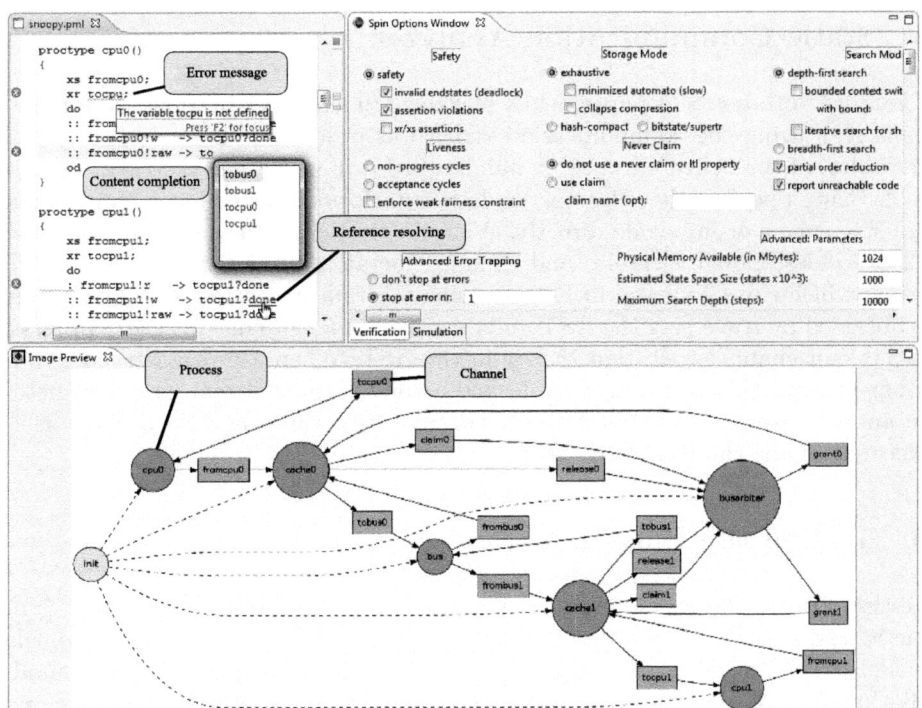

Fig. 1. Editor services, option window and dot graph

Editor Services

In Spoofax, the syntactic editor services can be fully specified using declarative editor service descriptor specifications [7]. Syntax highlighting, code folding and outline view are implemented to improve the readability, especially of large Promela models. These last two editor services are implemented in Spoofax by listing the sorts and constructors for which the editor service needs to hold. Another syntactic editor service is syntactic content completion. Based on static templates, at every moment a list of completion suggestions can be requested.

There are three semantic editor services in EpiSpin, being reference resolving, semantic completion and error checking. All of those are completely integrated in Eclipse. This means that error markers and error messages are shown instantaneously when an error is made. For reference resolving and semantic completion it is necessary to know about the identifiers present in the model. Therefore the first step of the analysis is to find all identifier declarations. This is done by defining a rule that maps the identifier name to its constructor for every declaration. When an instance of an identifier is clicked, the appropiate declaration is found by passing the name of the identifier to the rule. When content completion is triggered at a position where an identifier is expected, a list of all keys of the rule is shown. In Figure 1 a partial screenshot of Eclipse with EpiSpin can be found. Explanations are given in rounded boxes.

4   Static Communication Analyzer

The third author of this paper, while marking student work in Spin, often found himself drawing the communication structure (processes, channels and global variables) of the delivered work by hand; a task which can be taken over by this tool. Using rewrite rules, Promela code is transformed into constructors of another language or into code directly. With the Static Communication Analyzer, all processes, global variables and channel operations are displayed in a DOT graph which can be viewed in Eclipse using the ImageViewer[2]. This DOT code is obtained by traversing the AST and creating a node or edge for every process, variable or channel operation that is in the AST. When a process executes another process, this is shown by a dashed arrow. A channel sent as a parameter to another process and therefore existing multiple times as a local channel is pictured as one channel in the graph.

5   Testing the Plug-In

Testing EpiSpin has been done by syntactic testing and semantic testing. Syntactic testing is mainly done by feeding the parser with a lot of different Promela models from [1] and [9]. Since there is no full support for macro calls, all models that include macros are first preprocessed by the `spin -I` command and

---

[2] http://www.eclipse.org/evangelism/samples/imageviewer/

then parsed by EpiSpin. The editor services are tested during implementation by making a small test program for every rule that is implemented. Mutation testing [10] is used to obtain more test cases.

6   Conclusions and Future Work

We created a Promela editor with a Promela parser, various editor services and the possibility to call the Spin verifier and simulator. Additional tools such as the Static Communication Analyzer can easily be derived because of the use of a language workbench. The use of Spoofax makes it it easier to include future changes in the Promela grammar. We are currently looking into work-arounds for the limited support of macro calls.

EpiSpin can be downloaded from `http://epispin.ewi.tudelft.nl` (as a plug-in or as a stand-alone Eclipse distribution). It is not needed to have Spoofax installed since the required libraries are included in EpiSpin. This site will also show how the plug-in can be installed and used.

Acknowledgements. This research was supported by NWO/JACQUARD project 612.063.512, *TFA: Transformations for Abstractions.*

References

1. Beem: Benchmark for explicit model checkers, `http://anna.fi.muni.cz/models/`
2. Bravenboer, M., Kalleberg, K.T., Vermaas, R., Visser, E.: Stratego/XT 0.17. A language and toolset for program transformation. Sci. of Comp. Programming 72(1-2), 52–70 (2008)
3. FreeRTOS. The FreeRTOS Project, `http://www.freertos.org`
4. Holzmann, G.J.: Promela language reference, `http://www.spinroot.com/spin/Man/promela.html`
5. Holzmann, G.J.: The SPIN Model Checker: Primer and Reference Manual. Addison-Wesley Professional, London (2003)
6. Jhala, R., Majumdar, R.: Software model checking. ACM Comput. Surv. 41, 21:1–21:54 (2009)
7. Kats, L.C.L., Visser, E.: The Spoofax language workbench: rules for declarative specification of languages and IDEs. In: Cook, W.R., et al. (eds.) Proceedings of OOPSLA 2010, Reno/Tahoe, Nevada, USA, pp. 444–463. ACM, New York (2010)
8. Kovše, T., Vlaovič, B., Vreže, A., Brezočnik, Z.: Eclipse plug-in for spin and st2msc tools-tool presentation. In: Păsăreanu, C.S. (ed.) SPIN. LNCS, vol. 5578, pp. 143–147. Springer, Heidelberg (2009)
9. Promela database, `http://www.albertolluch.com/research/promelamodels`
10. Offutt, J., Ammann, P., Liu, L.L.: Mutation testing implements grammar-based testing. In: Workshop on Mutation Analysis (2006)
11. Rothmaier, G., Kneiphoff, T., Krumm, H.: Using SPIN and eclipse for optimized high-level modeling and analysis of computer network attack models. In: Godefroid, P. (ed.) Model Checking Software. LNCS, vol. 3639, pp. 236–250. Springer, Heidelberg (2005)

182   B. de Vos, L.C.L. Kats, and C. Pronk

12. Taverne, P., Pronk, C.: RAFFS: Model checking a robust abstract flash file store. In: Breitman, K., Cavalcanti, A. (eds.) ICFEM 2009. LNCS, vol. 5885, pp. 226–245. Springer, Heidelberg (2009)
13. Visser, E.: Syntax Definition for Language Prototyping. PhD thesis, University of Amsterdam (September 1997)
14. Woodcock, J.: First steps in the verified software grand challenge. In: Software Engineering Workshop, pp. 203–206 (2006)

DiPro - A Tool for Probabilistic Counterexample Generation

Husain Aljazzar[*], Florian Leitner-Fischer, Stefan Leue, and Dimitar Simeonov

University of Konstanz, Germany

Abstract. The computation of counterexamples for probabilistic model checking has been an area of active research over the past years. In spite of the achieved theoretical results in this field, there is no freely available tool that allows for the computation and representation of probabilistic counterexamples. We present an open source tool called DiPro that can be used with the PRISM and MRMC probabilistic model checkers. It allows for the computation of probabilistic counterexamples for discrete time Markov chains (DTMCs), continuous time Markov chains (CTMCs) and Markov decision processes (MDPs). The computed counterexamples can be rendered graphically.

1 Introduction

Due to the numerical nature of the used model checking algorithm stochastic model checkers are unable to derive a counterexample witnessing a property violation directly from the model checking process. The unavailability of counterexamples makes debugging very difficult, which constrains the practical usefulness of current stochastic model checking tools. The provisioning of such counterexamples requires addressing the following crucial issues:

- The definition of the *notion of a counterexample*: Since probability bounds are in most cases not exceeded by single execution sequences, stochastic counterexamples are formed by sets of execution sequences that jointly exceed probability limits [9,5].
- The *representation* of counterexamples: It has been proposed to either enumerate these execution sequences, or to represent them as graphs or algebraic expressions.
- The *selection of the traces* belonging to the counterexample: Heuristics guided search has successfully been used to select the counterexamples carrying most probability mass first.
- The *presentation* of counterexamples: Due to the large number of traces in the counterexample, a visual representation is required [3]. It has also been proposed to abstract probabilistic counterexamples into Fault Trees [12].

---

[*] The contribution of this author to this paper was entirely performed while he was with the University of Konstanz. Current permanent affiliation: Bosch Sicherheitssysteme GmbH, 85630 Grasbrunn, Germany.

A. Groce and M. Musuvathi (Eds.): SPIN 2011, LNCS 6823, pp. 183–187, 2011.

We present a tool, called DiPro, which we have designed and implemented in order to experimentally evaluate our algorithmic approaches towards counterexample generation in stochastic model checking. The tool implements the XBF algorithms to compute counterexamples as diagnostic subgraphs, using heuristics guided search [5]. Alternatively, it enumerates counterexamples using the K* algorithm, a heuristics guided on-the-fly variant of Eppstein's k-shortest-paths (KSP) algorithm that we developed [6]. When computing counterexamples for Markov Decision Processes (MDPs), DiPro uses an AND/OR tree data structure based approach [4]. Counterexamples are represented graphically, as proposed in [3]. While there exists a significant body of alternative work on the computation of counterexamples, e.g., [9,7], we are not aware of any other publicly available counterexample generation tool for CTMCs, DTMCs and MDPs.

2   Probabilistic Counterexamples

We briefly introduce the concept of probabilistic counterexamples, for a more detailed account see [5].

We call a path starting at the initial state of the system and leading to a state satisfying some state formula φ in some stochastic temporal logic, such as CSL [8], a diagnostic path. While in functional model checking a single path often provides valuable information for the debugging of the system, a single path is not sufficient in the probabilistic setting since the violation of a CSL property can hardly ever be traced back to a single diagnostic path. In almost all cases a set of diagnostic paths is needed to provide an accumulated probability mass that violates the specified probabilistic property. In CSL, an upper bounded property, for instance, can be expressed by a formula of the form $P_{\leq p}(\varphi)$. A counterexample for an upper bounded property is now a set X of diagnostic paths such that the accumulated probability of X violates the probability constraint $\leq p$. For a given model and an upper-bounded CSL formula, the set of diagnostic paths is usually not unique, and often very large. We propose the following criteria to be considered in the selection of the diagnostic paths that are to be included in the counterexamples:

- We prefer shorter diagnostic paths, that is paths with fewer transitions, over longer paths. This is justified by the observation that the shorter the path, the easier it is to interpret and retrace it in the model.
- We prefer diagnostic paths with higher probability mass to be included in the counterexample over paths with lower probability. This means that on the one hand we can keep the size of the counterexample small by considering few diagnostic paths that carry high probability each. On the other hand, executions with a high probability are also often more relevant when debugging the model.

These criteria have led us to use heuristics guided explicit state space search on the DTMC, CTMC or MDP models in order to include few, but high probability diagnostic paths into the counterexamples. XBF uses heuristic guidance to incrementally compute a counterexample in the form of a diagnostic subgraph. K* uses the KSP search idea in combination with heuristic search guidance to successively enumerate the most probable, which is an interpretation of shortness notion in KSP, diagnostic paths until the probability bound has been reached.

3   The DiPro Tool

The DiPro tool can be downloaded from the DiPro website[1]. The DiPro tool is open-source and released under the GNU general public license[2].

The DiPro tool can be used in a command line version, with a graphical user interface or as a library that can be invoked via an application program interface. All three version can export the counterexample in a text-file or in an XML-file for later usage. DiPro can be used to compute counterexamples jointly with the PRISM [10] and the MRMC [11] model checking tools. The graphical user interface of DiPro provides a wizard that guides the user from opening a PRISM or MRMC model file via the selection of a stochastic temporal logic formula to the settings of the counterexample computation. Finally, the counterexample is visualized.

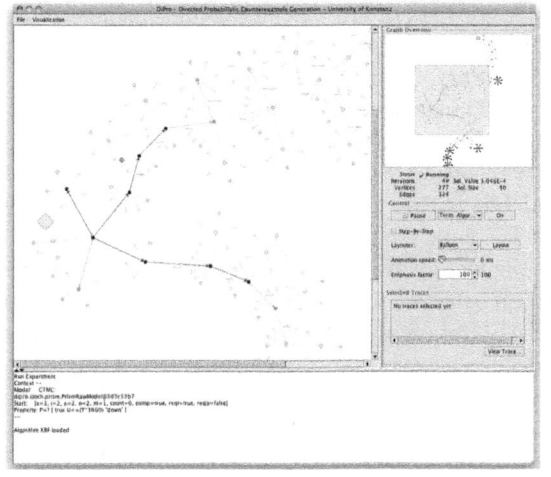

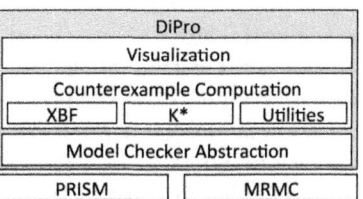

Fig. 1. DiPro graphical user interface   **Fig. 2.** DiPro architecture

Figure 1 shows the visualization and counterexample computation window of DiPro. In the upper right part of the window the counterexample is visualized as a graph. The visualization represents the counterexamples as a graph resulting from an unfolding of the CTMC, DTMC or MDP being analyzed. All paths belonging to the counterexample are colored in red, whereas paths not belonging to the counterexample are colored in blue. The states of the paths are represented

---

[1] http://www.se.inf.uni-konstanz.de/DiPro
[2] http://www.gnu.org/licenses/

as circles connected by arrows, which represent the transitions. All end-states of diagnostic paths are depicted as diamonds, the sizes of which correlate with the probability masses of the diagnostic paths ending in these states.

We envision DiPro not only as a stand-alone tool, but as being integrated in a tool chain, which is facilitated by its application program interface. In [12,13] we show how the counterexamples generated by DiPro can be used by other tools. This way we achieve an integration into the UML modeling world. We also enable counterexamples to be abstracted and represented as Fault Trees.

A pictorial overview of the essentially layered architecture of DiPro is given in Fig. 2. The *Model Checker Abstraction* provides all necessary interfaces to control access to PRISM and MRMC. The algorithms for the counterexample computation, together with data structures needed to store the counterexample and some additional utilities are included in the *Counterexample Computation* layer. The *Visualization* layer comprises everything necessary for the visualization of the counterexamples. DiPro is implemented in Java.

4   Case Study: Airbag System

This case study is taken from [1] and models an industrial automotive airbag system. The airbag system architecture consists of two acceleration sensors, whose task it is to detect crashes, one micro controller to perform the crash evaluation, and an actuator, called FASIC, that controls the deployment of the airbag. Although airbags save lives in crash situations, they may cause fatalities if they are inadvertently deployed. It is therefore a pivotal safety requirement that an airbag is never deployed if there is no crash situation. Suppose that the upper bound for an inadvertent deployment of the airbag within time T is p. In CSL, this property can be expressed using the formula $\mathcal{P}_{<p}(noCrash\ U^{\leq T}\ AirbagIgnited)$. Figure 3 shows one path in the counterexample visualization computed by DiPro. It starts at the initial state (1) and leads to an error state (4) after 3 transitions. We also see that a transition labeled with FASICShortage is the transition leading to the error state, and that the error state has a very high probability. To prevent the inadvertent deployment of the airbag we have to prevent the FASICShortage transition. This can be achieved by replacing the FASIC by an actuator that is more reliable. Extensive experimental evaluations of the algorithms implemented in DiPro can be found in [4,2,5,6].

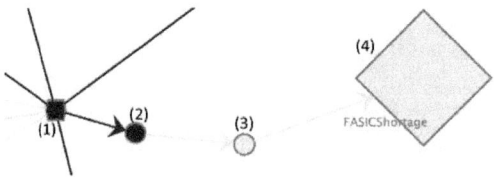

Fig. 3. Excerpt from the airbag system counterexample

5   Conclusion

We have presented the publicly available tool DiPro for the computation of probabilistic counterexamples for DTMCs, CTMCs and MDPs. In future work we plan to work on automatic generation of heuristics for the counterexample generation algorithms included in DiPro.

References

1. Aljazzar, H., Fischer, M., Grunske, L., Kuntz, M., Leitner-Fischer, F., Leue, S.: Safety analysis of an airbag system using probabilistic FMEA and probabilistic counterexamples. In: Proc. QEST 2009, pp. 299–308. IEEE Computer Society, Los Alamitos (2009)
2. Aljazzar, H., Kuntz, M., Leitner-Fischer, F., Leue, S.: Directed and heuristic counterexample generation for probabilistic model checking: a comparative evaluation. In: Proc. QUOVADIS 2010, pp. 25–32. ACM, New York (2010)
3. Aljazzar, H., Leue, S.: Debugging of dependability models using interactive visualization of counterexamples. In: Proc. QEST 2008. IEEE Computer Society Press, Los Alamitos (2008)
4. Aljazzar, H., Leue, S.: Generation of counterexamples for model checking of markov decision processes. In: Proc. QEST 2009, pp. 197–206. IEEE Computer Society, Los Alamitos (2009)
5. Aljazzar, H., Leue, S.: Directed explicit state-space search in the generation of counterexamples for stochastic model checking. IEEE Transactions on Software Engineering 36(1), 37–60 (2010)
6. Aljazzar, H., Leue, S.: K*: A heuristic search algorithm for finding the k shortest paths. Artificial Intelligence (2011) (accepted for publication)
7. Andrés, M., D'Argenio, P., van Rossum, P.: Significant diagnostic counterexamples in probabilistic model checking. Hardware and Software: Verification and Testing, 129–148 (2009)
8. Baier, C., Haverkort, B., Hermanns, H., Katoen, J.-P.: Model-checking algorithms for continuous-time Markov chains. IEEE Transactions on Software Engineering 29(7) (2003)
9. Han, T., Katoen, J., Berteun, D.: Counterexample Generation in Probabilistic Model Checking. IEEE Transactions on Software Engineering, 241–257 (2009)
10. Hinton, A., Kwiatkowska, M., Norman, G., Parker, D.: PRISM: A tool for automatic verification of probabilistic systems. In: Hermanns, H. (ed.) TACAS 2006. LNCS, vol. 3920, pp. 441–444. Springer, Heidelberg (2006)
11. Katoen, J.-P., Khattri, M., Zapreev, I.S.: A Markov Reward Model Checker. In: QEST 2005: Proceedings of the Second International Conference on Quantitative Evaluation of Systems, pp. 243–244. IEEE Computer Society, Los Alamitos (2005)
12. Kuntz, M., Leitner-Fischer, F., Leue, S.: From probabilistic counterexamples via causality to fault trees. Technical Report soft-11-02, Chair for Software Engineering, University of Konstanz (2011), http://www.inf.uni-konstanz.de/soft/research/publications/pdf/soft-11-02.pdf
13. Leitner-Fischer, F., Leue, S.: QuantUM: Quantitative safety analysis of UML models. In: Proc. QAPL (2011)

dBug: Systematic Testing of Unmodified Distributed and Multi-threaded Systems*

Jiří Šimša, Randy Bryant, and Garth Gibson

Carnegie Mellon University,
5000 Forbes Ave, Pittsburgh, PA, USA

1 Introduction

In order to improve quality of an implementation of a distributed and multi-threaded system, software engineers inspect code and run tests. However, the concurrent nature of such systems makes these tasks challenging. For testing, this problem is addressed by *stress testing*, which repeatedly executes a test hoping that eventually all possible outcomes of the test will be encountered.

In this paper we present the dBug tool, which implements an alternative method to stress testing called *systematic testing*. The systematic testing method implemented by dBug controls the order in which certain concurrent function calls occur. By doing so, the method can systematically enumerate possible inter-leavings of function calls in an execution of a concurrent system.

The dBug tool can be thought of as a light-weight model checker, which uses the implementation of a distributed and multi-threaded system and its test as an implicit description of the state space to be explored. In this state space, the dBug tool performs a reachability analysis checking for a number of safety properties including the absence of 1) deadlocks, 2) conflicting non-reentrant function calls, and 3) system aborts and runtime assertions inserted by the user.

Related Work. The idea of systematic testing of concurrent systems has been first explored by VeriSoft [2]. In recent years, the research community has significantly advanced the state of the art of practical dynamic analysis and produced a number of powerful tools for finding faults in concurrent systems. The CHESS tool [5] implements systematic testing for multi-threaded Windows-based programs. The ISP tool [7] implements systematic testing for distributed MPI-based programs. The MaceMC tool [4] implements systematic testing for distributed and multi-threaded programs written in the Mace language. The MoDist tool [10] implements systematic testing using binary instrumentation for distributed and

* The work in this paper is based on research supported in part by the DoE, under award number DE-FC02-06ER25767 (PDSI), by the NSF under grant CCF-1019104, and by the MSR-CMU Center for Computational Thinking. We also thank the members and companies of the PDL Consortium (including APC, DataDomain, EMC, Facebook, Google, Hewlett-Packard, Hitachi, IBM, Intel, LSI, Microsoft, NEC, NetApp, Oracle, Seagate, Sun, Symantec, and VMware) for their interest, insights, feedback, and support.

A. Groce and M. Musuvathi (Eds.): SPIN 2011, LNCS 6823, pp. 188–193, 2011.

multi-threaded Windows-based programs. Compared to these tools, dBug is the only tool capable systematic testing of unmodified distributed and multi-threaded systems. As such, dBug can be used for analysis of the plethora of existing concurrent systems designed for POSIX-compliant operating systems.

2 Tool

2.1 Architecture

Interposition Layer The interposition layer is responsible for monitoring and controlling the execution of the system under test. Notably, when a thread of the system under test is about to call a function which dBug seeks to control, the interposition layer transparently intercepts this call, suspends the execution of the calling thread, and informs the arbiter about this event. At some later point, the interposition layer receives a message from the arbiter which causes the calling thread to resume execution.

Arbiter. The arbiter is responsible for selecting the order in which concurrently intercepted function calls execute. The arbiter is a centralized entity that maintains a global view of the system under test. In particular, the arbiter uses a client-server architecture (depicted in Figure 1) to collect information about the threads running in the system and intercepted calls via instances of the interposition layer. At some point, referred to as the *decision point*, the arbiter infers that the system under test can make no progress without the arbiter resuming execution of some of the suspended threads. For example, when the number of threads in the system under test matches the number of concurrently intercepted calls, the arbiter knows it has reached a decision point. At that point the arbiter decides which of the concurrently intercepted calls should execute first.

Explorer. The explorer is responsible for navigating the repeated execution of the test to yet unexplored parts of the state space. In particular, after each execution of a test, the explorer collects information about all the decision points

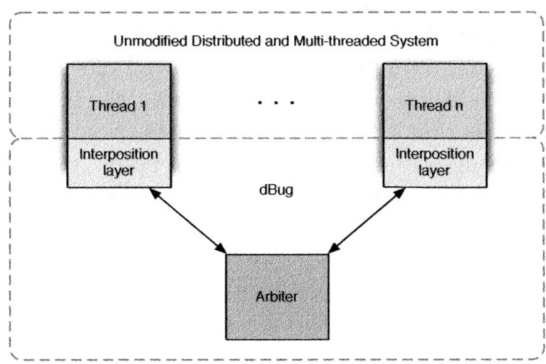

Fig. 1. dBug Architecture

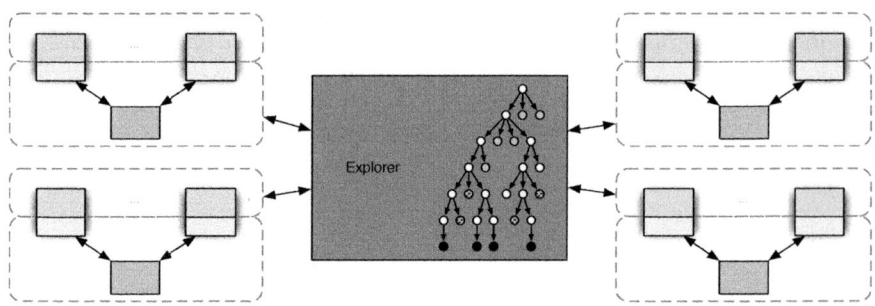

Fig. 2. dBug Exploration

encountered by the arbiter. This information is then used to gradually build a *decision tree* with nodes corresponding to decision points and edges corresponding to intercepted calls. The decision tree is in turn used to craft schedules for future instances of the arbiter to steer the execution down unexplored branches of the tree. Figure 2 illustrates how the explorer communicates with different instances of the system under test, while iteratively building the decision tree. To explore the decision tree, the explorer uses a stateless approach.

2.2   Functionality

Using the architecture described above, the tool performs a reachability analysis over the decision tree, while checking for a number of safety properties including the absence of 1) deadlocks, 2) conflicting non-reentrant function calls, and 3) system aborts and runtime assertions inserted by the user.

To check for deadlocks, the interposition layer intercepts function calls that are potentially blocking while collecting information that could influence whether a call blocks. Using this information, the arbiter can infer for each intercepted call whether execution of the call from the current state would block. For example, the arbiter keeps track of all threads and processes running as part of the system under test in order to infer if an intercepted call to `waitpid()`, `sem_wait()` or `pthread_join()` would block. A deadlock is detected when the arbiter reaches a decision point knowing all intercepted calls would block.

To check for non-reentrant function call conflicts, the interposition layer intercepts calls to functions that are not guaranteed to be reentrant (e.g. by POSIX standard [3]). The dBug tool checks if a decision point can be reached such that two intercepted calls correspond to the same non-reentrant function being called by two threads of the same process.

To check for assertion violations as well as more general system aborts such as segmentation faults, the interposition layer installs its own signal handlers. These handlers inform the arbiter about a delivery of a signal before the system actually crashes and then forward the signal to the original handler.

The current version of the dBug tool supports interposition of the POSIX process management, POSIX threads, and POSIX semaphores interface. For a detailed list of events intercepted by the interposition layer, we refer the interested read to the dBug User Manual available from the project web page [8].

2.3 Limitations

First, the tool might fail to discover a concurrency error that requires an interleaving of events at a finer level of abstraction than that of a function call.

Second, given that the problem of precise detection of a decision point (i.e. no forward progress is possible without resuming execution of one of the suspended threads) is undecidable, the tool sometimes resorts to using a timeout as a mechanism for detecting a decision point. If the arbiter incorrectly infers it has reached a decision point, the method might fail to cover the decision tree.

Third, even if decision points are detected precisely, if the system under test contains a source of non-deterministic behavior which is not controlled by the arbiter, the method might still fail to cover the decision tree. For example, the overhead imposed by dBug can skew the timing of events in the system, which can be a problem if control flow is time-dependent.

Lastly, the method assumes that a test execution terminates. Although it is possible to execute the method using dove-tailing to avoid getting stuck in an infinite execution, the method does not check for infinite loops.

3 Evaluation

In our previous work [9], dBug has been applied on a parallel file system and distributed key-value storage. More recently, the dBug tool has been used for systematic testing of implementations of a proxy web server created by students as their final assignment for *15-213 Introduction to Computer Systems*, a class offered by the Computer Science Department at Carnegie Mellon University.

The assignment asked students to create a proxy server that receives an HTTP request from a client, inspects the request header to find out the target server, sends the request to the server, receives a reply from the server, and sends the reply to the client. Additionally, the proxy was expected to service multiple requests concurrently and to service duplicate requests from a local cache.

To check student proxies, we would start up a local web server and the proxy and issue requests to the proxy using the `curl` utility. After eliminating 35 proxies that failed simple sequential tests, we were left with 80 proxies. To test the concurrent nature of these proxies, we would concurrently issue two identical requests and used dBug to systematically enumerate possible ways in which the concurrent events triggered by the test could occur. The dBug tool was configured to timeout after 60 minutes. The detailed experiment data for the results below are provided at the dBug project web page [8].

The dBug tool found concurrency faults in 25 of the 80 tested proxies, including a fault in the reference proxy written by one of the course teaching assistants. We confirmed the existence of all of these faults by mapping the traces generated by dBug into the source code of the proxies.

For 13 of the 25 faulty proxies, more than 60% of the executions witnessed by dBug were erroneous. We suspect that the reason why these faults went undetected by the programmers is because dBug, similar to Eraser [6], marks executions that could have gone wrong, but did not, as faults. For example, dBug flags an execution when two threads of the same process make concurrent calls to a non-reentrant function or when a free mutex is unlocked, irrespective of whether such behavior maps to an observable fault.

Lastly, we compared the findings of dBug to the code inspection carried out during grading of the assignment by experienced course instructors and teaching assistants. Surprisingly, the code inspection identified only 20% of the faults identified by dBug. On the other hand, unlike dBug, the code inspection was able to identify multiple data races that happened because of insufficient synchronization of concurrent memory accesses.

4   Conclusion

In this paper we have presented a novel tool, dBug, which addresses the challenge of finding concurrency faults in unmodified distributed and multi-threaded systems. The tool is an open-source project and is available for download from the dBug project web page [8]. As an on-going work we are working on extending functionality and improving efficiency of the tool. In particular, we are adding support for 1) interposition of events of the Linux sockets interface, 2) virtualization and control of time, and 3) state space reduction akin to [1].

Finally, while the experiment has been carried out independently of the 15-213 class, we are working towards making dBug an integral tool available to the education of programmers of concurrent systems.

References

1. Flanagan, C., Godefroid, P.: Dynamic partial-order reduction for model checking software. SIGPLAN Not. 40(1), 110–121 (2005)
2. Godefroid, P.: VeriSoft: A Tool for the Automatic Analysis of Concurrent Reactive Software. In: Grumberg, O. (ed.) CAV 1997. LNCS, vol. 1254, Springer, Heidelberg (1997)
3. Austin JointWorking Group. IEEE Standard for Information Technology- Portable Operating System Interface (POSIX) Base Speci cations. In: IEEE Std 1003.1-2008 (Revision of IEEE Std 1003.1-2004), vol. (7), pp. 1–3826 (December 2008)
4. Killian, C.E., Anderson, J.W., Jhala, R., Vahdat, A.: Life, death, and the critical transition: Finding liveness bugs in systems code. In: NSDI 2007: Proceedings of the 5th Conference on USENIX Symposium on Networked Systems Design and Implementation (2007)
5. Musuvathi, M., Qadeer, S., Ball, T., Basler, G., Nainar, P.A., Neamtiu, I.: Finding and reproducing heisenbugs in concurrent programs. In: OSDI 2008: Proceedings of the 8th Conference on USENIX Symposium on Operating Systems Design and Implementation, pp. 267–28 (2008)
6. Savage, S., Burrows, M., Nelson, G., Sobalvarro, P., Anderson, T.: Eraser: a dynamic data race detector for multithreaded programs. ACM Trans. Comput. Syst. 15(4), 391–411 (1997)

7. Vakkalanka, S.S., Sharma, S., Gopalakrishnan, G., Kirby, R.M.: ISP: a tool for model checking MPI programs. In: Proceedings of PPoPP 2008, pp. 285–286. ACM, New York (2008)
8. Šimša, J.: dBug Project, http://www.cs.cmu.edu/~jsimsa/dbug
9. Šimša, J., Gibson, G., Bryant, R.: dBug: Systematic Evaluation of Distributed Systems. In: SSV 2010: Proceedings of 5th International Workshop on System Software Verification (2010)
10. Yang, J., Chen, T., Wu, M., Xu, Z., Liu, X., Lin, H., Yang, M., Long, F., Zhang, L., Zhou, L.: MoDist: Transparent Model Checking of Unmodi ed Distributed Systems. In: NSDI 2009: Proceedings of the Sixth Symposium on Networked Systems Design and Implementation, pp. 213–228 (April 2009)

Author Index

GPSR Compliance

*The European Union's (EU) General Product Safety Regulation (GPSR)
is a set of rules that requires consumer products to be safe and our
obligations to ensure this.*

*If you have any concerns about our products, you can contact us on
ProductSafety@springernature.com*

In case Publisher is established outside the EU, the EU authorized
representative is:

Springer Nature Customer Service Center GmbH
Europaplatz 3
69115 Heidelberg, Germany

Batch number: 09478804

Printed by Printforce, the Netherlands